International Purchasing Handbook

JAMES M. ASHLEY

PRENTICE HALL

Library of Congress Cataloging-in-Publication Data

International purchasing handbook / James M. Ashley
    p.   cm.
Includes Index.
ISBN 0-13-251430-3
    1. Industrial procurement—Handbooks, manuals, etc. 2. International
business enterprises—Management. I. Title.
HD39.5.A84   1998
658.7'2—dc21   98-3195
                                              CIP

Printed in the United States of America

10 9 8 7 6 5 4 3 2 1

ISBN 0-13-251430-3

ATTENTION: CORPORATIONS AND SCHOOLS

Prentice Hall books are available at quantity discounts with bulk purchase for educational, business, or sales promotional use. For information, please write to: Prentice Hall Career & Personal Development Special Sales, 240 Frisch Court, Paramus, NJ 07652. Please supply: title of book, ISBN, quantity, how the book will be used, date needed.

PRENTICE HALL
Paramus, NJ 07652

A Simon & Schuster Company

On the World Wide Web at http://www.phdirect.com

Prentice-Hall International (UK) Limited, *London*
Prentice-Hall of Australia Pty. Limited, *Sydney*
Prentice-Hall Canada Inc., *Toronto*
Prentice-Hall Hispanoamericana, S.A., *Mexico*
Prentice-Hall of India Private Limited, *New Delhi*
Prentice-Hall of Japan, Inc., *Tokyo*
Simon & Schuster Asia Pte. Ltd., *Singapore*
Editora Prentice-Hall do Brasil, Ltda., *Rio de Janeiro*

Contents

CHAPTER 2

Using a Broker   *23*

CHAPTER 3

Importing on Your Own   *35*

*Pro Forma Invoice • Commercial Invoice • Consular Invoices •
Certificate of Origin • Article Marking for Origin • Dock Receipt
• Bills of Lading • Certificate of Insurance • Certificate of
Inspection • Packing Lists*

CHAPTER 4

Developing an International Sourcing Plan   *49*

CHAPTER 5

Cultural Issues: Barriers, Caveats, and Expectations   **65**

Learn the Language • Practice the Money Exchange System • Be Flexible • Be Empathetic • Know Some History • Be Protocol- and Etiquette-Conscious • Be Patient • Leave Aggressiveness At Home • Be Prepared to "Wine and Dine" • Take Your Time • Delay the Pricing • Take Plenty of Business Cards • Mementos of the Meeting Promote Harmony • Avoid Embarrassing Situations

Japan: Mother of All Tigers • Taiwan: Fastest-Growing Tiger • The Korean Connection • The Singapore Slingshot • Hong Kong Today and Tomorrow

The German Differences • The English Are Different Too • Euro- pean Generalizations • Northern Europe • The Other Europe • Russia and the Commonwealth of Independent States (CIS)

Israel

Brazil and Industrialization • Argentina: Closer to Europe

CHAPTER 6

Negotiation Strategies   **103**

CHAPTER 7

Contracting for the Goods   *123*

CHAPTER 8

Laws in International Business   *141*

CHAPTER 9

International Agreements and Associations *155*

CHAPTER 13

CHAPTER 14

ABOUT THE AUTHOR

James M. Ashley is an author, speaker, and consultant. His expertise spans the fields of purchasing, administrative quality, and foreign trade relations. In 1992 he coauthored (with Harry Hough of the American Purchasing Society) *The Handbook of Buying and Purchasing Management* for Prentice Hall. In addition, Ashley has written numerous articles for newspapers, newsletters, and magazines. As a trainer and keynote speaker, he has addressed such diverse groups as The Japan Society, the International Purchasing Congress, the American Society for Training and Development, the American Brush Manufacturers, and the International Bankers Forum.

In his extensive residency and travels to the Far East, Ashley learned several Oriental languages and served for two years as the program director of the Voice of the United Nations Command (VUNC) in Japan. For more than five years he was a contracts manager and chief negotiator for numerous component and assembly purchasing contracts for IBM in Japan, Korea, Taiwan, and Singapore. In addition, he was the personal computer division representative for international volume purchasing agreements for such commodities as chemicals, integrated circuits, and peripheral computer devices throughout Europe and the Far East.

Ashley is a member of the American Society for Training and Development and past president of the Gold Coast Chapter in Palm Beach, Florida. He is a Certified Purchasing Professional (CPP), on the Board of Directors of the American Purchasing Society, and vice president of the Florida Chapter of the Institute of Management Consultants and an Expert Witness (member of the Technical Advisory Service for Attorneys). He is most proud of being accepted as a member of the Deming Study Group for the Transformation and is listed in *Marquis Who's Who in Finance and Industry and Who's Who in America.*

When asked to provide a useful reference guide for buyers and purchasing managers on the subject of international purchasing, my first thought was, What a great subject. My immediate second thought was that every domestic sector in this country is exerting considerable pressure to export, export, export. The trade imbalance has weakened the dollar, caused unemployment, and generally thrown the country into chaos. My third thought, in light of this dilemma, was to look at the actual dollar value of the trade imbalance.

In 1993, the U.S. imported $827 billion worth of goods and services. It exported $755 billion. The difference of $72 billion is a less than 10% gap. Negotiation courses profess that any buyer with a minimum of skill should be able to come away from the table with at least 10% in savings. To further this premise, if buyers could effect a 10% cost savings across the board, the trade imbalance might be solved, hypothetically anyway. If you are interested in applying this solution, this book will help.

There are, however, extenuating circumstances to this business of global trade. The example above addresses only the right-brain theory, which relates to the economic and financial aspects. Turn on the left brain and start thinking of the social aspect of the globalization of economies, and an entirely different problem presents itself.

Robert Reich, secretary of labor under the Clinton administration, proposed a very interesting theory related to the de-communization of the Soviet Union, the fall of the Berlin Wall, and the opening of Eastern Europe. In his view, it was Levi Strauss, Bon Jovi, Jordache, and personal consumerism that caused the changes, not politics, diplomacy, and the Pentagon.

In the early 1980s, the eminent futurist John Naisbitt *(Megatrends)*, prophesied that the U.S. would be transformed from an industrial society to one of information, services, and technology. Nearly 20 years later, we find that the prophecy has come to pass. Information has become the be-all and end-all of virtually everything we do. Faxes have replaced the Western Union, cellular phones have replaced the two-way radio, and computer E-mail and the Internet have opened up the world in a way that science fiction moviemakers a generation ago could not have imagined. In many cases, the communication revolution has made the job of the international buyer a breeze. But as this book points out, caveat emptor—there is life beyond the fax. That life may have not yet caught up with the fast-paced American businessperson. In fact, many Asian and Middle Eastern marketers are ever more careful in their dealings in spite of those communications.

Another tangent on the subject of international purchasing involves the "soft skills" of the buyer. It is the "hard skills" in purchasing such as sourcing, documenting, negotiating, contracting, expediting, and so on, that one assumes every purchasing agent possesses after a reasonable amount of education, training, and service in the profession. Learning those hard skills may be accomplished with the guidance such books as *Handbook of Buying and Purchasing Management*.[1] *Import/Export: A Guide to Growth, Profits and Market Share* and *Import/Export Can Make You Rich* can provide you with the detailed technical knowledge to move goods from a foreign country through U.S. Customs and on to the consumer.[2]

But the soft skills may be the most important thing to perfect when dealing with other countries, other social groups, other cultures. Soft skills include the ability to recognize agreement, gain the confidence of your counterpart, and ensure a long-term relationship.

As recently as 1982 (according to A. T. Kearney), less than 5% of U.S. manufacturing firms counted a single foreign firm among their top five competitors. By 1992, 30% say that three of their five top competitors are foreign firms.

From a purchasing standpoint, where 50% to 70% of the cost of goods sold is purchased materials, there is growing evidence that international purchasing is here to stay and that American buyers must be aggressively competitive (globally) as well as the marketers.

---

[1] Harry E. Hough and James M. Ashley, *Handbook of Buying and Purchasing Management* (Englewood Cliffs, NJ: Prentice Hall, 1992).

[2] Howard R. Goldsmith, *Import/Export: A Guide to Growth, Profits and Market Share* (Englewood Cliffs, NJ: Prentice Hall, 1989); L. B. Lanze, *Import/Export Can Make You Rich* (Englewood Cliffs, NJ: Prentice Hall, 1988).

The Future World Economic Leaders

Korn/Ferry International and Columbia University business school in 1990 conducted a survey of 1,500 top managers world-wide. The report faulted American managers in the areas of multiculturalism and multilingualism. Surprisingly, only 2% of U.S. executives placed any emphasis on learning a foreign language.

The report further stated, "By discounting the importance of an international outlook, of multilingualism and of foreign assignments, our U.S. respondents gave expression to a parochialism that can only inhibit opportunity." American managers blamed their international problems on a lack of "qualified personnel."

The report also intimated that there will be a sharp decline in U.S. dominance in the international business world by the year 2000. In looking at the entire picture of manufacturing, services, investment, joint-ventures, and mergers, there was a feeling among less than 50% of international managers that the U.S. would remain a world economic leader. Fully 40% think Japan will take over that position.[3]

Tom Peters on Our Global Future

And tomorrow? Our networks of suppliers and producers and distributors and service companies and customers will be so tightly linked that we literally will not be able to tell one locale from another; it will all look the same on the computer screen. No political force can stop the arrival of the borderless economy. Be ready or be lost. As Peter Drucker told Business Month, *"If you don't think globally, you deserve to be unemployed, and you will be."[4]*

---

[3] Korn Ferry International and Columbia University.

[4] Tom Peters, *On Excellence,* Syndicated column.

CHAPTER 1

Preparing for Global Sourcing

In Japan in the mid-1960s, the dollar was worth ¥380 and a posh room at an international hotel on the Ginza could be rented for under US $50. Anyone who's been to Japan lately knows that's hardly the case anymore. What happened? Twenty years of industrial rebirth had brought Japan screaming and kicking into the 20th century with what some travelers have called 21st-century prices.

Along with the prices, however, came enhanced automation, quality, service, and a global mindset that was to put the rest of the industrial world back on its heels. By 1985, a mere 20 years later, gone were shoddy workmanship, rust-bucket automobiles, tacky plastic sandals, and cheap trinkets. Gone as well was the cheap labor. Assembly work wages had risen beyond those in the U.S. All wages in Japan had shot up. By 1990, per capita income in Japan was higher than it was in the U.S. But the cost of living also skyrocketed. A parking place for a car in Tokyo could cost over $1,000 per month.

Japan had made a quantum quality leap, thanks in part to the efforts of W. Edwards Deming and others who were an integral part of the rebuilding of Japanese industry following World War II. During the first 20 years or so after the war, Japanese industry was rebuilt literally from the ground up, with the latest technology. Automation, computers, and robots began to dot the Japanese factory floor as early as the 1960s—creating a significant reduction in the direct labor hours required to produce goods.

1

Some hypothetical but possible strategies of Japanese entrepreneurs on the basis of a 20-year plan include the following:

- 1945 to 1965: Rebuild factories with new equipment.
- 1965 to 1985: Enhance quality, reduce costs, capture world markets.
- 1985 to 2005: Become best in world class.

But Japanese strategists do not necessarily run on a 20-year plan. Their strategies may be projected way beyond that.

In the 1950s, Japan had become a world leader in cameras with Canon, Nikon, Minolta, and the like. By the mid-1960s, Japanese audio electronics (e.g., stereos and tape recorders) became a global standard. Sony, Toshiba, Panasonic, and Sanyo logos began to outsell Grundig, Telefunken, and Blaupunkt from Germany, and Scott, McIntosh, and Harmon Karden from the U.S. Thanks in part to the gas/oil crisis of the mid-1970s, small Japanese automobiles started their formidable march against the big three U.S. automakers. Today, the Japanese are making major export headway in such fields as computers, heavy machinery, and medical equipment. That's 50 years from a pile of rubble to world leader. All this while American industry procrastinated, faltered, became the underdog, and in some industries (e.g., televisions and VCRs) lost the ability to compete at all and ceased to exist. American buyers were obligated to source offshore.

This phenomenon is not unique to Japan. Other Far Eastern countries have since climbed on the bandwagon. Korea, Singapore, Taiwan, and Hong Kong have become known as the "four tigers." Now Thailand, Malaysia, the Philippines, and even Viet Nam have claimed fame as high-volume, low-cost producers. As the rest of the world creeps into various levels of industrialization and competitive advantage, it becomes obvious that the global market is here to stay. American buyers will be increasingly forced to look offshore for their needs.

WHY FOCUS ON THE PACIFIC RIM AREA?

Throughout this book, you will notice a propensity to focus on the Pacific Rim region, also called Asia, the Orient, and the Far East. This is simply because that's where the action is—of most of the international trade dollars anyway. Historians and trade experts have long noted the changes in the focus of trading in terms of ocean shipping lanes. During the first thousand years or so of the Christian calendar, trade routes centered on the Mediterranean Sea, plied by the Phoenicians and others. Carthage (Constantinople) was a major port and the gateway to the Silk/Spice Road. Later, with the Roman Empire, Italy became the center of the known world, and the Mediterranean routes continued to prevail.

With the colonization of the New World, trade lanes began to shift to the Atlantic Ocean and remained there for nearly five hundred years. Spain, Holland, and Britain dominated the shipping trade. Raw materials and crafts traveled east to Europe, and manufactured goods and immigrants traveled west.

The years following World War II saw the emergence of trade across the Pacific. International trade had always been there—mostly among the Asian countries—but it now began to move across the Pacific to the Americas. Trade figures from the early 1990s confirm that the dollar values of shipments across the Pacific exceeded those from European areas.

Therefore, in general terms, if you are going to be importing goods, it most likely will be from the Far East. Since World War II, this area has literally gone from rags to riches. The newly industrializing countries/economies (NICs/NIEs) have supplanted the agricultural and natural resource economic base with an industrial base, and with new state-of-the-art equipment and technology as well. Contrast that with the U.S. and Europe, both of whom continue struggling to replace outdated plants, equipment, and technologies.

There are still things going on in Europe, of course; particularly with the newly formed European Economic Community, the merging of East European nations into that matrix, and the newly independent countries of the former USSR. All these areas bear watching as possible sources.

Another reason for stressing Asia for potential sourcing is that the culture, sociology, and philosophy of that region is much different from the Euro-American way of doing business. European paradigms are similar to that of the U.S. (that's where we learned most of them) and the business traveler will find business methods less mystifying when dealing in that area than in the Far East.

It has been said that Asians communicate in a high-context manner as opposed to the Westerner's low-context manner. Simply put, the difference between low and high context can be summed up as follows:

High Context	*Low Context*
Harmony	Conflict, win/lose
Relationships	Business deals
Group/team dynamics	Individualism/ego
Listening/following	Talking/leading
Nonverbal	Verbal
Long-term	Short-term
Cautious	Risk-taking
Cooperative	Competitive

These descriptions are gross generalizations, to be sure. The point is to alert buyers and negotiators (and anyone else venturing to the Far East) that things are different there. Expect differences, learn to live with them, empathize with them, and develop strategies to deal with them, and you will be successful. There's no time to waste.

John Naisbitt in *Megatrends Asia* predicted that by the year 2000, "Asia will become the dominant region of the world; economically, politically and culturally." He further prophesied that China, known to the Chinese some thousands of years ago as the "Middle Kingdom," will again be at the center of it all.[1] That view is shared by the Chinese as well as was mentioned earlier in this chapter.

A final reason to seek long-term relationships with the Far East is that the area from India around the Pacific Rim to Japan consists of over three billion people—more than half of the entire world's population. It is the single largest, newly emerging conglomeration of consumers in the world. And they now have money to spend, thanks to all the exports they are sending to the rest of the world.

The U.S. has increased its importing from Asia substantially in the past dozen years or so. It remains to be seen what impact American marketers can have on exporting to the three billion emerging consumers to balance the trade figures.

---

[1] John Naisbitt, *Megatrends Asia* (New York: Simon & Schuster, 1996).

DECIDING WHETHER TO SOURCE FROM A FOREIGN COUNTRY

Before you decide to go outside the U.S. to buy anything, let's decide whether you really need to import at all. The following reasons for doing so are typical:

- To save money (lower total cost)
- To find a second source to protect continuity of supply
- To obtain higher quality than that available in the U.S.
- To obtain products that are not manufactured in the U.S at all
- To complete with others who are importing similar products
- To be a part of the big picture and show that your company is international by making ties to foreign lands

The last answer is probably the weakest. Without first getting a positive response to the first five reasons, just going overseas for the travel, the shopping, the thrill of it all, is a poor excuse. Chapters 2 and 4 will discuss, in detail, how to go about making these critical decisions. After all, dealing with another country is still not as easy as one would like to believe. As a prerequisite to importing, purchasing managers must also ask:

1. What recourse do I have if the foreign producer fails?
2. How can I be sure I will receive the right quality?
3. How do I ensure timely delivery?
4. What about unanticipated costs, fees, duties, and commissions?
5. Will I have to make large, long-term commitments?
6. How can I ensure that the foreign supplier will be there when needed?
7. What happens when the currency exchange rate escalates?
8. How do I sue the supplier for damages or nonperformance?
9. How do unions operate in the supplier's country?
10. What if there is a war in the supplier's country?

All this is not meant to intimidate potential importers. Just remember that when placing an order overseas, you must be prepared for a different way of doing business. The remaining chapters provide answers to these and many other questions that have been asked by novice as well as experienced importers.

HIRING AN EXPERT

Initially, you are probably having reservations about jumping into the international marketplace with both feet. If so, your best bet is to hire an import broker. The job of the import broker is to act as an intermediary between a buyer in this country and an overseas seller. A broker acts as an agent and accordingly charges a fee for these services—customarily a percentage of the cost of the goods. This fee is for the broker's knowledge and expertise as well as services in negotiating, preparing documents, communicating with the seller, and taking care of all the details necessary to make the deal go through at the lowest cost to the buyer.

In that regard, purchasing managers should hire a broker who is not only familiar with the country of origin of the products but who is also familiar with the products themselves. Accordingly, it would be unwise to engage the services of a textile import broker if you are sourcing computer parts. The details of brokering are covered in Chapter 2.

THINKING GLOBALLY

"We have to face it. [The United States is] no longer economically self-sufficient or capable of commercial isolation. International commerce is vital to American prosperity."[2] This statement says it all. The first thing managers need to know about getting into the business of international purchasing is how to think globally.

This should be easy for an American, who has grown up with a potpourri of immigrant influences from many parts of the world. But it isn't necessarily so. America has been described as a melting pot for the world's people dissatisfied with their lot. Virtually every town and city is made up of many national origins, national customs, and national mores. For exam-

---

[2] Lennie Copeland and Lewis Griggs, *Going International* (New York: Plume, Random House), 1985.

Case Study

In 1990, tycoon T. Boone Pickens purchased 21% of the stock in a Japanese auto parts company. He thought that because of his percentage ownership that he should be accorded a seat on the board of directors of that firm. In America that might be the case, but the Japanese like to limit their directors to Japanese nationals and shun influence from the outside. Mr. Pickens traveled to Japan and during a meeting of the board of directors exclaimed, in no subtle way, just what he thought of the way the Japanese were doing business. Naturally, his quest was a failure. Some reporters covering the story proclaimed that such arrogant displays of force could set Japanese–American relations back 20 years. Many Japanese from every industry remember this display of "ugly Americanism." Mr. Pickens could have used the expertise of a broker, consultant, or other intermediary to smooth communication given the cultural and business differentials.

---

ple, Jewish immigrants celebrate Hanukkah and Yom Kippur, Germans celebrate Octoberfest, the French honor Bastille Day, the Irish celebrate St. Patrick's Day, the Japanese have the Bon Festival, and the Chinese celebrate the Chinese New Year. Americans are not starved for diversity. The differences, however, go much deeper than a once-a-year celebration.

Knowing how a salesperson from another country thinks would be tantamount to being able to consummate a perfect purchase from that country. That may be difficult. If you have ever studied a foreign language, the teacher probably told you that when you begin to think in French, for example, you'll be well on your way to becoming fluent in French. Beyond that, the idea is to allow for international diversity, empathize with others' ways, make room for those differences in the way you conduct business, and above all avoid adopting the attitude that you are the buyer, it's your check, and you're always right. Demands like this will be perceived by others as arrogance, a trait that has negatively stereotyped Americans in the global marketplace.

That is not to say that people from other countries do not cause consternation by displaying their own ethnic idiosyncrasies, but the more room that is given for such diversity, the farther you will be along the road to a congenial long-term relationship with your international supplier. Cultural differences are covered in detail in Chapter 5.

ESTABLISHING LONG-TERM RELATIONSHIPS

It would be a real waste of effort to spend up to a year's worth of time and money sourcing, negotiating, contracting, and managing an offshore supplier only to discover that you have to do it all over again. It's bad enough when resourcing domestically. A good rule of thumb is to use a factor of 10 when calculating the costs of doing business offshore. Although the cost of the product may be less, outside the U.S. the cost of doing business can be 10 times greater. There are many tangible and intangible reasons for this, including the following:

- Travel costs associated with sourcing, negotiations, contracts, and management
- Shipping costs, custom duties, and insurance
- Intangible costs (e.g., delays in time to market, holdups in shipping, procrastination by the supplier in resolving issues, negotiations, engineering changes and communication headaches)

Even after considering these reasons, purchasing managers will often find that the aggregate, fully burdened unit cost for an item is still significantly less offshore than at home. If you continually find yourself changing suppliers, however, that may not be true.

UNDERSTANDING HOW FOREIGN SUPPLIERS THINK

If there is any constant in building and maintaining a relationship with an offshore supplier, it is the fact that the supplier's expectations will probably be radically different from your own. Foremost on the list is the expectation of time. In Asia, life has been plodding along pretty well for about 5,000 years. As the saying goes over there, "What's another year . . . more or less." Europe boasts a lineage of over 2,000 years or so, interrupted continually by war and changes of leadership. In the Middle East, businesspeople practice the most annoying habit of being out of the country when you (after a 12-hour flight) arrive for your appointed meeting. Time is not of the essence. (More on this in Chapter 5.)

Another aspect of time is the American propensity to view business in terms of fiscal quarters, profits, investment, and stockholders. Americans project this to offshore suppliers, who have a hard time dealing with the so-called Wall Street mind. Asian companies focus on market share, customer satisfaction and corporate longevity. To many offshore suppliers, the most important issue is the customer and his or her perception of quality and fitness for use. It is the supplier's opinion that if you take care of that, profits will flow. Incidentally, in most communist/socialist countries, present or past, the very idea of a foreign company making a profit from its labor is disgusting and forbidden by law (see Chapter 8 for a disccusion of intellectual property rights).

When Americans use the phrase *in the long run,* they have to inject real sincerity to overcome an offshore supplier's perception of a mere flippant remark. It is just this sort of perception of insincerity that outsiders have of many American business practices which include short term objectives. It was not always this way. Before World War II, the U.S. was pretty much self-sufficient. It manufactured almost everything needed at home and sold it at home. Just after the war, with the world's industrial base destroyed, the rest of the world was frantically buying from the U.S. By the late 1960s, however, the world's factories were rebuilt, and foreign imports began to creep in. U.S. suppliers found competing with low-wage imported products difficult, and many companies went out of business. This forced buyers to look elsewhere for their needs.

It was during this period that Hollywood produced the movie *The Ugly American.* Although the film's story line related to the pomposity of Americans in the political and diplomatic arenas, similar injustices were perpetrated throughout the business world as well. Americas are working even harder now to erase that stereotype through revised thinking coupled with renewed empathy for diverse cultures.

In contrast to the American fiscal–quarter–profit mindset, Asian and European companies plan 5 to 10 years. Visions are projected out 20 years and more. It is said that one American businessman, when confronted with his short-term thinking, asked his Japanese counterpart, "Well, just how far out is your strategic planning?" The reply, "Oh, about a hundred years." You must understand the religious practice of ancestor worship in Japan to

---

Case Study

Computers running at 100 MHz were unheard of in 1981, when IBM developed the first PC running at less than 5 MHz. Some predicted interference with FM radio broadcasting stations running at those frequencies (i.e., 87.5 to 104 MHz). Those fears were quickly overcome. In the early 1990s, you could buy a 100-MHz+ machine for half the price of the 5-MHz one in 1981. And in 1997, a basic 200-MHz computer could cost under $1,000.

---

even begin to grasp the meaning of this sort of long-term planning. Another such story comes from a Chinese official who proclaimed that "one day" China will be the number-one nation in the world. When pressed for a more specific time frame for this event, he matter-of-factly remarked, "Oh, in four or five hundred years." A mere 10% of their historical 5,000-year existence. Now that's long-term thinking. Let's take this issue of time and look at some ways to win the trust of offshore suppliers.

Long-Term Thinking

Business cases should be portrayed in terms of *years* at the very least. Show how things might be in 3 to 5 years. Have projections of market changes based on yet-undiscovered technology. Project your vision 10 years down the road. Even if your ideas might seem unbelievable today, long-term thinkers appreciate your ability to believe that you and your company will *be there* to challenge the future.

Time Is Money

This short-term-thinking idea is projected by Americans when only a few days are allowed for negotiations, meetings appear rushed, and participants feel as though they are a slave of the clock rather than a master of the relationship. You can overcome this perception at the first meeting by limiting the agenda to company overviews, relationships, introductions, meeting strategies, and entertainment choices. Allot a couple of hours for

Case Study

This author used the relationship (long-term-thinking) approach first in Taipei, Taiwan. My only overhead transparency for the first, 10 A.M., one-hour meeting looked like this:

- Introductions
  Supplier
  Buyer
- Company presentations
  Supplier
  Buyer
- Discussion of mutual visions
- Decision on location for lunch
- Adjourn

I was hardly out the door when my counterpart drew me aside and excitedly pronounced that he had never (17 years with his company) had a more wonderful first meeting. He wished that all Americans could be so accommodating to their needs. Interestingly enough, the supplier's last-day agenda transparency ended with "Location for Dinner!" And we all laughed together at our success in the meeting of the minds. As a footnote, the relationship is still alive and well nearly 15 years later.

this first meeting. Have each side provide information on company history, goals, customers, leaders, and visions for the future of the relationship. Show the supplier that extra time has been planned for individual discussions and express a willingness to extend your stay in their country (or arrange for extended meetings at your site) so that an agreeable and sustaining consensus may be set.

The first meeting with a new supplier is not the time to blast into discussions of costs, delivery, quality, specifications, and such. These actions merely confirm the other side's expectations of short-term thinking. As a contrast, if you have ever been pressured into a sale, and you were coerced to sign today or lose any hope of anticipated riches, you will get a feeling for how foreigners react to Americans in a rush.

Deadlines

Most other cultures do not believe in deadlines. They perceive deadlines as an ultimatum instead of a challenge. In most parts of the Middle East, however, a deadline may be taken literally, and you soon find the end (death) of your business there.

Asian business is conducted with more of a teamwork approach. Decisions involve dozens, sometimes hundreds, of diverse entities inside and outside the company. The Japanese may consult their suppliers, governmental agencies, international market analysts, research groups, or even consultants to reach a decision. All this takes an inordinate (by American standards) amount of time. You must be prepared for this and adjust your time frame for agreement accordingly. The good news is that once a decision is reached, all are in total and agreeable consensus, implementation is a snap, and the potential for discovering some unturned stones is minimal.

Therefore, it is to your advantage to develop your own long-term team. It will not be necessary to book airline tickets for two dozen or three dozen people however. With today's communications, you have all the necessary tools to arrive at the supplier's site with a hundred team members. You can caucus with them at any time and provide the picture of a united team to your supplier.

FIRST STEPS IN BECOMING INTERNATIONAL

First, purchasing managers must realize and admit that they may be far behind their foreign competitors in "globalese." In *Training and Development,* Steve Rhinesmith points to a study that indicates that U.S. executives are far behind their European, Japanese, and Latin American counterparts in valuing experience outside their company's domestic headquarters and in speaking foreign languages.[3]

---

[3] Steven Rhinesmith, *Training and Development* (Alexandria, VA: ASTD Press, 1991).

When you decide to "go it alone," it's always wise to make sure you have the necessary prerequisites. How is their business conducted? How do they negotiate? What are the pitfalls? What are the advantages? Much of this information can be learned from your experiences with an import broker. Because brokers are in business to make a profit, however, they probably won't tell you everything you need to know. After all, they are protecting their continuing business. You, therefore, must do some studying on your own.

Perhaps the most important difference in the way Americans conduct business and the way the rest of the world does is in face-to-face communication. As the costs of travel have escalated, especially for the middle-of-the-week business traveler, Americans have made significant use of every new high-tech device as soon as it is available. This means that pagers, fax machines, E-mail, overnight express mail, and video conferencing have taken a place in corporate communication. Nevertheless, as a former IBM manager once told me, "while a faxed picture may be worth a thousand words, a handshake can be worth a thousand faxes."

This is not to suggest that every meeting, every communication must be face-to-face. Many times, an initial meeting between buying and selling parties is sufficient to cement relationships for an extended period of time. Suppliers in the three major markets of the Far East, Europe, and South America all demand a degree of personal contact to provide the necessary ingredients for successful and cost-effective relationships.

Just as important as being there is understanding the rules of the game—their game. If, for instance, you are sourcing vegetables in Chile, it is helpful to understand the way agriculture is managed in that country. How is land owned? What about the farmer's associations? What part does the government play? How is produce brought to market, packaged, stored, preserved, and shipped? What environmental issues come into play (e.g., fertilizer or pesticide use, and field water outflows)? All this information may be available from Prochile contacts (see Appendix A). A trip to Chile that includes a tour of the farms where your purchases will be grown will greatly enhance your knowledge as well as provide valuable material for your negotiations and communications. Have a meal with the farm workers. Ask them what's happening. Even if you are purchasing through a broker or international distributor, such information will be useful in your purchasing efforts if only to provide a sanity check on pricing, quality, and delivery issues.

In the Far East, there is an unwritten prohibition for using the word *No*. No matter what context you use *no* in, it's a real deal killer. If you say no to another helping of rice it can be just as damaging to the relationship as saying no to a term or condition in the contract. Chapter 5 outlines some alternative responses to allow purchasing managers to indicate a negative response without actually saying the word. It's a strange custom to be sure, but it gives rise to the cliché that the Japanese never say no, which is very true.

THE IMPORT PICTURE

Exhibit 1–1 depicts comparative economic indicators of the U.S. and its major trading partners. What is interesting for purchasing managers to note is the relative comparisons of stability among the countries/areas listed. The lowest inflation rate is found in Canada and the highest is found in China. China, of course, is just coming out of communism into partial free-market capitalism, that is, from virtually no personal spendable income

Country	Real GDP [1]		Inflation rates [1]		Unemployment rates [2]		Government budget balances [3]		Merchandise trade balance		Current accounts balance	
	1994	1995	1994	1995	1994	1995	1994	1995	1994	1995	1994	1995
	<------Percent change from previous period-----><-------Billions of dollars-------><--% of GDP-->											
G-7 countries												
United States	3.5	2.1	2.6	3.0	6.1	5.6	-2.0	-1.6	-176.0	-194.0	-2.2	-2.4
Canada	4.6	2.4	0.2	2.1	10.4	9.6	-5.3	-4.4	11.0	20.5	-3.0	-2.5
Japan	0.5	2.2	0.7	-0.2	2.9	3.1	-3.5	-3.9	145.0	107.0	2.8	2.3
Germany	2.9	2.1	2.7	1.8	9.6	9.3	-2.6	-3.1	39.0	64.7	-1.0	-0.8
United Kingdom	3.8	2.7	2.4	2.9	9.2	8.4	-6.9	-5.0	-20.0	-24.8	0.0	-1.1
France	2.9	2.7	1.7	2.1	12.2	11.5	-6.0	-5.0	12.0	12.1	0.6	1.3
Italy	2.2	3.1	4.0	5.4	11.3	11.9	-9.0	-7.4	34.1	29.1	1.5	1.9
EU	2.8	2.7	3.0	3.1	11.5	11.1	-6.3	-6.1	63.9	13.0	0.3	0.6
OECD Europe	2.4	2.9	7.5	6.7	11.2	10.8	-5.8	-5.0	21.0	39.5	0.6	0.8
Mexico	3.6	-6.0	6.6	35.0	3.7	6.5	-21.0	-23.0	-17.8	-19.9	-7.8	-0.3
Total OECD	2.9	2.4	4.1	4.5	8.0	7.8	-3.9	-3.4	-9.4	-33.9	-0.2	-0.1
									<-------Billions of dollars----->			
China	11.8	9.5	21.7	15.5	n/a	n/a	n/a	n/a	-12.2	17.0	7.3	7.8
Taiwan	6.1	6.3	4.1	3.8	n/a	n/a	n/a	n/a	11.5	7.6	5.9	5.0
Korea	8.4	9.0	6.2	5.0	2.4	2.0	n/a	n/a	1.9	-9.9	-4.5	-9.9

[1] Percent change from previous year.
[2] Percent of total labor force.
[3] As a percent of GDP
Note: Trade and current account balances for China, Korea, and Taiwan are in billions of dollars.
Source : *OECD Economic Outlook*, 58, 1995; IMF *World Economic Outlook*, Oct. 1995, *International Financial Statistics*, Feb. 1996, and *China & North Asia Monitor*, No. 2, Feb. 1996. World Trade Oorganization (WTO) press release, press/44 Mar. 22, 1996.

Exhibit 1–1. Comparative Economic Indicators of the United Staes and of Specificid Major Trading Partners, 1994-95

into what we call consumerism. People make higher wages and buy things, the prices go up, supply and demand, a fairly new concept for China.

Other interesting categories are unemployment rates and trade balance. Low unemployment might mean that times are good and your supplier may remain stable. High deficits in the trade balance (e.g., between the U.S. and Japan) might mean that the U.S. government could levy high import duties (100% or more, as in the auto duty threat in 1995) on the very goods you will be importing from Japan. This will obviously cause you to change your plans quickly and radically.

Other economic comparison charts can be found in the *World Almanac* and publications of the International Trade Commission, the Department of Commerce, and the Customs Service. Another source to try is the Internet (see Appendix B for some Web addresses).

FINDING SUPPLIERS

Purchasing departments have used traditional means for identifying new sources for old products and initial sources for new products. Such publications as the *Thomas Register* and *MacRae's Blue Book* have been at the forefront of resources used in the sourcing process. Therefore, it is not surprising that many countries have adopted similar formats.

The *Taiwan Yellow Pages* is a typical sourcebook for that country. Many other countries also have such yellow pages. The Australian Trade Commission, for example, provides an annual update to their one-thousand-plus-page *Australian Exports*. These are available by writing to the appropriate embassy for the country from which you are interested in importing (see Appendix A). Chapter 4 contains more detailed information on sourcing.

DEALING WITH LANGUAGE BARRIERS

In the global marketplace, there are naturally many language barriers. First is the spoken word. When in France, speak French; when in Sweden, speak Swedish. You should at least be able to say hello, yes, no, and goodbye. You will undoubtedly be at the mercy of an interpreter much of the time if your supplier's counterpart does not speak English or another language in which you are fluent.

However, there are other languages as well. International shipping has its own unique language or set of terms and acronyms with which you may not be familiar. International insurance and currency exchange have a language all their own. In addition, long-term relationships, joint ventures, and investments all have their own individual terminology, much of which is quite different from that used in the U.S. The glossary contains definitions of these and other terms. Another good reference for industry-specific terms is the *Dictionary of International Business Terms,* a pocket-sized Barron's business guide available at most book stores.

Even the English language can be miscommunicated. Many everyday terms used casually in American business may mean just the opposite in some other country. For example, to "table" an issue in the U.S. means to put that issue aside for later consideration. In the United Kingdom, to "table" means to bring the issue to the forefront and discuss it immediately. Most are familiar with the cliché that in Asia *yes* generally means that the other party has heard you and understood the words you said. It rarely means, "Yes, I agree with or will do what you said."

Chapter 5 details many of the nuances of international parlance to the extent that you will be alerted to question, when necessary, the words and terms you hear and avoid getting caught in the trap of "assuming" the wrong meaning.

NEGOTIATING WITH OFFSHORE SUPPLIERS

"When in Rome . . ." The old saying applies to negotiations as well. When you are outside the confines of familiarity, you will quickly find that other people from other countries have other ideas regarding negotiations. Most suppliers from other parts of the world will initially perceive you as a novice, poorly informed, and not much of an international businessperson if you do not negotiate (at great length most likely) to procure the best price. Now we're not talking here about haggling or hard selling/hard buying. We're talking about intelligent, well-strategized, well-presented negotiation tactics—tactics that take into account the sometimes subtle differences in methods as you travel from country to country. Take, for example, the concept of time once again. You might think that a couple of days will be sufficient to cover all the issues and arrive at an amicable conclusion. The supplier, however, may have another concept of time.

Other differences you will encounter in the negotiation arena will be nonverbal, nonemotional, and ever-so-crafty. For you to be "streetwise" regarding such idiosyncrasies is to provide your company with the best

> **Case Study**
>
> *In the political arena, the negotiations that led to the end of the Viet Nam War provide a classic example of the concept of time as perceived in different parts of the world. The U.S. negotiator, Averell Harriman, and his staff rented a suite of rooms in Paris on a month-to-month basis. The North Vietnamese contingent, on the other hand, leased a large country estate for a year. With an option to renew!*

price while at the same time gaining the respect of your counterparts. Many of these methods are described in Chapter 5.

UNDERSTANDING PURCHASE ORDER RESTRICTIONS

The international paper chase is more than just dotting the *i*'s and crossing the *t*'s. The language differences become even more pronounced when you begin to read a written purchasing contract after it has been annotated or modified by someone from another country. But it's a little more serious in this instance than misspelling-riddled and grammatically convoluted instruction booklet that came with a foreign-manufactured product.

The supplier's team of contract people will wrangle for hours over the meaning of a particular word and its translation from several different reference sources. American legalese is difficult to decipher in many languages, and you may find that one single word winds up to be a complete phrase or sentence in Hindi or Chinese. The best source, if available, is a copy of Barron's guides to *Talking Business in* [the name of the supplier's country]. Even then, the supplier's language dictionaries might say something different, and you may have to alter the contract to obtain a consensus. Contracts are covered in detail in Chapter 7.

LEGAL ASPECTS OF IMPORTING

When you begin to talk about the laws, treaties, and agreements relating to international trade, you unearth a massive bowl of alphabet soup: GATT, NAFTA, WTO, ITC, CEBRA, ASEAN, and the list goes on and on. All these and more will be discussed in Chapters 8 and 9 to give purchasing managers a reasonable introduction to what American leaders and trade officials have done to ensure an honest and equitable passage of goods across borders.

The issue that is in the forefront of international trade as of this writing is the business of intellectual property rights. Countries such as China still do not fully recognize what they refer to as the "profiteering by individuals at the expense of the masses." Americans call the infringement upon a copyright or patent "counterfeiting." Other societies don't understand this. With all the pressure exerted on China to upgrade its human rights standards and comply with patent and copyright laws, China, as of 1997, still maintains most-favored-nations status with the U.S. But in 1997, intellectual property rights issues still rank high on the U.S./China disagreement list along with human rights issues.

Intellectual property rights are covered in detail in Chapter 8 because of the severe penalties associated with importing counterfeit goods.

ENSURING QUALITY

In Chapter 10, purchasing managers will learn that there is more to measuring quality than the difference between American Standards Association measurements (ASA) in inches and the British Standards Institute (BSI) metric system that is used by most of the rest of the world. You will be challenged by the depth and breadth of quality organizations and the fervor to excel that exists in much of the newly industrialized world.

Far beyond all this is the ISO 9000 series of standards for quality. Although many large American companies are still taking a wait-and-see attitude toward compliance with ISO 9000 specifications as of this writing, the rest of the world is hot on the trail of registrars to perform the necessary qualifications. More information about ISO 9000 can be found in Chapter 11.

VARIOUS INTERNATIONAL ROUTINGS, CARRIERS, AND DOCUMENTATION

What used to be a relatively simple task, shipping, has become a gargantuan industry of its own. Routings, consolidations, and FOB variables are a conglomeration of terms and choices. Purchasers are responsible for understanding tariffs (the rates trucks charge), terminal charges, dimensional weights, and LTL/LCL (less than truck/container load) shipments.

> **Case Study**
>
> *On a trip to Brazil to train purchasing personnel, I was afforded a tour of several factories of major industrial giants like Ford, Bosch, and Volkswagen. The thing that struck me immediately was the national origin of the personnel in a couple of the departments. The design and development engineering areas included many German descendants. In contrast, the quality control and assurance departments were staffed mostly by Japanese. Later I learned that the largest single community of ex-patriot Japanese was located in São Paulo, Brazil. The Brazilian industrialists seem to have picked what they thought were the best cultural origins for specific needs and either brought them to Brazil or trained them from local talent.*

Insurance in-transit is another issue that becomes increasingly more complicated in the international marketplace, so much so that thousands of cases have been tried in the courts and the results of rulings based on misunderstandings and misrepresentation of the rules fill volumes in legal libraries. Chapter 12 attempts to sort out these enigmas.

UNDERSTANDING CUSTOMS DUTIES AND TARIFF SCHEDULES

Perhaps nothing is more intimidating than having to pass through customs upon returning to the U.S. from an overseas trip. A friend of mine once told me that on his first brush with customs he was so nervous that they thought he might be trying to conceal something and he was detained for over 20 minutes while the customs agents went through his belongings with a fine-tooth comb. For the importer, it's not really that bad. If you have all your paperwork in order and provide all the necessary documentation to the customhouse broker, you will have few problems.

Customs duties are called tariffs (not to be confused with trucking tariffs, or rates). The important part of the customs business is to ensure that you are being charged the lowest rate allowable for the particular items you are importing. A small variance in the description of an item may make a very large difference in the rate you are charged. Even if there

Case Study

A preproduction shipment of computer monitors arrived with the customs documents. The goods had been classified as television sets, which qualified for a much higher duty rate. A quick call to the supplier in Taiwan (who, incidentally, manufactured TV sets as well) resolved the problem and resulted in a 40% cost savings on the U.S. customs charges.

is no duty on your items, however, there will be incidental charges that you will need to be aware of (e.g., merchandise-processing fees, federal excise taxes, and harbor maintenance fees). These terms are defined and discussed in Chapter 13.

MANAGING AFTERMARKET REPAIR AND WARRANTY

If you purchase products from Louisville, Kentucky, and there is a service problem, returning the defective parts to Kentucky would not be a problem. Shipping goods back to Indonesia for repair or replacement poses a greater dilemma. Most large overseas companies have anticipated that problem and provide domestic facilities for such needs. Some points to consider include:

- Who pays for shipment, reshipment?
- What is the turnaround time?
- What are the charges?
- How are engineering changes managed?
- How long will stocks of parts be maintained?
- What is "end-of-life"?

Chapter 14 addresses the most common problems that purchasing managers could encounter as importers and provides solutions.

PAYING FOR GOODS

Over the years, the methods of payment to suppliers out of the country have changed somewhat. Banking systems today are much more responsive when transfering funds in the global economy. Nevertheless, managers must be aware of the different means of paying invoices and the foreign exchange rate systems. Currency fluctuation is a major concern when dealing with many countries. Chapter 15 discusses the subject of international payment arrangements and specifics on how to effect the best terms for your particular needs.

CHAPTER 2
Using a Broker

Now that we're all excited about importing, let's get on the phone and start ordering stuff from China. Unfortunately, it's not that easy. First of all, purchasing managers must know something about the business of getting the goods from China to their receiving dock. And that's a big order. The following are just a few of the things to know:

- A little Chinese language (Mandarin and/or Cantonese dialects)
- Chinese government export regulations
- U.S. government import regulations, quotas, safety, and environmental requirements
- International trade laws and regulations
- U.S. Customs regulations, classifications, and tariffs
- International shipping regulations and terminology (e.g., FAS, CIF, ExWorks)
- Currency exchange regulations, rates, policies, and procedures
- Trademark and copyright laws

Regulations, regulations, regulations! If that seems like a mountain of knowledge, you're right. And that's just the tip of the iceberg. The purchasing manager must not only be knowledgeable in these areas but experienced and practiced as well. The ability to make informed decisions quickly is often crucial to ensure the safe, efficient, and legal flow of goods across international boundaries.

The obvious answer for the uninitiated buyer is to use an importer or engage the services of a licensed broker or trading company. Importers and brokers have years of experience with thousands of different commodities, situations, and problem-solving techniques. The small percentage they charge for their services may well be worth paying.

TYPES OF BROKERS

First, there are several kinds or combinations of brokers. These individuals or companies may be small or large businesses and may handle all the necessary activities the purchasing manager requires or specialize only in one or more areas. How a manager will select a broker depends on the manager's current knowledge and how much, if any, of the process he or she wishes to handle. When assessing capabilities, break the process down into smaller segments. Exhibit 2–1 shows the costs and responsibilities borne by the respective entities and assumes that the terms with the supplier are FOB supplier's port of export.

If you don't know how to invest in the stockmarket, you hire a stockbroker. In insurance dealings, you generally purchase a policy through an insurance broker. When buying a home, you will probably engage the services of a real estate broker. These brokers are all agents, subject to the law of agency, and are skilled in the subject matter at hand, familiar with the documentation, the fine print, and the individuals necessary to make a purchase smooth and uncomplicated.

An import broker mirrors this expertise in that he or she becomes the buyer's agent. There are no licensing requirements for handling the details of a purchasing contract; anyone who feels that they possess the necessary skills can do so. But be aware that customhouse brokers and freight forwarders must be licensed.

The job of an import broker is to help find sources of products for the buyer, develop and negotiate contracts, oversee the passage of the goods from the seller to the buyer, manage communication and cross-cultural diversity, establish banking liaisons, and generally perform all those things that the buyer does not possess the expertise or knowledge to accomplish.

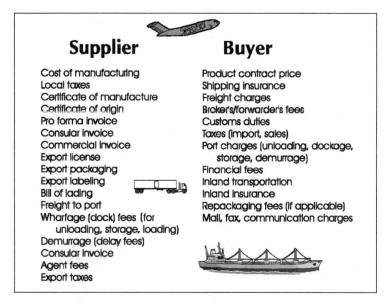

Supplier

Cost of manufacturing
Local taxes
Certificate of manufacture
Certificate of origin
Pro forma invoice
Consular invoice
Commercial invoice
Export license
Export packaging
Export labeling
Bill of lading
Freight to port
Wharfage (dock) fees (for
    unloading, storage, loading)
Demurrage (delay fees)
Consular invoice
Agent fees
Export taxes

Buyer

Product contract price
Shipping insurance
Freight charges
Broker's/forwarder's fees
Customs duties
Taxes (import, sales)
Port charges (unloading, dockage,
    storage, demurrage)
Financial fees
Inland transportation
Inland insurance
Repackaging fees (if applicable)
Mail, fax, communication charges

Exhibit 2–1. Importing Costs Analysis

If a broker handles customs matters, he or she must also be licensed by the U.S. Treasury Department as a customhouse broker. A customhouse broker is classified as an agent, and you will be asked to sign a customs power of attorney allowing the broker to sign papers on your behalf. Note that the onus of responsibility for the accuracy of all transactions as well as the actions and statements made by the broker in your behalf are *the purchasing manager's* ultimate responsibility.

BROKERS AND THE LAW OF AGENCY

As protection for the buyer, an import broker is subject to the law of agency. Therefore, the buyer, as the principal; and the broker, as the agent, have duties and responsibilities that are clearly defined by law. A buyer could be classified as an agent (i.e., purchasing agent) for his or her company as well and would thus be subject to the law of agency. However, once a broker is brought in as a second-level agent, things naturally get more complicated.

James Ritterskamp, Jr., in the *Purchasing Manager's Deskbook of Purchasing Law,* lists the following seven duties of an agent as established by law over the years:

1. Duty of loyalty to the principal
2. Duty of obedience to the instructions of the principal
3. Duty to perform with reasonable care
4. Duty to account to the principal
5. Duty to inform the principal
6. Duty of confidence
7. Duty to bring the necessary skills and training to the agency[1]

According to the Ritterskamp, duty of loyalty to the principal, the broker as an agent must act on the buyer's behalf, put aside all personal interests (and interests of the seller), and ensure that there is no conflict of interest involved in any dealings.

It is widely known that import brokers, while also serving as a representative of a seller, may be graciously entertained by sellers while in their country as well as when the seller is visiting the broker. There is little anyone can do to reverse this timeworn practice. However, as long as the purchasing manager is aware of this possibility; does the homework on pricing, quality, and delivery of products; and proceeds cautiously when a broker is overly anxious to use a particular source that he or she alone finds attractive, the manager should be fine. Those brokers who have a long and venerable track record usually do not get involved in such conflicts of interest, but it is always wise to check out sources yourself and not rely totally on the recommendations of a broker.

It is the common practice of some brokers to act as a dual agent. This situation occurs when a buyer expresses interest in a product the broker has dealt with or in a supplier with a longstanding relationship with the broker. A broker acting in this instance will ask you to sign a form called "disclosed dual agent." Because the agent is representing both the buyer and the seller, the agent finds him- or herself walking a tightrope.

---

[1] James Ritterskamp, Jr., *Purchasing Manager's Deskbook of Purchasing Law* (Englewood Cliffs, NJ: Prentice Hall, 1987).

Import brokers typically represent the buyer. Export brokers working from a particular country of origin typically represent the seller. You should establish early on whom the broker is representing. In the case of the dual representation, you need the dual agency disclosure.

A broker's duty of obedience to the instructions of the principal refers to the buyer's instructions. In this instance, you are the principal. All will be well if you periodically audit the documentation and establish that, in fact, all your directives were followed. Such things as freight carriers, port charges, point of passage of title to the goods, and packaging/packing requirements as spelled out in the contract with the broker must be followed to the letter. Most brokers will comply and realize that deviation from the contract terms subjects them to dismissal as the agent.

Exercising reasonable care is a given. No buyer wants to do business with a broker that continually makes excuses for sloppy paperwork, missed deadlines, faulty communication, or damaged goods. Brokers, or agents of any sort, for that matter, who continually make apologies or excuses for mistakes that occur during their performance of duties are obviously undesirable.

Accountability refers generally to the exchange of gifts and gratuities. A buyer is not to accept items from a broker as an incentive to do business with that broker. It is understood that this sort of activity goes on in other countries, and despite this book's directives to empathize with and understand the diversities that abound throughout the world, you must provide a high ethical standard for your company's business dealings. This goes not only for the agent/principal relationship as when dealing with a broker but for all transactions and supplier relationships as well.

Any personal gain for the buyer will eventually produce charges of a conflict of interest and may result in a company's dismissal of the buyer or even legal action. As an alternative, negotiate prices, costs, terms, and conditions on purchases in lieu of offered gifts and gratuities. As long as the benefit is to the company and not to the buyer personally, the business of gifts may be much more acceptable. Ritterskamp suggests that any such rebates or remunerations be made payable to the company to further protect the buyer's personal ethical standing.

The importance of the broker's duty to keep the principal informed is illustrated by the following case study. A broker's withholding of pertinent information to a buyer can be just as damaging as information withheld from a company by a buyer.

Case Study

During negotiations for a large electronics contract, the buyer for a Fortune 100 company was notified through personal in-country contacts that the CEO of the supplier who had provided the lowest negotiated pricing was able to provide such an attractive package because he was involved in gambling and other underworld activities. It was alleged that this supplier had connections to a money-laundering scheme and faced the possibility of criminal penalties, deportation, and the eventual closing of his company. The buyer, determined to enhance his position in his company through his negotiation skills, withheld this information. He believed that this sort of thing was common practice in the supplier's country and that there was little chance of any charges being filed against the supplier's CEO. As fate would have it, the company did close during the second year of the buyer's contract, and a frenzy to bring up another source for the product caused undue delays in customer shipments.

Confidentiality is of the utmost importance. Usually, the duty of confidence refers to handling intellectual property, trade secrets, and the like. A broker, as well as the buyer, must be careful when discussing proprietary information. There are few breaches of ethical practice that will get one in more trouble than impropriety in the use of another company's trade secrets. That goes for the formula for Coca-Cola as well as the source code for a piece of software.

Another twist to the duty of confidentiality is the business of circumventing the broker once the source of supply is known. Although you might not even think of such a thing, the business of international trade is complicated and loaded with individuals who would cut corners to make a buck. The informed broker will preclude being passed over with what is called a "noncircumvent clause." When you sign this document you agree to allow the broker to process the products for a specified time and restrain yourself from direct orders with the supplier. Obviously, this clause is in the best interests of the broker and protects his or her livelihood. Similarly, the duty of confidentiality enjoins the buyer from releasing to

> **Case Study**
>
> *A buyer contacts a broker for assistance in sourcing a special type of flowering plant for its retail chain of florist shops. The broker in good faith initiates a supply line from Costa Rica. The broker gives the buyer names and addresses so that the buyer may check out the supplier's credentials. Then the buyer goes to Costa Rica and sets up a direct contract with these suppliers, thereby bypassing the broker. This sort of activity does happen.*

other competing brokers the information (e.g., company names, trade secrets, intellectual property, etc.) given in confidence by the first broker.

It is assumed that buyers believe in and practice continual learning. Similarly, it is assumed that brokers possess the necessary skills and training to perform a quality service for the buyer. As for the purchasing function, two associations offer certification in the purchasing profession. The American Purchasing Society offers a certified purchasing professional (CPP) designation, and the National Association of Purchasing Managers offers a certified purchasing manager (CPM) certificate. Both require a written examination and that the individual engage in continuing education and periodic updates.

It is recommended that buyers scrutinize potential brokers through the Better Business Bureau, a credit bureau, and recommendations from existing customers of the broker or similar means as for any supplier. Be aware that many amateurs, beginners, and dabblers can be found in trading companies and brokerage establishments. You know that there are similar individuals in the business of real estate; import brokering is no different.

RESPONSIBILITIES OF A CUSTOMHOUSE BROKER

Although individuals who call themselves brokers may assume the general duties of an import broker, a freight forwarder, or a trading company, not all may perform the duties of a customhouse broker, who must be licensed and regulated by the U.S. Department of the Treasury. The customhouse broker is solely concerned with the documentation of the movement of goods into the U.S. from a foreign country and the payments of duties thereon to the U.S. government. That is not to say that a customhouse broker may not perform all the other duties; it's the license from the Department of the Treasury that sets the customhouse duties apart from the others. To obtain that license, the individual must pass two long and thorough exams on the Customs Regulations of the U.S. and the Harmonized Tariff Schedule of the U.S., and also undergo a comprehensive, in-depth character investigation.

Now we have a third agent in the importing chain; the buyer, the import broker, and the customhouse broker. However, if the buyer is managing the importing of goods, he or she may do so without the services of any of the others, including the customhouse broker. It may be expeditious to assume the duties of import broker and freight forwarder; however, it is recommended that the buyer retain the services of a customhouse broker for the company's own protection. Otherwise, the buyer will be required to post a substantial surety bond with the U.S. Customs Service to submit documentation. The bond must be made with a surety company (yet another agency in the picture) and usually requires a letter of credit with a deposit in cash, which in some cases may be up to three times the value of each shipment.

Another advantage of using the services of a customhouse broker becomes evident during the finite negotiations regarding classification of the imported goods according to the Harmonized Tariff Schedule (the rate schedule). More discussion of tariffs appears in Chapter 13.

If the purchasing manager's company is reasonably large and does a fair amount of importing, it might be advisable to have someone designated as an in-house customs agent and have that individual licensed. In addition to the necessary studying (which the buyer should perform in any event), the licensing fees are only about $300, and the exam is not impossibly difficult if one is adequately prepared.

A typical flow of the activities of a customhouse broker might be the following:

1. Receives a copy of the bill of lading or pro forma invoice
2. Prepares customs entry forms
3. Advises the buyer of applicable duties
4. Posts a surety bond
5. Submits documents to U.S. Customs Service

6. Coordinates with the shipper or freight forwarder

7. Clears goods with U.S. Customs

For more information about the U.S. Customs Service, see Chapter 13.

RESPONSIBILITIES OF A FREIGHT FORWARDER

Another licensed individual or agent in the importing chain is a freight forwarder. His or her primary concern is with the physical movement of goods either within or outside the country. The freight forwarder is versed in many areas of shipping including:

- Knowledge of sources and contacts
- Freight (e.g., ocean, air, and land) costs
- Insurance costs
- Carrier selection
- Consolidation of shipments (i.e., combining several shipments for several companies into one container)
- Containerization alternatives and fees
- Booking procedures
- Consular invoice fees
- Ocean bills of lading
- Dock fees and warehousing
- Duty charges
- Packing fees

In addition, some forwarders may be able to supply what are called "advanced services," including advice on market conditions, sources of supply, and translation and interpretation services. With these additions, forwarders become full-service agents. If they employ a licensed customhouse broker, they may be able to handle all your needs. Typically, these companies are concerned with ocean or air movement of goods but also handle overland shipments from Mexico, Canada, and other points in the Americas.

A freight forwarder dealing with ocean shipping must be licensed by the Federal Maritime Commission (FMC). For information on regulations and licensing requirements, contact:

Office of Freight Forwarders
Bureau of Tariffs, Certification & Licensing
Federal Maritime Commission
800 N. Capitol St. NW
Washington, DC 20573
(202) 523-5843

Air cargo forwarders are regulated by the International Air Transportation Association (IATA) in Montreal, Canada. The U.S. subsidiary is Cargo Network Services, Inc., and information may be obtained from:

Cargo Network Services
300 Garden City Plaza, Suite 312
Garden City, NY 11503
(516) 747-3312

The following represents a typical flow of procedures handled by a freight forwarder:

1. Receives goods from supplier
2. Consolidates buyer's shipments with others, if necessary, into single container units to the appropriate port of entry
3. Prepares the ocean/air bill of lading
4. Prepares customs forms
5. Books space on cargo vessels
6. Negotiates with steamship/air carriers
7. Provides for movement to port, wharfage, loading, and handling
8. Monitors loading of cargo
9. Tracks vessel/air carrier during voyage
10. Notifies buyer of arrival date and time

11. Expedites carrier delays in route
12. Invoices buyer for all charges

A freight forwarder should be contacted for information on costs and documentation as soon as the purchasing manager receives a quote or pro forma invoice from the overseas supplier. As with any supplier, get several quotes from forwarders, as routings and procedures may vary between agents.

RESPONSIBILITIES OF A TRADING COMPANY

Where trading companies differ from brokers and forwarders is in the fact that by virtue of their name, they provide a full-service function usually at no fee to the importer. They charge the exporter and of course are representing the exporter's interests. In addition to the normal and customary duties of international trade, trading companies offer marketing, sourcing, and financial services. In addition, in countries with many years of trading experience, such as Japan, trading companies have provided the necessary catalyst to form mutual-benefit industry groups in food processing, petrochemicals, and other raw-material-dependent industries. They assist in the management of offshore ventures—especially in the newly industrializing countries—and provide sources of financing and peripheral investment. Trading companies have further combined their efforts to contribute to large-scale projects such as infrastructure improvements and major factory construction (e.g., China's largest ethylene plant).

Japanese trading companies, not consumed with business dealings in and out of Japan, now provide services between second and third countries without involving Japan. A Japanese trading company might therefore be a choice for sourcing anywhere in the Far East or even other countries where it may have expertise or connections.

Trading companies get involved in environmental and social concerns as well. Many companies are, for example, playing leading roles in promoting recycling and developing alternative energy resources, and are closely involved in the preservation and rehabilitation of tropical forest ecosystems.[2]

---

[2]JETRO, report on the role of trading companies in international commerce.

SELECTING A BROKER

Engaging the services of an import broker is like selecting any supplier, and the same checklist used for that exercise should be used for this. In addition, be aware that the best choice is probably not located in your area. Remember, we are talking here about an *import* broker—not necessarily an officially licensed U.S. customhouse broker. Survey several agencies, looking specifically at such issues as:

- The firm's length of time in business.
- The experience level of its employees.
- The size of the organization.
- Its levels of certification and licensing requirements.
- Its credit references (through D&B, TRW, Equifax, Better Business Bureau, Chamber of Commerce).
- Whether it is currently doing business in your country of interest.
- Whether it is currently doing business in your commodity.
- Names of existing customers as references.
- Types of products it is currently importing.
- Services it offers (e.g., customs documentation, freight forwarding, warehousing, and financing).
- Communications available to it (fax, telex, E-mail. Telex capability is still important. Many foreign companies and agencies still rely on telex).

As a postscript to all this agent and broker confusion, it isn't really all that bad. With a little homework, you should be able to come up with a full-service agency in or near your location that will be able to handle all your needs.

A good place to start sourcing an agent is your local classified phone directory. Depending on your location, you will most likely find listings for customes brokers, freight forwarders, and importers. Contact your chamber of commerce or a large trucking company for referrals. Also try your regional U.S. Customs Service office (see Chapter 13).

CHAPTER 3

Importing on Your Own

Should a purchasing manager decide to launch into importing on his or her own, the first things to consider are the negatives, the pitfalls, and the risks. The international marketplace accommodates its share of dishonest people and companies. As there are scams in the U.S., there are scams abroad. In other instances, quite common in many areas of the world, you may discover that your brand-name merchandise is counterfeit.

You will quickly discover that in many parts of the world, bribery is the normal and customary method of doing business. This unsavory practice is a one-way street to disaster. Once initiated, the price always goes up. In addition, a host of international policing agencies deliberately set up sting operations just to catch unwary foreign businesspeople. Many times it is the foreign government or its own personnel who perpetrate the bribery. Latin American countries have a long history of such practices.

Another caveat in the international marketplace is the cost of travel to and from the supplier for the buying personnel, engineers, and others. Large Far Eastern cities are the most expensive travel destinations in the world. A midrange hotel room in New York might cost $200 a night. In Tokyo or Singapore it can cost $500 or more. The alternative is to stay at what is called a domestic hotel, as opposed to an international hotel. The bad news is that the domestic accommodations provide something along

Case Study

During the early 1980s, those who were manufacturing personal computers were all in the race to purchase every available semiconductor chip that could be produced by the existing supplier base. At one point, IBM had requirements for over 150% of the world's capacity for certain chips. Needless to say, many third-party companies were willing to sell IBM anything that resembled the required part number. Unsolicited calls offering chips were received in the purchasing department from all points of the globe.

One particular caller offered 64K DRAM (memory) chips in great quantities. The parts were properly qualified and stamped with the necessary manufacturer's name and country of origin. The quantity available was substantial, and the delivery could be airfreighted within 24 hours. The price was extremely high, however, almost three times the street price for the same product—if it were available.

The agent for the supplier was calling from an office in Ohio and assured that all was legal. He said that the company that had purchased the parts in Singapore lost its backing and had to shut down the operation, and therefore found itself stuck with this unusable inventory worth hundreds of thousands of dollars.

At the request of the purchasing manager, an IBM buyer from the Ohio area was dispatched to the agent's address. When the buyer arrived, he found a vacant lot and later learned that a forwarding instruction was given to the post office to reroute or forward mail from this address to a post office box in New York. The telephone had also been set up on remote call forwarding, done in cases where there is no physical phone location. (This is common for businesses who desire a local toll-free phone number for the convenience of customers who live outside the calling area.)

Finding this, the IBM buyer called the supplier's agent for an explanation. Upon learning what the buyer had discovered, the agent abruptly hung up.

Case Study

Manufacturers of high-tech products tend to require specific parts made by specific suppliers (single-source supplier). Such was the case with the IBM PC. Engineers had determined that only certain chip manufacturers possessed the quality necessary to become an IBM supplier. Accordingly, samples were always requested from any source of supply (e.g., distributors, agents, or resellers) other than the original manufacturer.

One such sample set of National Semiconductor chips, shipped from Indonesia, arrived at IBM for inspection. From microscopic inspection of the interior silicone chip, astute engineers quickly determined that these chips were not National Semiconductor chips. Indeed, the outside of the chip package had been re-marked by an Indonesian packager. Always request samples and check their authenticity.

the line of a $10-per-night U.S. hotel room located in a less-than-attractive part of town.

Travel agents today are well equipped to provide itinerary estimates for almost any place in the world. Do that homework and apply the costs multiplied by the best-guess number of trips and personnel, then add that to your overhead cost estimates for the product. All these problems, however, can be overcome. And hundreds of billions of dollars worth of imports arrive at U.S. docks every year, so one would assume that importing problems are minimal or that they can be dealt with given adequate knowledge and preparation.

DOCUMENTATION

In the business of documentation, the first thing to remember is that you are not the judge. The bank, the customhouse broker, U.S. Customs, and the freight forwarder all will be the judges. If the paperwork is incomplete and inaccurate, the goods will be delayed, or worse, returned to the supplier, maybe at a cost to you. You get the bill, but you don't get your parts.

Case Study

Mexico established the maquila dores program in 1965, which allowed industry to import U.S. parts, duty free, manufacture products and ship back to the U.S. and/or other countries. Thanks to the this program, many American companies set up shop in Mexico during the past 20 years or so. Much of the product was shipped to the United States across the border. To assure a speedy trip through Mexican customs, each truck had to pay a fee not listed on the customs documentation merely to move the truck up in the waiting line. The bigger the truck, the more expensive the cargo, the farther up the inspection queue one wished to be placed—all cost more. Fees from $20 to $100 per truck have been charged.

Such fees must be hidden by the supplier in the overhead costs of doing business. In some cases, such fees coupled with other unofficial payments can make the imported product noncompetitive with similar products manufactured in the U.S.

Additionally, refusal to pay said fees can delay shipments for days, with the consequence of additional costs in wait time for truck and driver.

Pro Forma Invoice

In Latin, a *pro* ("in") *forma* ("form of") invoice is simply a communication in the form of an invoice. Usually, a pro forma invoice is a response to a request for quotation (RFQ) or even a request for information (RFI). This might be a little unsettling when all that was requested was a catalog. Not to worry. The only official invoice is a commercial invoice, discussed later. The term *"pro forma invoice"* has a very loose meaning and can be used for anything from a faxed response for pricing to a request for capabilities, to a request for banking action to establish a letter of credit (see Exhibit 3–1 for a sample invoice).

Note, however, that agreement to the pricing, terms, and conditions of a pro forma invoice can denote a type of contract just as if you agreed to RFQ terms and conditions in a formal contract. Be careful. Make sure you agree on every detail on every part of the paper. Treat it as a response to

Abalone & Company

234 Main Street
Taco City, 06002, Mexico D. F.
Phone: 123-5687

Pro Forma
Invoice

SOLD TO:		
ADC Company		
34 Your Street		
Anytown, 12345, USA		

INVOICE NUMBER	97016
INVOICE DATE	02/05/97
OUR ORDER NUMBER	8965ABC
YOUR ORDER NUMBER	12587
TERMS	COD
SALES REP	J. R. Sanchez
SHIPPED VIA	OCEAN FREIGHT
TERMS	FOB, New Orleans

SHIPPED TO:
ABC Company
34 Your Street
Anytown, 12345, USA

QUANTITY	DESCRIPTION	UNIT PRICE	AMOUNT
120	Fine, clean, abalone shells	$5.00	$600.00
	Inland freight estimate, packing and forwarding		114.00
	FOB New Orleans		739.00
	Estimated ocean freight		125.00
	Estimated marine insurance		40.00
	CIF, Taco, Mexico		$904.00
	Individual shells wrapped in bubble pack. Packaged 10 per box		
	in popcorn.		
	12 boxes total 48 cubic feet		
	Gross weight: 75 lbs.		
	Net Weight: 60 lbs.		
	Shipment can be made 3 weeks after receipt of order.		
	Payment terms: Irrevocable letter of credit		
	We certify this pro forma invoice is true and correct.	TOTAL	$904.00
	J. R. Sanchez		

Exhibit 3–1. Typical Pro Forma Invoice

an RFQ, and you should be fine. Many international businesspeople use the pro forma invoice as a basis to begin negotiations.

On the other hand, you may request a pro forma invoice and get only a catalog with pricing information. But you can go on from there. Oddly enough, the importer may have to provide a pro forma invoice in the absence of a commercial invoice to clear goods through customs. It doesn't matter who provides the documentation to customs, but it must completely and honestly describe the shipment, costs, charges, and contents. A commercial invoice submitted at a later date may be checked against the pro forma invoice for validity and conformity.

A checklist for contents of a pro forma invoice includes the following:

- Description of the product being imported
- Unit price
- Terms and conditions of sale
- Terms and currency of payment
- Duration of validity of the offer (pricing, terms, and conditions)
- Freight and insurance charges
- Delivery schedule (shipping time, carrier type)
- Weights, packaging, etc.

Commercial Invoice

The commercial invoice is the bill. It could be merely a copy of the pro forma invoice if the original terms were agreed upon. This document will be used by the U.S. Customs agents to identify the product, the bank to release funds, and so on. A commercial invoice entering the U.S. must be in English or have an English translation attached. If necessary, freight forwarders generally provide this for a small fee.

A checklist for contents of a commercial invoice includes the following:

- Name and address of the seller
- Name and address of the buyer
- Date of invoice
- Description of the product
- Method of transportation
- Terms of payment
- Insurance terms
- Customs declaration
- Packaging and shipping markings
- Quantity of product
- Quantity of packages, crates, or containers
- Unit price of product

- Currency agreed on
- Gross weight of shipment
- Net weight of products
- Terms of sale
- Fees and commissions
- Consular invoice
- Freight costs

The accuracy of this particular document is of the utmost importance. Any irregularity in the invoice may be cause for grief from several agencies later on. Most of the items required may be self-explanatory, but some may require clarification.

Description of the merchandise. Merchandise must be described, in English, as it would in the country of origin or exportation. Next, it must be as described on the Harmonized Tariff Schedule. If the product is unidentifiable by U.S. Customs, you could incur untimely delays in delivery. The quality of the merchandise may have an effect on the duty. For example, diamonds may be imported in numerous forms. There are miners' diamonds, carbonados, industrial, unsorted, unworked, sawn, cleaved, or bruted. Check the tariff schedules against the customs charges. You are allowed to make an appeal for reclassification after receiving the customs paperwork.

You should also ask the supplier to provide obvious identifying marks, labeling, or stamping that will assist a customs agent in locating the item on the tariff schedules. Markings should appear on exterior packages (e.g., boxes, bales, bags, and crates). All descriptions must be in English.

Weights and measures listed can be those of the supplier/exporting country or those of the U.S. It's better to provide both. There are four ways to weigh a shipment:

1. *Gross weight* is the total of the goods and all packaging including export crating and containerizing.
2. *Tare weight* is the weight of the internal or product packaging.
3. *Net weight* is just the goods; in the case of bananas, for example, the weight of the bananas without the box.
4. *Legal weight* is the total of net weight plus tare weight.

When dealing with samples or prototypes that are to be imported at no charge, the fair and reasonable value must be included by the exporter as if the buyer were going to purchase that item. Many companies have a policy of not accepting free samples. That may be a good idea.

Currency declarations other than in U.S. dollars must indicate the current exchange rate (as agreed to in the letter of credit or other form of payment) conforming with the rates published by the Federal Reserve Bank of New York. If there are ancillary costs, those other than the unit price of the product, these must be listed in detail. Such items might include engineering charges, setup charges, tool-and-die work, molds, and patterns. Any subcontracted charges not rolled into the unit price must be identified by name of contractor, country of the subcontract, and charges incurred. Other charges might be crating, cartage, demurrage, storage, commissions, and broker fees.

The invoice must list only merchandise that is included in this individual shipment. The exporter must not include information on split orders, backorders, blanket orders, and the like. If the exporter shipped a thousand pieces on a particular boat on a particular day, only that should appear on the commercial invoice.

Consular Invoices

A consular invoice will probably not be required for an importing company; they are generally used only to export items into another country—specifically South or Central America. The consular invoice is provided on a form by the country's consulate. The only time a purchasing manager may see this document is if the product was made in more than one country.

Certificate of Origin

In the case of products or parts of products that could possibly originate in a country that is under some form of embargo or other restriction by the U.S., a purchasing manager will have to request a certificate of origin from the supplier (see Exhibit 3–2 for a sample certificate). An example is cigars from Costa Rica. Because the U.S. has an embargo on Cuban cigars, the supplier must authenticate that the cigars did not originate in whole or in part in Cuba. This document is customarily rendered by a chamber of commerce or a resident counsel in the country of export.

With the advent of the North American Free Trade Agreement (NAFTA), a new certificate of origin (for shipments greater than $1,000 and originating in one of the NAFTA countries) was issued because of the "special tariff treatment" described in the agreement and to preclude the potential Costa Rica/Cuba problem discussed above. The intent behind this certificate is to determine where the *materials* that the products were made from originated. The classifications are lengthy (i.e., five volumes) as the possible percentages of parts making up the product are endless—like 20% from China, 30% from Japan, 3% from Taiwan, and on and on. It is the supplier's obligation to provide the required documentation for this certificate.

Article Marking for Origin

In addition to the certificate of origin, the marking on the article must conform to U.S. Customs laws. The name of the producing country must be labeled in English in a conspicuous place as legibly, indelibly, and permanently as the nature of the article permits. This may seem like another outrageous bit of legalese, but simply means that when you look at the bottom of your coffee cup you see, for example, "Made in Japan."

Failure to comply with marking may mean as much as a 10% penalty of the total customs duty due in addition to the expensive task of marking every article under the supervision of U.S. Customs or returning the goods to the supplier.

Exceptions to this requirement include articles not intended to be sold, certain components used in combination or included in U.S.-manufactured products, articles that cannot be marked without damage, certain antiques, and articles manufactured more than twenty years previously. A complete list of exclusions may be obtained from the U.S. Customs Service.

Dock Receipt

This document provides a continuation of the paper trail from an inland carrier to the ocean/air carrier. The exporter or forwarder provides this documentation, and the dock personnel will note a dock storage location before completing. The dock receipt transfers accountability from one carrier to another and is very important should the goods be misplaced, stolen, or damaged while waiting to be loaded aboard the vessel or aircraft.

Certificate of Origin

Shipper/Exporter

_____

_____

_____

Consignee

_____

_____

_____

The undersigned declares that the following mentioned goods shipped
on the date of _____
via _____
consigned to _____
are the products of the country of _____

Description of goods

_____

_____

_____

Signed and dated this _____ day of _____
by _____
for _____
a recognized Chamber of Commerce in the country of _____

Exhibit 3–2. Typical Certificate of Origin (NAFTA)

The original copy of the receipt is generally held by the dock or port, and
a copy is forwarded to the ocean/air carrier.

Should you contract for ExWorks, or FAS (free alongside ship), this
document is of utmost importance, since the goods may be stored on the

dock for some time and could get lost—and you now hold title to and responsibility for the goods. The dock receipt might also include a ware-housing receipt and certificate of entry and exit from a free-trade zone or other location where the goods were stored and signed for.

Bills of Lading

A *bill of lading* (*to lade* means to place; for example, on board a carrier) is the contract between the supplier/exporter and the carrier (Exhibit 3–3). An inland carrier usually calls this document a *waybill*; an air carrier an *airbill* or *air waybill*; and a ship will use an *oceanbill*. Besides being another piece of the paper trail, the bill of lading provides documentary evidence of title to the goods, a receipt for the goods, and a contract for their carriage or shipment. There are two types of bills of lading, defined by their terms of negotiability or who owns what and at what point in time.

A straight bill of lading is not negotiable (transferable). The document consigns the goods only to the importer or the importer's designated party. In effect, the bill of lading transfers title and ownership of the goods at this point from the exporter to the importer. Straight bills of lading are printed on white paper.

A shipper's order bill of lading is a negotiable bill because the document in and of itself constitutes a title to the goods. If the bill is not signed by the consignee or importer, then the supplier, or its bank, still holds title to the goods. This bill may be bought, sold, or traded while the goods are in transit. You could find this sort of bill used for many types of financed transactions. The shipper's order bill of lading is printed on yellow paper. Ocean and truck bills of lading may be either straight or shipper's order bills of lading. However, air, courier, and postal bills of lading are never negotiable. These carriers accept only straight bills of lading.

Bills of lading are an integral part of the business between the importer's bank and the supplier's bank and crucial to releasing funds. The importer's bank will release funds only if the bill of lading is marked "clean on board," signifying that no exceptions were noted by the carrier at the point the goods were loaded onto the carrier.

A "stale" bill of lading is one that has not been expeditiously pre-sented to a bank for payment under a letter of credit or other financial arrangement. Typically, the bill of lading is faxed or air-expressed to the

Tropical SHIPPING
Worlds of Service

GENERAL AGENT: BIRDSALL, INC.
P.O. BOX 106837
RIVIERA BEACH, FL 33419-0683
(561) 881-3900 OR (305) 687-8767

Tropical Shipping International, Ltd.
Bill of Lading
NON NEGOTIABLE - NON ORIGINAL

SHIPPER/EXPORTER	DOCUMENT NO. 1234567
ABC MARINE SUPPLY, INC. 123 WHARF DRIVE ANYTOWN, USA	BOOKING NO.
CONSIGNEE (NOT NEGOTIABLE UNLESS CONSIGNED TO ORDER) GATEWAY MARINE PIER 2 ST. GEORGES GRENADA WI	FORWARDING AGENT - REFERENCES
NOTIFY PARTY	EXPORT REFERENCES INVOICE# 765487
	ALSO NOTIFY

EXPORTING CARRIER (VESSEL) RITA	PORT OF LOADING PORT OF PALM BEACH, FLORIDA
PORT OF DISCHARGE (& DELIVERY) GRENADA, WEST INDIES	ULTIMATE DESTINATION GRENADA, WEST INDIES

PARTICULARS FURNISHED BY SHIPPER

MARKS AND NUMBERS	QUANTITY	DESCRIPTION OF GOODS	GROSS WEIGHT	MEASUREMENT
		EMERGENCY PHONE #: 800-424-9300 QUANTITY: 1 CTN		

MISC:SHIPPER'S WEIGHT. CARRIER'S CUBE.
    TOTAL SHIPMENT CONSISTS OF 18 PCS. 17 PCS ONBOARD THIS VESSEL, 1
    PCS. (HAZ CLASS) TO FOLLOW ON SUBSEQUENT VOY - DUE TO INCOMPATIBILITY O
    HAZARDOUS MATERIALS.
MARKS: NO LEADING MARKS
        SHP#97145824
        SPICE ISLAND MARINE
        PO BOX 449
        ST GEORGES GRENADA
        SHP#97145827

EQUIPMENT:	NUMBER	SEAL NBR		PIECE	TEMP	HAZ
	TRIU901205-2	NA		1		YES
	TTRU261321-5	NA		16		YES
ACCESSORIAL CHARGES:			B/L PROCESSING	25.00		
MULTI TALLY	30.00		INSURANCE PREMIUM	34.96		

DESTINATION GRENADA, WEST INDIES

FREIGHT COLLECT X	FREIGHT TO BE PREPAID	BILL TO:			ACCESSORIAL CHARGES
ITEM NO.	WEIGHT	CUBIC FEET	RATE	FREIGHT	
GRE 32	43	3	4.8	168.70	
					FREIGHT CHARGES 168.70
					ACCESSORIAL CHARGES 89.96

Subject to Tropical's terms & conditions for carriage. See WEBSITE for more information

INSURANCE VALUE 3,495.97

In witness whereof, the carrier by its agent has affirmed to (number) 1 bills of lading, all of this tenor and date. One of which being accomplished the others to stand void.

Received, subject to the classification, tariffs and clauses in effect on the date of the issue of this ocean bill of lading.

For Tropical Shipping International, Ltd.
0925 1603   By its Agents
PROF.NBR:000

(STOWAGE CLAUSE)
GOODS IN CONTAINERS OR TRAILERS AS WELL AS ANY MOTORIZED VEHICLE MAY BE CARRIED ON DECK AT THE CARRIER'S OPTION IN ACCORDANCE WITH CLAUSE THIRTEEN (13) HEREOF.

These Commodities, Technology, or Software were exported from the United States for ultimate destination (above) in accordance with the export Administration regulations. Diversion contrary to U.S. law is prohibited.

Birdsall Inc. as agent for Carrier Tropical Shipping Company.

**TOTAL U.S.   258.66

BILL OF LADING
1234567

Exhibit 3–3. Typical Bill of Lading

bank as soon as the goods are aboard the vessel. This ensures that the documentation arrives before the shipment. If the goods must sit at the port of import, additional charges may be assessed over and above those agreed to in the letter of credit. Naturally, the bank will not want to alter the documentation and the buyer will not want to incur the additional charges. And receipt of the goods may be delayed until the financial obligations have been satisfied. Therefore, the purchasing manager must set up a check-file, tickler, or suspense file to ensure that the importer or its bank receives copies of the bill of lading on or within a day or so of the notified shipping date.

Suppose your supplier will be shipping FOB to your plant. First, you may route by sea to a U.S. port. Then the goods will be transferred to a barge up the Mississippi River to, say, St. Louis. From there they are loaded on a rail car and transported to your freight station, where a truck continues the shipment to your loading dock. The through bill of lading, or combined transport document, covers all carriers.

A "foul" bill of lading (not a type of bill of lading but a condition noted on the bill) is one that states that the goods were damaged, broken, or inadequately packaged. Should the carrier mark the bill as foul, he or she is obliged to notify either the shipper or the receiver of this fact before loading the goods. This brings us to insurance forms.

Certificate of Insurance

Freight forwarders generally provide insurance for their shipments at an additional fee to the importer. The importer may, however, opt to provide its own insurance and if so, will have terms with the supplier other than cost insurance, and freight (CIF). Maybe cost and freight (CF). But it is customary that he who pays the freight, pays the insurance. Like everything else, there are different types:

- *All Risks*. Covers the shipment from the supplier to the buyer's dock. It provides coverage for damages or total loss. It does not, however, cover loss due to war, strikes, riots, or civil disturbances. These may be added to the policy for a very low cost.
- *With Average*. Covers total or partial loss while physically on board the major carrier only. It does not cover inland transit, storage, dock site, or loading.

- *Free of Particular Average.* Covers a total loss on the major carrier only, such as a plane crash or sinking of the ship. There is no particularly great cost savings between this type and all-risk coverage.

Insurance documentation is not a big deal but will be required by the bank as closing documentation for the buyer's financial arrangements. Insurance is discussed further in Chapter 12.

Certificate of Inspection

Although the buyer may desire to have the product inspected and certified by either the supplier or a third party, the bank may require such a document before releasing funds. It can contain any combination of inspections, tests, calibrations, or test-running of machinery.

Packing List

In the business of international trade, there is virtually no difference between this document and the one enclosed in the little plastic pouch on any shipment. But the information must match that on all the other documents relating to that particular shipment.

CHAPTER 4

Developing an International Sourcing Plan

To get an idea of how to develop an international sourcing plan, consider this example. As the purchasing manager for a retail chain, you have just received a requisition for an unusual computer card assembly. You have a specification package from engineering that leads you to believe that the product is fairly sophisticated in that it includes some of the latest technology, requires a large amount of testing and agency approvals, and will cost over $100 each to manufacture. You anticipate a large long-term order following the approval of samples. The annualized cost of the orders will exceed $50,000 (criteria that, according to your purchasing operating procedures, will require an approval decision from several different departments in the company). Your mission: Where to buy this product?

The general procedure you will use to source internationally does not vary greatly from sourcing domestically. But the purchasing manager must be organized and thorough. (Note: The company may not have the resources to provide a sourcing exercise of the breadth and complexity indicated here. Nor may it have the need to commit large sums of money to a foreign supplier. In either case, the purchasing manager may choose not to include all the items indicated below. The manager should be aware that this method illustrates a comprehensive sourcing strategy and implementation.) The following are the eight stages of supplier selection:

1. Identify users, desires, competitive products, and competitive sources.
2. Develop a request for information (RFI).
3. Survey potential bidders.
4. Develop a business case (make versus buy).
5. Assemble a source review board.
6. Develop a request for quotation (RFQ).
7. Evaluate the bids.
8. Present recommendations to the source review board.

In this example, we are going to assume that you are asked to supply the highest-quality, lowest-cost product. The marketing department tells you that you will have short lead times. You decide to use the team approach for sourcing and review to make sure that all parties are informed of the progress of your sourcing effort at the same time and that misinformation and surprises will be kept to a minimum. Some suggested parties to include on the source review board are

- Buyer
- Procurement manager
- Materials manager
- Program/project manager
- Manufacturing or process engineer
- Quality manager
- Finance
- Contracts administrator

The first step is to identify the product and determine who the users of the product will be, who currently makes a similar product, where it is made, and what the good and bad features of the product are. You will be looking for statements such as the following:

> "The ABC Company sells one made in California. It's too expensive."
> "The XYZ company gets theirs from Malaysia. There are lots of returns due to bad workmanship. But it's cheap."

"Main Street Inc. makes one that uses old technology. They sell a
   lot."
"Technology for this product is moving rapidly; we need a high-tech
   supplier that can retool quickly if necessary."

The objective is first to use your own internal resources to set a base
for your sourcing. At this time, do not take too seriously any derogatory
comments about a particular company or area of the world from which a
particular product has come. Do your homework and establish your own
benchmarks. For example, what may have been poorly manufactured by
one company in Malaysia for one customer in the U.S. does not necessarily mean that *all* products or companies from Malaysia are bad. With this
basic information in hand, your next step is to find companies that are
capable of manufacturing the product.

FINDING INTERNATIONAL SOURCES

Where do you find international sources? The *Yellow Pages*, of course. Most
countries with worthwhile manufacturing bases have some organization
that lists or promotes their products. Many use the *Yellow Pages* (not
related to the telephone book), which can usually be ordered from trade
associations of particular countries for free or for a small handling charge
(see Appendix A). Some countries publish trade directories. These publications are printed on better paper and may cost from $50 to over $100.
The good news is that libraries in larger cities tend to carry a selection of
all these directories, which you can access, of course, for free. Also try
looking for sourcing information at a country's trade headquarters.
   Another option is to call or write the embassy or consulate with
offices here in the U.S. A list of these can be found in Appendix A. This
procedure generally involves having your call bounced around several
times because each country handles trade in a different way. You will
eventually get directed to the right office. This procedure might be a good
way to establish a pre–request for information database for sourcing. In
compiling information for this book, this author sent out nearly two hundred letters to embassy addresses listed on a commercial CD-ROM phone
book. The resulting return mail filled a whole 28-inch file drawer.
   Subscribing to a trade magazine is also a solution. Virtually every
trade has a magazine, and most are free, especially to buyers. To find out

what magazines cater to your commodity needs, ask your suppliers of similar products. Each magazine will include a card for a free subscription.

To find even more information, go to your library and ask the reference clerk for a copy of the *Standard Rate and Data Service/Business Publications* (published monthly by SRDS, a Macmillan company). Typically, this source list rates for potential advertisers, but it also lists every magazine, periodical, and newsletter that accepts advertising. Therefore, your needs may be listed in this book along with where to get the publication, what the publication costs, circulation figures, and more.

For example, companies that sell software to service companies to manage their dispatch, help desk, service personnel, product specifications, and customer contracts advertise in trade publications geared toward the service industry. These publications can be found in the section on automatic data systems. Publications related to the grocery trade can be found in the section on grocery.

The chambers of commerce or the (country name)/American Chamber of Commerce can be a sourcing resource. You can generally get the telephone number for the Taiwan Chamber of Commerce, for example, through international telephone information.

Trade Associations are another great resource. If you live near a port such as Miami, New Orleans, Jacksonville, New York, or Los Angeles, there is probably an import/export association there. You can find a listing for such associations in *Gayles Directory of Associations*, available at most libraries, or ask someone whose job is related to the port activity. You might even have a world trade center nearby. For instance, there is one in Miami and in Fort Lauderdale.

Going online is yet another source. Organizations that promote trade (e.g., the Small Business Development Centers; universities; and trade associations, centers, and missions) have online connections to databanks or CD-ROMs that will allow you to do a global search for a particular commodity. Increasingly, you can get a surprising amount of information through the Internet. New marketing home pages are entering the Internet daily. Using various search engines and some well chosen keywords you may be able to access a large number of competitive companies. Or use any web browser and just type in the name of the country. You will be amazed at how much information is available. Once you find the information you need, you can print anything you see for future reference. The following is an example of information that was obtained by just typing "Costa Rica" in the search box of America On Line's Internet "Web

Exhibit 4–1. Sample Internet Source Information

Crawler." Of the first 25 choices, I chose "Business in Costa Rica by the Costa Rica Internet Directory." What followed was over 30 pages of selective information (see Exhibit 4–1). I even learned the particulars of banana packaging and chemicals that are used to clean the packing plant floors. Quite an education for a few minutes online.

A final source is newsletters. Many associations and trade centers both here and abroad publish newsletters and periodicals that contain advertising and articles about companies in their area of interest. There is the *Hong Kong Digest, Caribbean Basin Initiative Business Bulletin, Trade Winds* (Taiwan), *Malaysian Trade News, Investment News Update*, and *Trade and Culture* (Denmark), and many more.

DEVELOPING A REQUEST FOR INFORMATION (RFI)

Before you start sending out requests for quotations to new prospective suppliers, a request for information (RFI) will enhance your understanding of each company as it relates to their capabilities and objectives (see Exhibit 4–2). By using an RFI, you will eliminate the need to compile information on useless quotes.

Use all the data gathered about potential suppliers, draft a simple letter outlining your needs, and request that the supplier respond within two weeks. All you are trying to establish at this time is the potential com-

The ABC Company

Dear Supplier,

The ABC Company is looking for manufacturing sources for specialty flatware sets. Our standard specifications call for two knives, three forks, three spoons, and various serving pieces. The material will be stainless steel with and without specialty handles. We will require a stamping process with high-quality hand-finishing. Designs will be furnished by the buyer, and annual quantities are anticipated to be 50,000 to 75,000 sets.

Our company has been in the housewares business for over 40 years and has an established distribution chain. We target the middle of the retail pricing area and sell mainly through department and specialty stores, with a few commercial accounts.

Enclosed is a brief survey form we request that you complete. Additionally, any information you wish to enclose such as an annual report, current product sheets, or catalogs would be helpful.

Please include in your response estimated lead times, manufacturing technology, capabilities and capacities, process experience, and employee expertise.

Note: This is only a request for information, and no purchase orders will be issued as a result of this process. Business is awarded only after a competitive request for quotation. Please respond by January 15, 19___ with your capabilities to provide the requested items.

Yours truly,

Jane Buyer

Exhibit 4–2. Sample RFI Letter (translated into the language of the supplier—send both the English and the translated versions)

pany's basic capabilities. Do not send detailed specifications at this time, especially if they contain sensitive or proprietary material. You may secure a confidential disclosure agreement from the company later if it becomes a request for quotation candidate. Just give the supplier a general idea of your requirements and quantities.

Some suppliers will respond with a letter and a catalog. Others may send a 25-pound overnight box. The volume of each individual response is an indication of the eagerness of the supplier for your business—a fact that can be positive or negative. After making an RFI, you will obviously have more information than you had after the verbal polling of your colleagues, and you will be ready to compile the necessary requirements for an RFQ.

Of course, if you are intending to import ready-made items, a simple request for a catalog will probably suffice. Once you decide which items you want to import, it is of the utmost importance to request samples in advance of any orders or RFQs. The simple fact is that photographers always have a way of making products look better in pictures than they are in real life.

COMPILING A REQUEST FOR QUOTATION (RFQ)

Going to a supplier in another country necessitates an especially detailed and comprehensive request for quotation/bid/proposal (RFQ, RFB, RFP). Leave no stone unturned. The ability of the supplier to produce to your specification and at a price you can live with are just the tip of the iceberg. Depending upon the necessities of your business, the following are things to know if you are going to be awarding manufacturing business:

- Supplier organization, objectives, strategies, and attitude
- Length of time in current business
- Financial strength
- Employee stability and union affiliations
- Quality practices and controls (ISO 9000?)
- Manufacturing-process controls and charts (statistical process control)
- Calibration of equipment, assembly, and testing
- Condition and age of plant and equipment

- Material flow, process flow, and materials management
- Security procedures
- Housekeeping, maintenance, and repairs
- Expertise, availability, and longevity of the workforce
- Use of subcontractors
- Materials suppliers and purchasing procedures
- Availability of peripheral services
- Inventory turns per year
- Machine/manufacturing capacities
- Warranty, repair, spares, and replacement capabilities
- Other customers of the supplier

These items have been generalized here and must be made more specific for your particular needs or process requirements. In addition to this information, you must include:

- Cover letter with list of attachments
- Product specifications
- Quantity/schedule requirements
- Quality specifications and requirements
- Approved and/or single-source material supplier list
- Price/quantity matrix
- Packaging, crating, handling (make sure you ask for shipping weights and cubic dimensions so that you can factor shipping costs from different locations in the world)
- Multiple shipping quotes—example—FOB supplier's dock and ExWorks (this is so that you can compare international shipping cost quotes from supplier and your own broker or freight forwarder—see Chapter 12)
- Methods of payment
- General and administrative information
- Response to RFQ date

Once you have compiled all the necessary paperwork and reviewed the information, try to get the entire package translated into the native lan-

---

Case Study

While negotiating a contract with a Chinese company, I noticed that each participant from the other side came to the table with a Chinese/English dictionary. Not wanting to be left out, I placed my Barrons, Talking Business in Chinese, *dictionary on the table. Whereupon the Chinese leader responded, "So, you have problems with Chinese like we have problems with English?" "Dui [yes]," I responded. "Now we both are on equal ground," he said.*

---

guage of each different supplier's country. That's a big order. But doing so may make the difference between problems later and a smooth relationship. Just ask yourself, if you received an RFQ in Spanish, and you have only a working knowledge of the language from two years of study in high school, how would you respond to that RFQ? Again, while many foreign businesspeople may seem fluent in English, they are speaking only the words they know. Your RFQ will include a plethora of terms and spellings they do not recognize. Some of the unknowns will be questioned, others will be glossed over, in hopes for the best. That will not be the best for you.

EVALUATING RESPONSES TO THE RFQ

In response to your RFQ you may receive a packet of information, pricing, and notes on your terms and conditions. However, from many countries you will often receive a pro forma invoice (see Chapter 3). The supplier is not assuming that your RFQ was an order and billing you for the goods. The pro forma invoice is found typically in international trade and is considered a standard response to pricing information and shipping data including weights and measurements. The real invoice is called a commercial invoice.

A pro forma invoice may be initiated by the buyer to provide information to freight forwarders, customs, or banking entities. In other words, it is a sort of dummy or model invoice that describes all that is necessary for the procurement and movement of goods. If and when the buyer decides to issue a purchase order with that supplier, he or she will need the pro forma invoice to obtain an import license, funds transfer, customs quotations, and the like.

Initially, foreign suppliers usually compile their response to an RFQ in their language, then it is translated into English. Other items that may be different or in error in an international response to an RFQ are

- Irregularities in English grammar
- Conversion of American measurements into metric
- Alternative suggestions to an approved material supplier list
- Design changes to allow for faster/better manufacturing

After receiving all this information, you should start compiling it into an analysis matrix. When you look at all the variables involved you may want to schedule a Bidder's conference. The purpose of this meeting is to allow a representative of the bidding company to meet with you and discuss his or her response to the RFQ. Such a conference is valuable to make sure that the bidding supplier fully understands the terms and conditions of the anticipated business relationship as well as the scope of work and the product itself. In some cases and in the interest of time, this meeting includes all the bidders on the list, but a meeting of this kind is not recommended, especially with a group of offshore suppliers.

If the value of the contract warrants, and the company has the resources, it is advisable to to reconvene a source review board. The object now of the source review board is to arrive at a consensus of opinion regarding doing business in a foreign country. A source review board may also be used for a contract with an American company. In any event, for large dollar commitments and for the prospect of long-term relationships, such a consensus will ensure a smoother relationship, both within the company and with the supplier.

If you are preparing the RFQ responses for a source review board or just for a superior's review, include a thorough plan, documentation, and evaluation of the bids. Use the format of a business case. Here are some of the issues to address:

Supplier selection criteria.   How was information obtained on the foreign suppliers? What was the rationale used to narrow the list from the RFI stage?

Candidate selection for the RFQ.   Summarize the RFI process and the steps taken to whittle down the list of candidates.

Supplier business considerations.   Include financial stability, past experience, capacity and schedule requirements, quality, technical acceptability, resources, and workforce information.

Product cost considerations.   After responses to the RFQ are received a better picture may be seen of the acquisition or manufacturing costs for the product. Now the buyer is in a better position to suggest second, alternative, or additional sourcing. One or more of the parties to the RFQ may suggest alternatives in the manufacturing process, materials, testing, and such. This is especially true of suppliers from the Far East. These companies have always seemed to be overly anxious to be helpful in the entire process of supplying products to their customers and ultimately yours. It's that "customer focus" thing that consumes much of Far Eastern marketing executives. If they feel that there is a glaring inconsistency in a particular area related to cost, quality, manufacturability, or specifications that will cause them problems or you money, they will be only too anxious to point that out to you.

Another important area of costs that must be considered is the ability of the supplier to recover development costs. Because most foreign suppliers are accustomed to doing business within a long-term relationship, they have factored such costs over a much greater time frame than the buyer has. For a high-tech product, your company may anticipate a life span of 3 to 5 years. The supplier may be thinking of 10 years or more for amortization of costs. Discuss projected end-of-life times with each supplier and make them fully aware that all costs must be included within that time frame.

Also consider alternatives in case your product doesn't sell or the technology moves too quickly, as in many computer and communication products. What will your company's or the supplier's liability be if orders are reduced or canceled, or even if the entire contract is terminated? See clauses addressing these factors in Chapter 7.

Your company's financial people may be interested in a cost estimate of the total program over time. Marketing may be interested in unit costs versus projected volumes, cost reductions over time in case of increased demand and production, and price action milestones. Manufacturing engi-

Case Study

While in Japan negotiating with the top choice of supplier for a new product, the supplier's engineering manager pointed out to the negotiating team that the so-called hybrid (some old, pin-in-hole components and some new surface-mount components) construction of the card assembly would cause extra processing steps, take extra time, and cost extra money. During the interim between the submission of the RFQ and this first meeting, the supplier's engineers had redesigned the card to include only new, high-technology, surface-mount components. According to their engineers, the assembly time and test time could be reduced, rework should be minimal, and costs to the buyer's company might be reduced up to 30%, depending on approvals of final redesign (notice the supplier's use of the terms could, should, might—*these words are carefully chosen from extensive translation research). The supplier further assured our team that the changes would be made within the time frame allotted and not affect the first-product ship date.*

This unsolicited suggestion from the supplier was a boon to the marketing team members, allowing them to anticipate providing retail suggested price reductions even before the product was officially announced.

neers may want to access cost reduction considerations like learning curves, process or machinery enhancements, and materials acquisition plans. All these issues can be discussed at this early point in the acquisition process by the source review board.

Acceptance criteria. Provide a review of the pre-RFQ objectives for price, delivery, costs, quality, and so on. Make any necessary adjustments or comments that have surfaced as a result of your analysis of the potential-supplier responses. Items that can be included in this area are a description of the supplier's quality plan; registration with ISO 9000; process, assembly and testing procedures; postdelivery services (e.g., for returned products); nonconforming materials; service strategies; and warranty and after-warranty strategies.

Deliverables schedule.   Outline the time scale or matrix for deliverables, including prototypes, samples, approvals, first-product shipment, and ongoing production schedule. Include method of shipment and costs associated therein.

Attachments.   Include the latest copies of all pertinent documentation, including the following:

- Engineering specifications
- Quality plan
- Reliability plan
- Design agreement (where necessary)
- Manufacturing agreement
- Spare parts agreement
- Postwarranty agreement
- Confidential disclosure agreement (where necessary)

Signoffs.   Provide a sheet listing all the parties on the source review board, with signature blanks for the parties to indicate final approval of the sourcing decision.

USING A WEIGHTED STATISTICAL ANALYSIS

If you have experience with weighted analysis, you can create a matrix of pertinent items from the RFQs and assign a weight to each. Granted, such a mathematical or statistical approach for arriving at a sourcing decision is rare, but the extra time spent compiling such an analysis up front will save many hours of wrangling at the conference table when making a decision later. The principles used to formulate this analysis can be found in the seven basic tools of a quality program such as Total Quality Management (TQM) or Total Quality Control (TQC).

Exhibit 4–3 depicts an example of a situation that you may encounter at the source review meeting. Using raw totals only, three suppliers (B,C, and D) all seem to qualify at first glance. What usually happens is that personal opinions or the strength of a single member will sway the vote for a particular supplier. If the team members all agree beforehand that the

Weighting	2	2	3	4	4	5		
Ratings						Pricing		
1-POOR	<$10M	<5 years	Low	Poor	<80% on-time	Target ++	$117.00	
2	$10M -$25M	6-10 years			80-85% on-time	Target +	$105.00	
3	$26M - $50M	11-15 years	Medium	Good	<86-90% on-time	Target	$100.00	
4	$51M - $100M	15-20 years			<91-95% on-time	Target -	$97.00	
5-EXCELLENT	>$100M	>20 years	High	Excellent	<95% on-time	Target - -	$92.00	

	Total Supplier Revenue	Time in Business	Technology Level	Quality Plan	Delivery History	Quoted Price	Raw Totals	Wtd. Totals
Supplier A	2	2	3	2	3	5	17	62
Supplier B	4	5	4	1	5	1	20	59
Supplier C	2	2	5	3	4	4	20	71
Supplier D	5	5	3	1	3	3	20	60

Note: The formula for weighting is to multiply each of the scores by the category weighting number and add the results.

Exhibit 4-3. Weighted Statistical Analysis of Suppliers

qualities of the supplier as listed are accurate and that the weighting is accurate, one supplier in this example stands out above the rest.

Given only the information from the RFQ, you would tend to award the contract to supplier A as the low bidder. After putting the information into the matrix, and computing raw totals, you would probably award the contract to the low bidder of B, C & D, supplier D. By weighting the qualities based on how important the various issues are to the relationship as a whole, however, you come up with supplier C.

Again, to make such a statistical approach work, you must first have consensus on the formulas, weights, and grading numbers. This approach certainly reduces discussion time during a sourcing decision.

All of the information given can be readily obtained, except perhaps delivery performance in the case of a new supplier. In that case, seek referrals to other customers of the supplier to see if you can obtain that data.

Feel free to include different or more categories in your analysis (e.g., nonrecurring engineering costs, shipping costs from different global locations, communication ease between companies and languages, travel costs for you and your team, and engineering consulting). All such items can have an impact on the total cost in dollars and time for your company and certainly can have an impact on the decision-making process.

CHECKING OUT A SUPPLIER

Obtaining a Dun and Bradstreet report on a foreign supplier might not give you the information a purchasing manager needs. The U.S. Department of Commerce has a branch called the Commercial Service, which provides a world trade data report for about $75. Browse the Internet at www.ita.doc.gov/uscs for contacts and phone numbers or call 1-800-STAT-USA. Similar to a D&B, it contains information on principals, financial history, product lines handled, and much more. Opinions regarding the general reputation of the firm or problems it may have encountered are advanced in the report.

CHAPTER 5

Cultural Issues: Barriers, Caveats, and Expectations

After observing some of the basics of the "hard skills" of international sourcing, it is time to look at the "soft skills." The soft skills are the foundation for communicating with a source in any another country by any means, whether in person, by phone, by fax, or through the Internet and E-mail. The old adage that first impressions are lasting impressions is ever so true when crossing the cultural line. Outside the U.S., the so-called good-ol'-boy network ceases to exist, backslapping is forbidden (in most countries), and everything written or spoken will affect, in some measure, the outcome of the transaction. This chapter covers some of the most obvious, and damaging, customs that are different abroad along with some historical trivia that may explain why these differences exist. *NOTE:* None of the cultural comments contained herein are meant to be derogatory or detrimental to the specific culture mentioned. The information is intended as a guideline for understanding actions and reactions to the way things are.

An all-important prerequisite is for the purchasing manager to admit that he or she may have become somewhat sheltered and oblivious to the differences, the diversity, and the workings of business in other countries. "Haven't been there . . . haven't done that" is a good mentality to adopt. This allows one to be more open to information.

Although other countries have, for the past few generations or so, come to the U.S. to buy, the U.S. is now going outside its borders to buy.

Senator J. William Fulbright once said that Americans suffer from what he called "cultural myopia." Although Americans readily admit a lack of understanding of another's language (e.g., say Japanese or German), they outwardly try to deny any lack of understanding of other areas of difference.

Purchasing managers must be aware that in the business of international sourcing, people will almost always have different and sometimes seemingly strange agendas. A company's choice of a buyer (or other representative) to manage foreign sourcing is crucial to its success.

As one hypothetical example, consider a buyer whose hidden agenda is merely to shop in Paris or on the Ginza in Tokyo or just see the sights.

Case Study

A Fortune 100 company decided to open a sales office in Beijing in the mid-1980s. It sent several of its more adventurous senior marketing people, along with their families, to China for a 1- to 2-year stay. Within 30 days, one family returned to the U.S., leaving the employee in Beijing. By the end of 6 months, most families were back home, and the office was moved to Hong Kong within a year.

It seems that there were precious few English-speaking people in Beijing. The families would congregate at the Sheraton Hotel several nights a week for dinner just to engage another American in conversation. Additionally, the office was opened in the spring of the year, a time when the winds blowing across the Gobi Desert pick up tons of yellow dust so thick that many wore a surgical mask to fend off the choking, gritty pollution. Other unexpected adversities reported were the inability to buy common American foods in the stores, the almost impossible task of finding one's way around the city, and electrical interruptions several times a day. One recent report in Newsweek *said that the Sheraton Hotel in Beijing used more electricity in the previous year than the rest of the entire city, where population is over five million.*

One returnee said that he now had a great deal of respect for reporters, ambassadors, and other diplomats who seemed to spend most of their life living in other countries—and he thought they were out there having fun!

Be wary also of the individual who, bent on success, is merely interested in getting the job done quickly and hurry back to the office to play politics or boast of his or her international prowess. In most instances, the work of procuring goods overseas is never as easy as one would like it to be and most assuredly will take much longer, require more effort, be fraught with more roadblocks, and eat up more time than expected. But the rewards can be great if one succeeds. Even more damaging is sending a representative to a foreign country for six months or more, with or without his or her family, only to find that the representative just hates living without the expected conveniences and friends.

PREPARING FOR FOREIGN BUSINESS TRAVEL

Learn the Language

It is important for purchasing agents traveling abroad to learn the language—at least enough to get by on the street, order meals, ask directions, find help in an emergency, and create small talk with foreign counterparts. Start with, "Hello, how are you." The host will greatly appreciate attempts to assimilate into his or her culture, and the purchasing agent will have created a good first impression.

Learning bits and pieces of the host supplier's language and culture may supply the extra few points needed to be accepted as a good person and a good company with which to do business. One doesn't have to be fluent in the language—as few as 25 words relating to greetings, weather, time, or dining will stand the buyer in good stead, not only in the conference room but in traveling as well. Knowledge of major cultural events, famous local birthdays, or religious holidays will indicate an interest in what the host believes to be important. After all, the average Japanese businessperson has spent years learning English, the meaning of Washington's Birthday, and the Fourth of July.

Practice the Money Exchange System

Understanding the basics of a country's money exchange system is critical, because the purchasing agent is going to be buying goods for his or her company in this country. If the buyer has great difficulty in using their

Case Study

During the late 1980s and early 1990s, the Japanese yen (¥) fell precipitously against the U.S. dollar from around ¥180 = $1.00 to less than ¥100 = $1.00. A traveler during that time would experience a great delay in the processing of credit card charges (including his or her $300-per-night hotel room) for up to three months so that the hotel could recoup the latest, greatest exchange rate. The business traveler who had submitted travel expense report would be faced with additional costs of up to 50%, requiring a supplemental reimbursement from the company—not easy to do in many cases.

money on the street, tackling the costing and pricing intricacies of a purchasing contract will be nearly impossible.

Even if the contracts are written in U.S. dollars, as is generally the case, the history of the stability of the country's currency will become an issue, and the purchasing agent must be aware of it. Take Brazil, for example. From 1986 to 1990, the inflation rate at times reached 30% an hour. Yes, per *hour!* Even the name of the money changed several times (*cruzeiro* to *cruzado* to *new cruzado* to *real,* today's unit), and the government, in defense of the issue, began dropping zeros off the value of the currency. During one two-year period, six zeros disappeared from the Brazilian currency. That means that if you had a 1,000,000 (one million) cruzerio note stashed under the mattress since 1986, it would now be worth about 1 (one) real in today's currency. In Argentina, the exchange of the austral caused such consternation that manufacturers would take orders for parts only to find out that the contracted sales price was less than half the total factory cost on the day of invoicing. They, in turn, asked buyers to pay more for the product.

One may find indications of foreign strategies and tactics even in comic books. Asians in general take their comics more seriously than Americans do. It is common to find business and international matters lampooned not only on the editorial pages of the newspapers but in comic books. These come in the traditional rag paper format we are accustomed to as well as soft-cover and hard-cover versions. In the U.S., we have such political and business satirists as Scott Adams, Gary Trudeau, and Mike

Shotaro Ishinomori, Japan Inc. (Nihon Keizai Shimbun, Tokyo, 1986); translated by Betsey Scheiner (Los Angeles: University of California Press, 1988).

Exhibit 5–1

Peters. In Japan, there are hundreds of such writers and cartoonists drawing on business and government for their material. (This cartoon appeared when the Yen exchange rate was about ¥180 = US $1.00.)

Be Flexible

In other countries, there are always unforeseen obstacles, in spite of the amount of training and preparation one might have received. Some common surprises are the size and duration of the traffic jams, the taste of

---

Case Study

I noticed that even after repeated forays to the Far East from the eastern U.S. time zone that I would awaken several times during the night wanting an immediate breakfast. At three in the morning, this can be a dilemma even in the best of hotels. Since every room in every country seemed to have a hot-water thermos for tea, I could make some instant coffee that I brought along, but that didn't help the hunger pains. The munchies from the in-room refrigerator were not only expensive ($5–$7) but not my idea of breakfast. So on the second trip I made sure that I stocked the room with plenty of pastries, juices, and such, so that I could eat when I wanted.

---

the water (and the food), the slowness of the other party's decision-making process, the softness or firmness of the hotel bed, the 3 A.M. hunger pains, and other time zone idiosyncracies.

It is common in the Far East for the negotiations to take twice as long as expected, or more. In the Middle East, the important players expected to be at the conference table may not even be in town at the appointed time. In view of this dilemma, the purchasing manager should always convince the company to purchase a full-fare airline ticket in anticipation of a change in itinerary. One can usually find a hotel room, but without a full-fare (alterable at no extra charge) airplane ticket, the purchase of an additional one-way fare home may be the only option.

Be Empathic

Empathy is not sympathy. I like to think of sympathy as feeling sorry for someone and empathy as feeling happy for someone. Although not particularly true from the Websterian standpoint, this explanation fits well when having empathy for another culture and its people. Empathy is the ability to be open-minded to the diversity of the world. Empathy is celebrating diversity. Empathy is never, ever, telling a person from another country, "Well, that's not the way we do it back in the States."

Case Study

This writer was invited to a dinner party at a sales manager's home in China. The menu included a boiled chicken. The weather was delightful, and there was a definite air of conviviality around the predinner dim sum *platter. As the chicken arrived and was placed at the center of the table, I took a deep gulp. It was presented like a pile of cord wood, obviously hacked to bits with a traditional Chinese cleaver. Splinters of bone were everywhere.*

As I dallied with my soup, I observed the locals eagerly dipping their chopsticks into the morass and merrily chewing away, spitting the bones onto the lawn with wild abandon. As best I could, I maneuvered around the obvious bones, and the chicken was delicious. When confronted with an errant sliver, my hosts spit it out. I thought of the watermelon spitting contests I once had with my cousin one summer. And I spit. After all, spitting in some cultures is a sociologically accepted thing. I can remember that my mother was not too sympathetic with the seed-spitting activity, but I can empathize with the Chinese spitting bones.

Know Some History

Imagine for a moment that it takes 2 weeks for a Chinese company to negotiate a contract. It may take 2 years for a factory to implement a change in human resources policy. In addition, it may take 20 years or more for mainland China to get over Maoism and accept capitalism. Twenty years is just a click in time for a country whose history goes back some 5000 years. This appreciation of history will help you understand and perhaps be empathic to why the pace of life seems so slow to us.

Be Protocol- and Etiquette-Conscious

The smattering of Emily Post you may have been exposed to during your lifetime and such procedures as which fork to use for which dinner course will seem trifling when you encounter the structured protocols followed in

Latin America or Europe. Europeans do not switch the fork and knife after cutting a piece of meat. Hands are always kept in view and on the table—never in the lap. At an Asian table the host always is seated facing the main entrance/exit. Arabs kiss when greeting one another. In Thailand, one does not touch another's head.

The Chinese concept of feng shui is ever present in many aspects of Far Eastern life. Feng shui is the ancient Chinese art of aligning buildings, furniture, and objects so that they are in harmony with nature and their surroundings and therefore will bring good luck. Don't be surprised if your Chinese host asks to rearrange the order of the documents on the table or the seating arrangements in the conference room.

Social status is measured differently in other parts of the world. In the U.S., one's status tends to be measured by position in a company and the area of the city in which one lives. In Latin America, inherited family status is important. In the Middle East, it is money; in Western Europe, it is the schools attended; and in the Far East one is measured by corporate affiliation.

The phrase *buy American* is truly an indigenous Americanism. Once you leave the borders, it's anybody's game. For all the marketing and prodding and politicking Americans have used over the past few decades to ensure best relations with Saudi Arabia (a very influential member of OPEC), the contract to build a new U.S. embassy in Riyadh was awarded to a Korean construction firm, not a U.S. one.

Asians, in general, tend toward the positive in all aspects of their life. They have a well-known habit of never saying no. Americans, on the other hand, are well known for their blunt negatives. Since the word *no* can kill a deal and ultimately a relationship, here are a few tips on alternatives to use in a situation of disagreement. Remember that these situations might normally be handled with "No, thank you," or "We cannot," or "Never!" Just omit the negative word.

Asian Salesperson:	"Will you join us tonight for dinner and drinks?"
American Buyer:	"I'm sorry, but I have another engagement."
Asian Salesperson:	"Can we delete this portion of the contract?"
American Buyer:	"It may be difficult to convince my company." [Then later.] "My people have great resolve in keeping the clause."

Asian Salesperson:	"Have some more [drink, food]."
American Buyer:	"Thank you, I'll try some more." [Then, after trying, admit you are full.]
Asian Salesperson:	"Will you be staying next week?" [a test of *your* time limit for the negotiations or talks.]
American Buyer:	"I really should be returning on the tenth, but we'll see."
Asian Salesperson:	"Do you like raw fish [sushi, sashimi]?"
American Buyer:	"I'll try it, but I prefer it tender cooked."

There is an old expression, "You have to read between the lines." This is further exemplified by the following case study.

Case Study

During the signing of the Structural Impediments Initiative (designed to use excess Japanese profits to improve Japan's infrastructure rather than to buy up American companies, golf courses, and real estate) between President George Bush and Prime Minister of Japan Toshiki Kaifu in Houston, Texas, the prime minister was asked by a reporter if he was supportive of the agreement. The prime minister responded with "It may be painful to implement" once back in Japan.

The inference here is that his signing of the agreement was merely to save face with the American president and that little or nothing would be done to fulfill its contents back home. It's just another example of how Asians will skirt a negative response even though they know full well that "no" is their response.

Along with the protocol issue, it would be a positive move for the purchasing manager to find an introducer. The selection of who should make the introduction must be addressed with as much effort and detail as should negotiation strategy. The manager should use all the contacts he or she can and then look for still more. The selection will provide the highest possible credibility to one's company and to one's self. The introducer must also retain the highest possible credibility to the parties with whom the purchasing manager wishes to do business. This ombudsman is the manager's entry ticket to the event, without whom he or she may appear as a gate crasher. This agent will be very useful in Latin America and the Middle East.

Be Patient

The purchasing agent should plan to spend a long time fulfilling his or her mission. That goes for the Middle East as well as the Far East. In Europe, things usually happen pretty much according to plan. In Japan, for example, managers have been trained in some form of the art of bushido, the ancient code of the samurai. Bushido teaches patience and forbearance and is somewhat linked to the training and discipline of such martial arts as tae kwan do and karate. From this code also comes the practice of bowing, maintaining harmony, stoic endurance, consensus, and love of country. When a negotiation seems to have gone on forever without any appreciable progress, that is the perception of an American. In the eyes of a Japanese, things may be progressing just fine. Even in times of ostensibly insurmountable disagreement, a Japanese spokesperson will say, "Things are proceeding just wonderfully."

Leave Aggressiveness At Home

Humbleness is next to godliness in most of the world. And where humbleness may not be obviously practiced, such as in parts of South America or the republics of the former Soviet Union, restraint will set one apart from others and make cause for the other side to take a second look. Think like a diplomat—a good diplomat.

For decades, Americans have repeatedly been characterized as conceited, arrogant, and pushy in their dealings all over the world. In the movie *The Ugly American,* Marlon Brando portrayed a U.S. diplomat with much the same temperament. What was shown as unacceptable behavior then is still unacceptable today, in the Far East in particular. The maintenance of harmony is a requirement of the first order in Japan and China. A major Japanese company will reject any deal, no matter what the anticipated benefits of it, if it feels that the chemistry between the parties will not work or be able to sustain a fiduciary long-term relationship.

Be Prepared to "Wine and Dine"

In the U.S., many companies have instituted codes and restraints regulating socializing between business entities. Even the IRS has greatly reduced the amounts that are deductible. Most large companies have well-documented policies on gifts and gratuities of any kind, while others frown upon the practice of any social activity and refuse to reimburse employees who feel obligated to respond in kind.

You are the host in America, and your guest suppliers will expect the same business treatment from you that their company insists that you receive while visiting their country. It's a "catch-22." Nightspots in the Far East tend to be lavish and very expensive. A dinner at your local hotel will probably not suffice. Far Eastern travelers enjoy cultural events, theater, music, and sports. So a box seat at a football or baseball game may be just as appropriate as a night on the town. Educate your management on these entertainment facts and see if you can be allowed to reciprocate with your suppliers.

As you travel eastward across Europe, the propensity for drinking and the percentage of alcohol increases dramatically from the wine in France to the beer in Germany to the vodka in Poland and Russia. If you are a moderate drinker, play the sipper. If you don't drink at all, you may find that a reference to an assumed liver problem will be readily understood by most Eastern Europeans and Russians.

Take Your Time

In Japan, people-finding takes precedence over fact-finding, image over substance. At a meeting of two very large companies, one American, one Japanese, not even the agenda may be shown or discussed until the third meeting, maybe four days into the relationship.

However, this rule does not always apply. In Scandinavian countries, small talk and protocol are kept to a minimum or are nonexistent, except in Norway, where a slightly more personal tack is taken by negotiators in their quest for relationships.

The term *relationship* has a more than passing meaning. Americans teach their salespeople that "customers do business with people they like." Buyers don't always follow these rules and beliefs, however. This is ever so true in the Far East. To know the other side in Japan relates again to bushido.

In most Persian Gulf countries as well, lengthy preliminary meetings (sometimes two or three) to establish relationships may precede any discussions on the particular product or contract. Information on the attendees, their management, their company, their industry, and more may be on the supplier's agenda. The purchasing manager should be prepared to supply volumes of data in this regard. Oddly enough, don't be surprised if you are asked about the quality of your trip by many different people at the meeting—more than once from each person.

Delay the Pricing

Money talk should be delayed as long as possible. The substance of the negotiations must be totally understood and accepted before any mention is made of price or cost. A Chinese supplier will be offended if the price of the item takes precedence over their pride in the function or quality. When selling to Japan, the price is of little importance if the product is unacceptable. That goes true for buying as well.

The buyer who opens with, "Your price is too high," in Europe, has confirmed the other side's perception that that is a hot button. Leading with cost in South America, one's tactics may be perceived as *fait accompli,* and the initial low bid may be dramatically eroded. Anything the buyer asks for after driving total costs down will include a cost escalation factor from the other side.

Take Plenty of Business Cards

In the Far East, business cards will be delicately arranged on the table in front of each member of the Japanese or Chinese team and looked at every time a member of the buyer's team speaks. They will be registering all that is said, the name of the speaker, the way in which it is said, and the level of harmony exuded by that speaker. They will go home with a mental picture linked with the speaker's business card, a picture that will be important during their consensus discussions later.

In Europe and especially Russia, former Soviet republics, and the Middle East, telephone directories are highly abbreviated and often hard to come by. Personal names and phone numbers are conspicuously unlisted in many cases. Classified directories (American yellow pages) just do not exist in many countries except through trade organizations. Your collection of business cards will be your only guide.

It is traditional to have the reverse side of a business card imprinted with the buyer's data in the language of the country of the supplier. Nothing is more embarrassing than having the representative from the other side turn over a card and find it blank. The impression is that you didn't think enough of the supplier or his culture to provide a translation. Translations and typesetting of business cards may cost as little as $25 and are available in most larger cities in the U.S. as well as by mail order. Cards can also be translated and printed (usually overnight) in most large international cities—ask the hotel concierge. It's a small investment that will make a large first impression. After all, you expect to receive their business card in English, don't you?

Mementos of the Meeting Promote Harmony

Mementos of the meeting are typical in most countries. Given out just before you leave, a small token will help your counterparts remember the good times. Choose gifts that are uncommon in that country. Good scotch, whisky, wine, or perfume can be purchased from the in-flight duty-free shop and delivered with your baggage. American handicrafts or small artworks reflect an interest in culture. Tee- or sweatshirts that reflect the names of important places or events can be a learning experience for the participant's children (Disney World or national parks, for example). A buyer who has done his or her homework should know sufficient information about the people with whom he or she is meeting to choose an appropriate gift.

Avoid Embarrassing Situations

Notwithstanding the years of wars in Europe or the episodes of overt violence in Taiwanese and Japanese legislatures Americans must look beyond. Americans must understand that Europeans have been a closely knit cross-cultural group of trading nations for over a thousand years. They have ways of working things out (the latest is ISO 9000).

The concept of working together may be epitomized by the business of growing rice in Asia. Without cooperation and harmony at the lowest levels, people would not eat. These concepts are steeped in thousands of years of history. Although Americans have been unique and pretty much led the world in social and industrial progress, they have, maybe because of that, tended to become complacent to the wants, needs, and desires of others.

Never openly chastise or downgrade a member of your own group, or the supplier's, for that matter. This is another way of maintaining harmony, which has been mentioned before, but must be stressed again and again. Harmony is the key to success. The intricate carvings in a Chinese temple bears witness to years of working together and attention to detail. The simpleness of a Japanese garden is the epitome of the lifestyle in Japan. If you break the pattern of the sand or upset the harmony of the rocks, your mission is over. As the saying goes in the china shop, "You break it, you bought it!" You may sadly return home to try again another day.

You might be surprised, however, in the Russian and the former Soviet republics to find the other side highly emotional. The classic appearance by Nikita Kruschev at the UN many years ago, when he removed his shoe and banged it on the podium to make a point is an example. Russian negotiators somehow just don't feel they have accomplished anything without at least one or two episodes of slamming their books closed and stomping out of the conference room in a huff. Not to worry. It's all part of the cultural business. You must remember that right now, they may need you more than you need them. All will sort itself out if you persevere.

FROM THE SILK ROAD TO THE SILICON ROAD

Prized commodities from the Asian continent have whetted the appetites of the rest of the world for centuries. Silks and spices, linens and porcelain, ivory, jade, and tea have kept the caravans and superfreighters busy. Today, it's jeans, sneakers, and silicon. The Orient has come of age.

The word *Orient* is derived from the Latin *oriens,* or direction of the rising sun or east (*occidere,* direction of the setting sun or west gives us the word *Occidental*). If there was ever a time for rising, the Far East has certainly taken advantage of the global marketplace. From the rice paddy to the assembly line, Asian workers, armed with Confucian work ethics, have provided the world with a vast array of machinery, electronics, tools, automobiles, textiles, and more.

Let's take a look at the major players in this phenomenon.

THE FIVE TIGERS

Japan, South Korea, Taiwan, Hong Kong, and Singapore are traditionally known as the five tigers (Singapore being the latest addition to the original four). This appellation seems to have come out of ancient Oriental culture but in reality it refers to the aggressive strength of these countries in overcoming the adversities of many years of colonialism, war, and occupation. Needless to say, these countries have proven themselves as world-class competitors in countless areas of manufacturing. Other newly industrializing countries (NICs) such as Malaysia, Thailand, Indonesia, Philippines, and even Viet Nam now are following the lead of their sister tigers and becoming tigers in their own right. Maybe there will soon be 10 tigers?

Japan: Mother of All Tigers

Like the Phoenix, Japan has risen from the ashes stronger and more formidable than before, with a new weapons arsenal—products to trade. Since most everyone knows of the prowess of Japan in the areas of innovation, quality, and customer focus, it would be superfluous to enumerate here the advantages of importing from Japan. The purchasing manager will no doubt receive little help from American agencies, both government and private, who are currently trying to reduce the trade deficit with Japan (about $50 billion). These agencies are on an export, export, export *to* Japan track now.

The good news is that for the past decade or so, Japan has been offloading many of their earlier manufacturing commodities. Japanese automobiles are now made in the U.S.; electronics in Taiwan and Korea; computer parts in Taiwan, Singapore, and Thailand. There are Japanese joint ventures all over Mexico and Latin America. Japan at home seems to be bent on the new directions of the latest, greatest technology such as robotics, biomedical, aircraft, and space.

This has created a so-called domino effect around the Pacific Rim, where, as technology becomes old in one country, it is picked up by countries with just a little less experience than the former. As an example, televisions and computer monitors moved from Japan to Taiwan in the 1980s, even though Japan produces most of the world's CRT tubes for these items. In another example, South Korea "picked up the pieces" in the consumer electronics markets. Gold Star, Samsung, DaeWoo, and others began to prosper in kitchen, workshop, and audio equipment. Singapore accepted the title of the world's largest maker of hard-disk storage devices for computers. And Thailand, once a poor agricultural kingdom, now supplies cable and card assemblies. So as Japan has led, others followed.

Taiwan: Fastest-Growing Tiger

Of all the countries in the Far East, the Republic of China (ROC), better known as Taiwan, has been the most enthusiastic in promoting economic relations with and imports from the U.S. as well as their exports.

Taiwan, in 1997 the sixth largest trading partner with the U.S., imported a total of $20 billion worth of U.S. goods. We imported nearly $30 billion from them.

At a Pacific region forum on business and management communication in 1992, Dr. Ryh-Song Yeh, a professor at Simon Fraser University in California, stated that from the 1980s to the 1990s, economic prosperity in Taiwan was enhanced by increasingly liberalized government regulations, lowered import barriers, and the reduced role of government in enterprises. During this stage, the science and technology factors for producing intermediate products were emphasized. At this time, because of more foreign exchange reserves, the quality of life improved, wages were higher, and industries were upgraded. In 1990, the agriculture sector became much less important, accounting for only 4% of gross domestic product, while the industry and service sectors accounted for 42% and 54%, respectively. Taiwan has become an industrialized economy.

Taiwan also boasts the world's largest cash reserve, over $66 billion, higher than Japan's $63 billion. Some of this money is used to expand its manufacturing base in other countries. Mexico and Central America are prime targets for offloading excess manufacturing capacity.

Among Taiwan's statistics that favor trade are an even distribution of wealth, low inflation rate (0.4%), low unemployment rate (1.4%), high foreign currency reserves ($66 billion), no government budget deficit, low foreign debt ($2 billion), and a high individual savings rate (over 35%).

The director general of Taiwan's Board of Foreign Trade, K. S. Sheu, said in 1990 that "Taiwan is mounting 'concerted efforts' to rectify the balance of trade with the U.S." Of all the U.S. trade deficit countries, Taiwan has reduced the imbalance the most.

Since Taiwan is not recognized officially by the U.S. (the Peoples Republic of China took over Taiwan's seat at the UN in 1971), it has no embassies or consulates here. The easiest way to learn about Taiwan is to contact the Taipei Economic and Cultural Office (TECO). (See the listing in Appendix A.)

Many states have trade offices in Taiwan. Florida opened theirs in 1992 at the Taipei World Trade Center. Since Florida tends to lead the country in coordination efforts with Central and South America, the Taiwan office will also serve as a bridge with Taiwanese manufacturing investments in Honduras and Guatemala.

Initially it is not necessary to travel across the Pacific to identify and feel out suppliers. Through the TECO, a purchasing manager can establish whether or not his or her company's product or service is available in Taiwan, who the major companies are, and what specifications they are offering. All the preliminary requirements can then be accomplished through the mail or by fax.

As with any foreign market, personal contact is vitally important. To succeed, a manager can hire the services of an in-country ombudsman, and an export broker or trading company. Having an in-country Mandarin- or Taiwanese-speaking go-between will greatly aid in the success of the relationship. By the time you have made your first trip to Taiwan you should know who will best serve this purpose.

When you do travel to Taiwan, plan your itinerary well in advance. During certain periods, hotel rooms are booked several months in advance. The trip will take you about 30 hours, door-to-door from the eastern U.S. You will have plenty of time to brush up on a few Mandarin phrases from a traveler's language book, a definite asset.

Plan also to see some of the fabulous sights in Taiwan: Sun Moon Lake, the National Museum, Chang Kai-Shek Memorial, Taroko Gorge, the Alishan Forest. A member of the Taiwanese group you are meeting with may enjoy showing you these treasures. This is also a great way to show your hosts the interest you have in the country of which they are very proud.

Centuries ago (around 1590), Portuguese explorers named this island Ilha Formosa, Beautiful Island. *Taiwan,* in Mandarin, means "terraced bay." Throughout history, this little island has been invaded and occupied by Genghis Khan, the Dutch, the Spanish, and the Japanese. Today, Taiwan is a major economic power in the Far East. Buyers and importers will surely be rewarded, not only in business, but in knowing its marvelous people.

The Korean Connection

Although not quite as adept as other Asian counterparts at trade relations or as accomplished in the areas of innovation and quality, South Korea nevertheless has taken its place as a world-class supplier. *The Economist* listed South Korea as the 17th-largest economy in the world in 1989. By the mid-1990s, nine South Korean companies were included in the International Fortune 500, four in the top 100.

In 1992, South Korea was America's 13th-largest trading partner. The trade deficit with South Korea was a mere $2 billion. During the rebuilding of South Korea (1955–70), South Koreans were accustomed to buying American, and the many U.S. aid plans and promotions brought American goods to all. In the early 1990s, however, a "Don't Buy American" attitude began to permeate the country. Department stores took household appliances off the floor. Comic books and newspaper editorials began to run stories about the bad effects of American imported foods. South Korea was certainly voicing its individuality.

Unlike Taiwan, the Koreans mounted a coordinated protectionist plan, hoping to make sure that Korean products remained on top of the domestic buyer's list. Market share, not financial gain, is of the utmost importance to Koreans. Another factor, still not widely admitted to by Asia watchers, is the fact that both the Chinese and Japanese inflicted gross injustices on the Korean people for most of this century. Now that China and Japan have become world trading magnets, the Koreans are bent on outdoing their former adversaries.

Much of the protectionist furor has simmered down in the late 1990s, but misguided government plans seem to have hindered rather than helped the momentum of South Korea toward world-class status. Quality has suffered. Pricing competitiveness has waned. Other problems encountered by buyers include late deliveries and difficulty in implementing engineering and quality changes, as well as warranty and replacement part availability.

Korean negotiators are far different from those from the rest of the Pacific Rim countries. They are very aggressive, tough to convince, and doggedly pursue their own agendas in spite of the Asian tendency toward long-term-relationships. Koreans insist on a 51% share in all joint ventures, probably because of their former bad experiences with domination by colonialist-type foreign-manufacturing enterprises.

Related to the tendency of Asian companies to operate as a team with group consensus and their concern with saving face is the question of ultimate responsibility. In Korea, if the group succeeds, the group gets credit; if it fails, the manager is to blame. In the rest of Asia, the group generally takes the kudos as well as the fault. Contrast this with the American way, where if the team succeeds the manager takes the credit, while failure is attributed to the team.

Koreans still like to get everyone involved, however. All concerned individuals and departments get a copy of the buyer's terms and conditions (again, the importance of providing a translated copy). This is called *pummi* when all are asked to provide input into the decision-making process. Unlike with the Japanese tradition of consensus, a Korean decision uses the input from others, but a few top executives filter the final decision down to the negotiating parties. Hence, decisions tend to come more quickly in Korea because fewer actual decision makers are involved.

Much of the direction of industry is promoted by the Chaebol, a consortium of 50 of the largest industrial conglomerates. The Chaebol holds the trade strings as a unified entity sort of like Keiretsu in Japan, except that in Korea, where many of the top companies were formed by a select few individual entrepreneurs (Daewoo, Samsung, and Hyundai were all founded by one person), the unity is much closer.

As a result, South Korea has been plagued by strikes, unnatural wage hikes, rising unemployment, inflationary housing costs, and a reduction of venture capital necessary to recoup from prior adversities. A word to the buyer: approach this area with caution.

Korean negotiating strategies and tactics are similar to those of the Japanese and Chinese, but the decision-making process is generally faster. This may be due to the fact that most large Korean companies are fairly young and are still managed by the founding team.

Whereas the Japanese practice the art of bushido in their negotiating and management interactions, the Koreans follow *kibun*. Kibun comes out of a Confucian-Buddhist ethic that teaches that individuals should be driven by personal feeling, mood, attitude, and mental state. This induces a more ego-driven relationship with others, whereas the Japanese are more group-oriented. Korean managers are more often seen with large private offices, company cars, and walls emblazoned with corporate certificates of achievement. One columnist recently referred to the Korean businessman as an Asian traditionalist riding the trade wave in a Cadillac limousine. That is to say that while culture is of the utmost importance in personal and business transactions, a Korean will want to prove to the world that he or she, too, is a part of the global trading boom.

Knowledge of the Korean culture is crucial to the long-term business relationship. Dr. Rosalie Tung (University of Wisconsin) has said, "In dealing with Chinese and Japanese counterparts, knowledge of cultural differences will not guarantee success, but a lack of cultural awareness could be a principal factor for failure." Koreans go one step further: knowledge of the culture and language is imperative to success. But don't talk about the North!

The profit motive, as in most of the Asian companies, takes a backseat to market share. As noted, in Korea, the push is even greater for market share. Since they are 20 years or so behind tigers such as Japan and Hong Kong, Koreans must try harder and forgo profits longer. The term *dumping*, once ascribed to the Japanese, is now directed toward Korean companies in such areas as semiconductors, consumer electronics, and appliances.

Japanese and Chinese employees exhibit close ties with their company, and within these cultures, lifetime employment is the norm. Korean employees, however, identify with their fellow employees than with a particular company. This is due to the fact that regional clanship and attendance at common schools, both high school and college, form the criteria for who gets hired at a certain company. It is not unusual for 60 to 75% of the employees at a very large company to have their roots at a particular high school or college.

Women's rights still have a long way to go in South Korea. It would be unadvisable to send a female negotiator or team leader to a Korean contract session. Unfortunately, she will not receive the attention she should, and her gender could have a negative impact on the entire relationship. Sad but true.

The Singapore Slingshot

Singapore has become a jewel. This tiny city-state (224 square miles) is smaller than New York City, has only about three million people, yet generates a gross national product of over $50 billion. Singapore is heavy into electronics and computer parts and provides over 60% of the world's hard-disk storage devices for computers. Singapore has become the fastest-growing, most-educated high-tech producer on the Pacific Rim in just 20 years. "A slingshot into the 21st century," said T. B. Koh (Singaporean ambassador to the U.S.) during a trade mission of the Association of South East Asian Nations to Miami in 1990.

Founded, or expanded so to speak, by Sir Thomas Raffles in 1819, Singapore existed as a British colony until its independence in 1965. It exported rubber and palm oil from one of the world's largest ports for over 150 years. Just 30 years ago, Singapore was among the poverty-stricken, barefoot countries of Southeast Asia. Today, per capita income exceeds that of Great Britain. The literacy rate is nearly 100%; in the U.S., it barely exceeds 80%. One Singapore businessman told me that since Singapore has no natural resources (even its water must be imported), the only thing it has to build on is its citizens' brains. A scant generation since my first visit to Singapore in 1965, the city has supplanted the beer can–roofed slums with gorgeous high-rise apartments, glass skyscrapers, and pristine roads and streets. Even the famed Raffles Hotel, named for Singapore's founder, had a recent facelift.

In the early 1980s, the Economic Development Board (EDB) decreed a nationwide wage hike. This action, later recanted, caused a pause in the galloping investments by other nations in the economy. The EDB quickly realized that for an importer to accept a higher price, the product had to have higher value. Thereby, a massive industrywide training program was mandated that included quality, productivity, technology, and, of course, the sciences. All workers from entry-level assembly to the CEOs went back to school. From Singapore companies to those owned by others, everyone went on the fast track. Thousands of workers were sent to Japan and the U.S. to accelerate the learning. The EDB asked the companies with facilities in Singapore to help with the push. Such international companies as Philips (Netherlands), IBM, Apple, Sanyo, and Browen-Boveri (Switzerland) invested in training centers. The governments of Japan, Germany, and France also set up technical institutes with the help of the EDB. Such government help in the area of training and upgrading the skills of workers is unparalleled in any part of the world, not to mention the accelerated timeframe.

Through such efforts, a new world-class center for quality and productivity emerged with all the bells and whistles of statistical quality control and high-technology innovation. Japanese and German companies with interests in Singapore even sent home-based workers to find out how the training programs were implemented and brought back with them many new paradigms for their own plants.

On another front, Singapore's universities tripled in enrollment and course offerings. Research and development centers mushroomed, and independent training schools abounded. One researcher stated that today, tiny Singapore graduates more engineers than the United States.

This enhanced training began to show up in high quality products in a few short years. In addition, local engineers began to innovate beyond the expectations of the investing company. Rework and scrap rates declined dramatically, lot-sampling testing became a less frequent necessity, inventories were greatly reduced, and just-in-time began to mean receive parts this morning, build this afternoon (a much compressed theory than that known in the rest of the world). It is no wonder that Singapore has come to be known as the Silicon Island.

Hong Kong Today and Tomorrow

Hong Kong seems almost forgotten in the excitement of the "race of the tigers." Even smaller than Singapore, this is an island of a mere 35 square miles. A British crown colony since 1841 as a result of the Opium Wars, Hong Kong was supplemented by about 350 square miles of the New Territories, leased from China by Britain in 1898 for 99 years. Kowloon and Stonecutters islands make up the rest of the territory. When these leases ran out in 1997, the entire British holdings reverted to China. As of this writing, there is still much speculation regarding the security and future of this financial capital of the Far East.

Hong Kong possesses another of the world's great seaports and for most of its history served as a transshipment point for the Chinese mainland. Following the formation of the People's Republic of China in 1949 and during the Korean conflict in the early 1950s, all trade from mainland China was under an embargo by the UN. What did flow into Hong Kong were tens of thousands of Chinese industrialists and workers fleeing Mao Tse Tung's Cultural Revolution. Because of this, Hong Kong transformed itself from a shipping port to a light-manufacturing center. Within 20 years, large financial institutions, seeing the resurgence of the Asian economy, chose Hong Kong, with its laissez-faire attitude, for their offices, making the colony a world financial center right behind New York and London. The *Asian Wall Street Journal* is published there.

The years from 1949 to Mao's death in 1976 marked a period of Chinese isolationism and xenophobia. Hong Kong remained effectively walled off from the mainland. Richard Nixon's trip to China in 1972 facilitated the normalizing of relations and formal recognition of China. Deng Ziaoping then focused China toward increased trade and investment, albiet with a very watchful eye. This resurgence of manufacturing in China boosted Hong Kong back into the role of a transshipment point from the mainland.

SOUTHEAST ASIA: THE NEW FRONTIER

Southeast Asia is made up of 10 countries, and the Association of South East Asian Nations (ASEAN) accounts for only 7. (See more on ASEAN in Chapter 9.) The remaining 3, sometimes referred to as Indo-China, are Burma (Myanmar), Cambodia (Kamputchea), and Laos. The governments of these nations are still more authoritarian than those of the other ASEAN countries and are socialist in nature. Their industrial prowess is minimal, and their trading is generally among themselves and with China. One might liken the differences between the Indo-China nations and ASEAN to the differences between North and South Korea. The former tends toward isolationism, an agrarian economy, and avoiding the mainstream. For that reason these nations are not addressed in this book as possible sources, but eventually they will probably take their place in the ASEAN union.

The ASEAN group of countries has shown interest in becoming a part of the global economy through ongoing and never-ending trade missions to major world cities in search of everything from exports and imports to joint ventures and investments. The increasingly prosperous ASEAN economies boast a gross domestic product approaching 10% per year. The exception is the Philippines, which has grappled with recent natural disasters like an earthquake and a volcanic eruption coupled with a modicum of political unrest.

Indonesia boasts the world's second-largest seaport after Rotterdam, Holland. This advantage plus the designation as a free-trade zone has made Indonesia a major trading player as a where value-added manufacturing soon boomed.

Malaysia, by virtue of its prosperity and stability, has earned a reputation as one of the most favorably placed nations in Southeast Asia. The country is the world leader in the production of raw materials such as natural rubber, palm oil (60% of world supply), and tin. Of late, Malaysia has added to this list cocoa, petroleum, and natural gas. Apart from being a major producer of primary commodities, the country is also a producer of a whole range of quality manufactures and semimanufactures. Malaysia is among the world's major suppliers of air conditioners, electronic components and parts, textiles and apparel, and a host of foodstuffs.

The Philippines is a country still in transition. Plagued by rebel groups (the Huk Bala Hap, the Revolutionary National Alliance, and the Moro National Liberation Front) in the countryside and the uneasiness related to the recent political problems of former president Marcos, industry still is making forward strides. The years 1986 to 1988 were marked by a positive growth rate between 3% and 6% during the Aquino administration, but as industry began to grow, massive shortages of electrical power stymied progress.

The recent forced exodus of U.S. bases like Subic Bay and Clark Airbase appeared, on the surface, to be a detriment to progress and international relations. On the contrary, Clark is being resurrected as a resort area to include theme parks, golf courses, hotels, restaurants, and even a retirement village. With help from Malaysian billionaire Lim Goh Tong and Taiwanese billionaire Jeffrey Koo, Subic Bay is being converted to an industrial park. Such notables as FedEx and Reebock have already staked their claim to plants and facilities.

Also on the positive side, President Fidel Ramos has led the reform movement to make the country more competitive. By 1994, electrical power shortages had been virtually eliminated in metropolitan Manila. Large expenditures in infrastructure have modernized the cities and freed the industrial parks of electrical blackouts. He further instituted programs that broke up family-owned monopolies and reduced graft and corruption in the international trading markets. Newly acquired foreign investments include Avon products and Proctor and Gamble.

In 1994, the U.S. was the leading export market, accounting for a 38% share of total exports from the Philippines.

Singapore, covered earlier in this chapter as one of the tigers, is the self-proclaimed economic leader of ASEAN. Its financial centers and educational institutions draw from the group countries in great numbers.

Thailand is rushing to join the other tigers in commodities such as consumer electronics and light manufacturing. Remember the Siamese King who hired the British teacher, Anna, to make sure that his children were educated enough to be respected in the world? Well it's happening again. Thailand, still a kingdom, is importing experience and expertise to assimilate what manufacturing it can from countries that have graduated to the next step in technology and manufacturing-process control.

Brunei Darussalam derives 90% of its revenue from oil. The ruling Sultan of Brunei is listed by *Forbes* as one of the 10 richest men in the world. Newly independent (1984), the less than half a million people seem content to ride with the tide. As a source of energy and foreign investment for the association, Brunei maintains a quiet seat in ASEAN.

Viet Nam, newest member of ASEAN (July 1995), is probably the most surprising upstart in the Asian community. Ravaged by some 75 years of wars and insurgencies, the communist government in Ho Chi Minh City (Saigon) has privatized most of the industry through *doi moi* (renovation) and opened the doors to foreign investment. In 1994 alone, more than 100,000 small retail business licenses were issued. In that same year, BMW moved in with an assembly plant. Despite the normalization of relations, American investment has been somewhat delayed due to the postwar MIA issue, but other countries swarmed through the open doors.

In state-led economic development, in general, it is said that the artificial distribution of resources is apt to be a cause of inefficiency. But such a system also has certain advantages. It facilitates the achievement of economies of scale and the accumulation of technology through intensive investment by the state into selected industries and regions. In the case of Viet Nam, however, it has not completely shifted away from an inefficient socialist economic system and an unclear decision-making process regarding economic development.

EUROPE: EAST AND WEST

Within the newly formed European Economic Union (EEC) there has been standardization on the one hand and a tenuous grasp on certain individual characteristics of nations on the other. ISO 9000 (Chapter 11) has worked wonders in the areas of a single quality standard and other organizational facets of the manufacturing world. Still remaining to be solved are a universal monetary standard, some legal contractual differences, and, of course, the cultural differences.

Remember that Europe is a collection of states that did not come together as did the U.S. To maintain their identities, each country developed unique qualities that would deliberately set them apart from the others.

Most Europeans are strongly individualistic in their personal as well as business life. This individualism is tempered, however, with a modicum of cultural and social ideology. That is to say, status, rank, and position are important facets of the interrelationship among people and countries. Also to be contended with are differences between objective and subjective reasoning.

Facts and objectivity win out over emotions in most instances, even when emotions (in eastern countries especially) may flare up during a discussion. One exception may be the southern countries of Italy, Spain, and Portugal, where participants in a negotiation tend to lean more toward the subjective sides of issues.

Technical information is readily accepted in Europe, probably due to two world wars effectively won with the infusion of American technology and strategies. It is the legal and contractual side of the negotiations that may be difficult for Europeans to accept at face value.

The German Differences

A possible exception in all these generalities is Germany, which is still trying to outlive the ambitions of its misguided rulers of three "reichs" that invaded their neighbors and generally created chaos. From the Holy Roman Empire First Reich to Otto von Bismark's Second Reich and on to Hitler's Third, the focus was on empire building. Maybe because of this past, Germans still tend to be suspect of outsiders. They maintain a strong allegiance toward some central authority and a demeanor that provides little room for individuality or feelings. They are very serious negotiators, and comical or flippant attitudes and jokes are not acceptable. The same goes for their personal life such as family, pastimes, and such. Again, in Germany, business is business. If there is an exception to these rules, let *them* lead the way.

Needless to say, you would be cautioned from mentioning anything related to war, Jews, and past German leaders as these topics are of great concern to today's Germans. Talk about beer instead and you'll be a winner.

German businesspeople are generally skeptical of anything new or untried, or that hasn't been invented there. They don't like exaggeration of claims that have an unstable basis of fact. They are highly structured organizationally, and although laws proclaim equal rights, social strata are like a multifaceted organizational chart without connecting lines.

The recent lifting of the Berlin Wall has opened a floodgate of immigrants from the east. Despite the fact that many of these immigrants are German by descent, they have endured a generation of differences under Soviet control, no longer possess the same work ethics or skills, and are considered by many as gypsies that overburden the employment lines.

The English Are Different Too

Somehow Americans often have the impression that because the English language is spoken in both the U.S. and U.K., they know and understand the English ways. Not necessarily so. The English can operate within a very closed, stubborn, and intractable society. Once the British set their mind to something, it's hard to sway them. By the same token, they are almost completely objective on the issues and rarely offer a subjective opinion.

To complicate all this, the British tend toward individual decision making while at the same time remaining supportive of group or company wishes. They follow traditional norms and at times can be viewed as old-fashioned in their thinking. In that light, these opinions and beliefs are communicated directly, albeit sometimes brashly, when they feel circumstances dictate.

The English are proud of their historic sites. Set aside time to visit as many as you are able and ask your hosts to recommend some.

Be aware that the ethnic portions of these islands off the coast of Europe are extremely proud of their heritage. While the English might refer to Scotland and (northern) Ireland as part of Britain or the U.K., Scots prefer to call themselves Scots and the Irish are Irish.

Due to its location in the North Atlantic, the islands can be often drizzly, rainy, and misty. Plan on bringing an umbrella for those times that you will be walking or waiting for a taxi.

European Generalizations

Most Europeans as well as Asians write dates with the day first, month second, and year last: 05 December 97 or 5/12/97. This can be very important in deciphering correspondence and keeping an appointment calendar.

Europeans tend to take their vacations in the summer, usually in July and August. Furthermore, entire companies and some industries completely shut down so that everyone is away at the same time, eliminating the need for someone to cover for someone else during vacation time. One August, while in France, I found that, aside from the grocery, the bakery and entertainment, virtually everything in the city was closed. Additionally, in many countries, offices close early on Fridays.

Regarding language, an American purchasing agent may feel inadequate when his or her counterparts are speaking in four or five languages. It is common in European schools to study two other languages in addition to English. That makes four all together.

Professional achievements are acknowledged. A buyer who has an advanced educational degree should add that to his or her business card. Save all business cards, as telephone directories are hard to come by and many numbers are unlisted; these may be the only reference.

Northern Europe

By northern Europe, the reference is to Scandinavia in particular, which includes Denmark, Norway, Sweden, and Finland. These governments are organized along the lines of social welfare and are highly concerned with environmental issues. In discussing an issue, Danes, for example, might first be interested in the impact on all the people, the environment, and their nationalistic ideologies. In Sweden, the purchasing manager might find an inordinate amount of attention applied to the impact of an issue on a subcontractor or supplier. In that regard, it can be said that when conducting business in this area of Europe, the manager must be cognizant of the egalitarian mentality and show empathy for other points of view.

These socially oriented countries are mostly middle class, with minimal distinction between living conditions, income, and benefits. Compared with most other countries, the gap between the entry-level wage and the salary of the corporate CEO is much less.

Because of their proximity to Germany, the Scandinavians are very independent, objective, and fact-oriented, and tend to spend a great deal of time on details seemingly insignificant to Americans. In business meetings they get right to the point and are not prone to subjective ideas. They resist humor, tangenting from the issues, or what they may consider trivial conversation. The so-called American hype marketing approach is not appreciated by these countries.

Like the British, Scandinavians tend to be more serious and reserved, show minimal emotion, and focus on the business at hand. Accordingly, they may spend an inordinate amount of time during meetings just thinking. If there is a long silence from the other side, don't jump in and fill the void with conversation; be patient. Use the sales technique—after you ask for the order, shut up.

Although there are a lot of similarities within the Scandinavian countries, there are also differences. Norwegians, for example, are somewhat more informal and may bypass certain protocols for expeditious reasons. However, this is not to imply that they are lax; they are on the contrary very businesslike.

The Other Europe

The Eastern countries, closed off for a generation or so, have only recently reopened. From Poland on the Baltic Sea to Bulgaria on the Black Sea, the area under control of the former USSR has been an enigma. Because of their proximity to Russia and the domination factor, many of their business practices tend toward Russian standards.

Hungary seems to have emerged as the manufacturing leader of the area following the end of the cold war. Formerly agricultural in nature, Hungary boasts over 40% of gross national product from manufacturing. The government opened up formerly state-owned businesses for sale or lease to private entities. By 1994, over 50% of businesses had been privatized. An act passed by the parliament in 1995 was designed to accelerate this process.

It is difficult, even with six months notice, to get a hotel room in Budapest. Many companies buy blocks of rooms for their foreign visitors.

Unlike the rest of Europe, which is somewhat structured and hemmed in by history and culture, East Europeans have become increasingly open and eager to do business in their new-found freedom. You will find Hungarians surprisingly, and sometimes embarrassingly, direct. They express feelings and emotions openly and let their true side show.

In the Czech Republic you will find a propensity toward German business practices. The slow, methodical analysis of large numbers of facts characterizes the progress of negotiations. Conversely, personal topics such as home and family are also welcomed.

Poland has also been driven by the new privatization of business and industry, and there has been a rapid growth in entrepreneurial spirit and a rise in free-enterprise mentality. Heavy manufacturing is being slowly rebuilt with modern equipment, and the banks and businesspeople are eager to do business. It might facilitate relationships to understand that Poland still maintains a very male-dominated business world. The sending of female negotiators may not be in a company's best interests.

To facilitate communications in any of the former Eastern countries, it is advisable to obtain a local agent, who can expedite business affairs. The advantage of having this agent is that in each country the rapid transition of rules, laws, and regulations is almost impossible to keep up with unless one is there every day.

Russia and the Commonwealth of Independent States (CIS)

The Russians are still struggling through their own transition to a free-market economy. Real money is scarce, and many government employees (including doctors, miners, and others still under state employment) do not get paid for months at a time. Possibly because of this, or just the traditional demeanor of the Russian people, they seem to be temperamental, argumentative, and like to walk out of meetings in a huff.

Business matters in any of the CIS countries can be difficult. Laws and expectations are continually changing. Since the demise of communism and the totalitarian central decision-making authorities, businesspeople are looking for new authorities for guidance but are naturally very cautious. They may not be tuned in to what a buyer may consider obvious, standard, or accepted business principles and practices. For example, the legal and banking professions as we know them were virtually nonexistent in most of the former USSR.

Agreement may be hard to come by, and the very thought of a compromise may be abhorrent to a Russian. Rather, find a way to present your needs within a framework that will allow the other side to visualize concessions on *your* part. And be prepared to play hardball.

As in Japan and the Middle East, where *yes* does not necessarily mean *yes;* in Russia, *no* probably does not mean an emphatic *no*. Its just that *niet* ("no") has become such a common word in these countries that you might

---

Case Study

This author served as a consultant to a firm interested in setting up banks in the Ukraine. During a meeting that included representatives from the Ukrainian-American Credit Union (in the U.S.), we were made startlingly aware of the monumental task ahead of us. One team member remarked, "The first question you have to answer for the people is 'What is a bank?' Then we can proceed to other matters."

---

feel like a toddler having everything you do admonished by a mother saying no.

Because the logistics and infrastructure of the CIS are in such chaos as of this writing, a purchasing manager will find on-time delivery of anything is rare. Even restaurants seldom have all the items listed on the menu, and stores are perpetually out of almost everything. Shipments do come in, but within hours stock is sold out.

As an exception to the shortages mentioned above, vodka seems to be ever present. The Russians are heavy drinkers, and straight vodka instead of water or wine is traditionally drunk with meals. Remember to sip judiciously and leave some in your glass, as an empty glass will be refilled and a new toast made.

THE MOSLEM MIDDLE EAST

The Middle East has been a center for trade for thousands of years. The silk and spice roads passed through this area on the way to Europe a thousand years before Vasco da Gama circumnavigated the tip of Africa in 1497. These people know trade and may look upon Americans as rank amateurs in the business of bartering, negotiation, and logistics.

The Middle East is the cradle of Islam, a religion practiced throughout the world but focused mostly from northern Africa to Indonesia. A devout practitioner of Islam, called a Moslem, will call a break in the meeting to perform his twice daily prayer ritual.

One common Islamic belief is that the soles of the shoes are the farthest point away from Allah (the Islamic equivalent of God). A knowledgeable foreigner would not show the soles of the shoes by crossing his or her legs, as this would be considered offensive to a Moslem.

Another bit of cultural diversity is the separation of the use of the right hand and the left. The left hand is considered unclean (most Moslem countries are arid, and water for washing is at a premium). Accordingly, the stigma persists, and you would be wise to not reach for items with that hand or, more importantly, to touch anyone or eat with that hand, even if you are left handed. Another hand problem is with the "thumbs-up" gesture used in Europe and America signifying "OK," "great," or "A-1." In the Arab world this is highly offensive.

Case Study

During the American hostage crisis in Iran, then secretary general of the UN Kurt Waldheim arrived in Tehran to assist in their release. When asked by a reporter what he thought his chances of success were in facilitating the release of the hostages Mr. Waldheim raised his right hand above the crowd in the traditional Austrian fashion with the thumb up. The crowd, believing this to mean an obscene gesture, stoned the official limo as it exited the airport.

Pointing (using the index finger) is generally not done in Moslem countries. Furthermore, the Western "come-here" gesture of crooking the finger or hand upward and toward one may be considered an obscene sign. Rather, Middle Easterners use the palm down, all fingers waving together and inward in this instance, such as for hailing a taxi. Nodding one's head for yes is the same, but shaking the head from side to side means that you do not understand rather than disagree. To indicate the negative, an Arab tilts his or her head backward, raises his eyebrows, and looks down his or her nose. This may also be accompanied by the sound "tsk."

The Moslem world forbids alcoholic beverages, although there are places, such as certain international private clubs and hotels, where these may be served, but only in some countries. Make sure that you do not invite a Moslem to these places. Meetings do not begin with the traditional coffee as in the U.S.; they end with coffee.

When making business decisions, it is not unusual for a Moslem to launch into a discussion of the impact on Islamic beliefs. Beyond this, the decision-making process, although painfully slow, is collective in nature, and individual and personal issues are usually set aside. As in Japan, *yes* rarely means the affirmative. It merely signifies that you are probably on the right track and have received interim agreement, pending further facts.

The Islamic sabbath is on Friday, and businesses may take their two-day weekend on Thursday and Friday or Friday and Saturday. Midday is a time of rest and prayer, so many offices will be closed from around, 1 P.M. to 5 P.M., and then resumes work in the early evening until 7 or 8 P.M. The business day is only six hours, and meetings are best arranged in the mornings. Evening appointments, in the cool of the night, are also common.

Just a word about punctuality. In this area of the world, you must be prompt for appointments. The same is not true for your counterparts, who will generally be late or not show up at all. Many times this happens with no explanation or apology. They may even be out of the country. In light of that, a purchasing manager might be wise to schedule only one appointment per day, with time set aside for rescheduling.

Relationships are key. An agent or intermediary to facilitate an introduction is advised. In many countries, having a local agent is mandated by law. Most Middle Eastern countries require a written invitation from the buyer's in-country host to obtain entry. The buyer will also need an exit permit to be allowed to leave the country.

The Arab world practices a physical closeness that may unnerve many Americans. During conversations, Arabs may stand frighteningly close to you. Kissing the cheek when greeting and holding hands among men is a sign of friendship and universally accepted. If you find yourself heading out of the conference room hand-in-hand with your host, you have probably made a superb impression and sealed a sterling business relationship.

Remember that women in Islamic countries are still oppressed by Western standards. American female team members traveling to these areas should choose conservative clothing, high necklines, long sleeves, and skirts below the knee. Worse, special police called Matawain earnestly enforce the dress code, and even a foreign woman with too revealing a hemline may find her exposed legs flogged with a camel whip right on the street. Beware.

For men, not surprisingly, some of the same restrictions apply. Even if the weather is very hot, which it usually is, donning a tank top and shorts for a trip to the market is not proper or tolerated in most countries. To protect oneself from the sun in the Middle East, most of the body is covered with light-colored, loosely fitting garments. Bring baggy clothes.

All decisions in the Arab home are made by the husband or other male. And all business and advertising must be directed toward men.

Case Study

The Singer Sewing Machine Company decided to export to Saudi Arabia a few years back. Their advertising showed an Arab woman happily at work on her machine, and the text proclaimed all the fine stitchery that could be accomplished with a Singer. Sales were very disappointing. As a last resort, the Singer Company engaged the services of a local advertising agent, who promptly informed the company of the error in the direction of its appeal. New advertising was designed showing an Arab male describing the quality and efficiency in the repair of his garments. Sales rose immediately. Men make the buying decisions in Moslem countries.

Israel

In Israel you will find two major religious entities, Moslems and Jews, plus some Christians. The competition between the first two groups is no secret, and differences seem to be in the news daily. In that light, political conversations should never be initiated by Americans. Furthermore, never discuss Israel in other Arab countries. At the risk of being chastised by readers, I would have to advise against sending a team member of Jewish faith to an Arab country. It cannot be stressed enough, the volatility of the Arab–Israel differences.

The Jewish sabbath is Saturday, and the traditional work week runs from Sunday through Thursday. Remember that Islamic businesses are closed on Fridays for the same reason. Plan to conduct business from Monday through Thursday in Israel.

As opposed to Moslems, Israelis tend to be more individualistic and opinionated. They can be very open and sometimes emotional.

LATIN AMERICA

Practically all of Central and South America was conquered by the Spanish starting shortly after the arrival of Columbus, the exception to this being Brazil, which was colonized in 1500 by Pedro Cabral for Portugal, and a sprinkling of smaller countries settled by the Netherlands, British, and French. Indian cultures such as the Aztec, Mayan, and Incan were replaced with Spanish culture. Most Mexicans today are mestizos or part Indian and part Spanish. During the following 400 years or so, entire economies were changed from hunting and gathering to agriculture and thereon to industry and service under Spanish influence. Most of the business methods stem from same cultural origin.

Internationally accepted standards fall apart in Latin America. A purchasing manager can anticipate a lack of promptness, incessant and seemingly unexplainable delays, a lack of attention to detail, and difficulties in accepting a fact as a fact.

Long before the North American Free Trade Agreement, Mexico devised a way to encourage business ventures in that country to boost employment. Beginning with the U.S. border towns of Tijuana, Nogalas, and Juarez in 1965, the government popularized what it called *maquiladora* operations. Literally translated, *maquiladora* means "corn-ration" or "sweatshop wage." The object was to attract U.S. businesses to import U.S. parts, use cheap Mexican labor to assemble goods, and export back to the U.S., all without any tax or restrictions like a foreign trade zone. Thousands of such factories sprang up along the border and expanded southward to Monterrey, Guadalajara, and beyond.

Brazil and Industrialization

Probably the most industrial country in South America is Brazil. It is also the country in the most economic turmoil. São Paulo and the surrounding countryside of Campinas and Sumaré are the focus of manufacturing, with huge facilities with such names as Ford, Volkswagen, Philips, and IBM.

There are three distinct classes in Brazil, widely separated from each other economically. The rich are few but conspicuous in their wealth. The working class seems to be able to manage, in spite of the rampant inflation and devaluation of the currency. The *fevaladoes,* or what we might refer to as ghetto people, live in abject poverty. Hundreds of seemingly homeless children ply the streets of major cities stealing and picking pockets at will. Guard your money and jewelry very closely. Better yet, leave all jewelry at home and wear a $10 watch.

Brazilians tend to be more interested in facts and objective reasoning than most of the rest of Latin America. This may be due to German and Japanese influences, which are extensive in the industrial sector. The largest single community of expatriate Japanese anywhere in the world is in São Paulo with over one million Japanese among its 16 million inhabitants. The Japanese workers can be found in the quality departments of almost any company. German workers may be found in the design and engineering departments.

When sourcing in Latin America, you will find that agreement is easily acknowledged but plan on little change being made. Even in the case of engineering-process changes, it is possible that six months later you will find that nothing has changed. One way to expedite such situations may be to devise a method whereby the changes are arrived at by the local engineer. Then the implementation may be swifter.

Some reasoning for this phenomenon may be due to the educational system, which spends little time on social interaction, creativity, and logical thinking. Learning is by rote and facts; methods and principles are memorized and fixed. Anything new or novel may be wondered at but in the long run shunned as outside their known and accepted norms.

Personal relationships are key, culminating in many intertwined networks of cliques within which all business and personal matters are shared.

Argentina: Closer to Europe

Perhaps the only other country in Latin America that doesn't follow the generally accepted "Spanish influence" theory is Argentina. As opposed to the mestizo Indian/Spanish mix of most of the population of Latin America, Argentina has been settled by Europeans, mostly Spanish and Italians. Intermarriage with native Indians has been rare. Even their Spanish language is tempered by a heavy Italian-like dialect and is unlike any other Spanish in the hemisphere.

Argentines are apt to be less subjective in their reasoning than other Latin Americans. The general Latin American paradigm of a long decision-making process is further expanded by the practice of requiring multiple signatures at practically every level on virtually every decision. This bureaucratic nightmare may cost a purchasing agent several trips to accomplish the necessary business.

The raising of livestock and associated industries has made Argentina a major source for packaged meats. Reasonably large auto and ship-building industries lead the manufacturing sector, which now accounts for about 25% of gross national product.

OTHER COMMUNICATION DIFFERENCES

Carrying the dos and don'ts to the next step, let's look at some things that, while they may seem positive in an American setting, actually call for just the opposite reaction in a foreign venue.

Case Study

Negotiators were sitting around the conference table in Scotland, just beginning to get to business. The Scottish host said, "I guess we should table this computer contract."

"Wait just a minute," said the American. "That's the whole reason we came all the way over here."

The internationally streetwise Scotsman just laughed. "In Scotland, to table something means to put in 'on the table'; not your American meaning to 'put the matter off' until some later time." All laughed. A point had been made.

In Canada, there are two cultures, English and French. Since this is a highly charged situation in most of Canada (especially in the French-based province of Quebec), the purchasing manager must be careful not to mention politics in any way. However, in deference to the probable inclusion of French members of any Canadian supplier organization, recognition of this diversity may be helpful to the buyer's cause.

A minimal gesture could be a simple "bon jour" along with "good morning" and ending with "thank you" and "merci." But again, refrain from instigating a cultural or political discussion at any cost. In any country, it is wise to "ask before you leap," even if you think you think you know what's happening.

Case Study

President Ronald Reagan was on a state visit to Mexico during his term in office. During his address (in English) to the Mexican people, he was somewhat amazed that there was little or no reaction to his statements of cooperation and a bright outlook for the future of Mexico. Following his speech, a well-dressed Mexican from the head table then addressed the crowd. Unlike President Reagan's speech, this one was punctuated by numerous outbursts of applause and cheers from the audience. Since the other members of the head table were also applauding, Reagan did so as well.

After several instances of applause, the Mexican president leaned over to Mr. Reagan and said, "I wouldn't do that if I were you." "Why not?" responded Reagan.

The Mexican president whispered, "Because that gentleman is translating your speech."

Despite your best efforts, you may find yourself in an embarrassing position while in another country. The best thing to do is apologize profusely and let the matter be. After all, I'm sure that you could name several instances where a foreigner has found him- or herself in an embarrassing position regarding language or customs while visiting the U.S.

Be patient and tolerant of cultural differences. There is a little-known example of Asian patience and forbearance which I will relate here as it appeared in *The Art of Negotiating,* by Gerard I. Nierenberg:

> Franklin D. Roosevelt used to tell a story about the Chinese use of forbearance, based on 4000 years of civilization. Two coolies were arguing heatedly at great length in the midst of a crowd. A stranger expressed surprise that no blows were being struck. His Chinese friend explained, "The man who strikes first admits that his ideas have given out."[1]

---

[1] Gerald I. Nierenberg, *The Art of Negotiating.* (New York; Pocket Books, 1981).

CHAPTER 6
Negotiation Strategies

Most individuals enter into the international negotiation arena poorly prepared for the diversities they will encounter. They attack the issues a priori, so to speak. The term *a priori* is defined as reasoning based on theory instead of experience or experiment and before examination or analysis. This is sort of a right-brain or creative approach, as opposed to the left brain or logical mind. This approach tends to work pretty well in the U.S. When crossing borders, however, there is no substitute for knowledge and experience.

Businesspeople in the rest of the world are far more experienced in the art of negotiating than Americans are. This experience ranges from the intricacies and mystery of the Chinese puzzle to the prolonged haggling that goes on in the Middle East. For those unwilling to learn and become part of the international negotiating scene, the price can be high. Buyers must be continually open to new approaches and the indigenous intricacies of the international negotiating game.

Rule number one: don't ever assume that you can "wing it" at the negotiating table. For example, suppose you are going to negotiate in Thailand. Do you speak any Thai? Do you know the history of the country? Do you understand the various religious and foreign influences that have shaped Thailand over the past thousand years or so (e.g., China, Britain, France, Japan, and America)? That's pretty comprehensive. You will find that the strategies of the Thai negotiator are just as intricate. The purchasing manager must formulate a plan of attack, including the following steps:

- Inventorying abilities
- Planning a strategy
- Developing product knowledge
- Researching suppliers
- Forming a negotiating team
- Defining a cost model
- Documenting tactics
- Planning for the long haul

INVENTORYING ABILITIES

Not everyone is a seasoned, high-class negotiator. That's all right. A good negotiator, however, possesses certain distinct qualities. Some of these can be learned, but those that are natural and consistent with the individual will be an invaluable asset and return rich rewards for the company. A good negotiator, especially one who ventures outside the comfort of his or her own country, will have the following traits:

- Patience
- Preparation
- Practice
- Perseverance
- Amiability
- Quick thinking
- Competitiveness
- Initiative
- Reliability
- Stamina
- Flexibility

Patience is at the top of the list for a reason. A negotiator who is constantly on the offensive and is in a hurry to get to the bottom line and return home will ultimately find that he or she was shortchanged in the process. Every author on the subject of international diversity notes that Americans are impatient, blustery, and many times rude. Suppliers from all parts of the world have told me personally that they expect little from Americans, and they are usually right. Remember the movie *The Ugly American?* In that movie, a U.S. diplomat ingratiated himself at the expense of intercountry relations. That stigma follows Americans everywhere— sometimes even in the U.S. itself.

There are probably some good reasons for that stigma. The East, from China to Israel, boasts of a history some 5,000 years in the making. To them, the clock moves slowly and the calendar even slower. We recently celebrated the 200th birthday of the U.S. as an independent country. That's just a tick of the clock in India or China. There is a definite difference in the concept of time.

A foreign supplier may anticipate a negotiation of several days or weeks. An American purchasing manager may have an airline ticket that requires him or her to leave by the end of the week. One option is to present the facts, garner some important information, and then continue the negotiation via fax and phone on returning home. Those buyers who can convince their company to "stay as long as it takes" will get the best pricing and terms.

Preparation is paramount for performance. Again, leave nothing to chance. The purchasing manager should read as much information as possible about the supplier's country. He or she should learn about its history, religions, financial information, per capita income, and laws. Has the country experienced a war in the past hundred years? What was it about? What influence did it have on the people or changes that it might have caused?

The manager should learn some language. It will not be necessary to become fluent by any means. But a sprinkling of the native language will go a long way to smoothing the path to agreement. The American that says *dzao an* (good morning) or *xhe xhe* (thank you) in Beijing will have narrowed him- or herself into the top 10% of Americans who know any Chinese at all. That person will have made his or her best first impression.

The other important part of preparation for the buyer is to write down all the things he or she hopes to gain during the negotiation and the least that will be accepted. A window of opportunity should be established. Variables can be plugged into a matrix as follows:

	Quote	*Best*	*Accept*
Unit Price	$365	$300	$340
Lead Time	8 weeks	5 weeks	7 weeks

The manager will want to write down things he or she thinks the supplier will ask for and be prepared to respond with preauthorized alternatives. For example, based on earlier conversations the buyer thinks that the supplier may want to use a particular component, maybe made by a company that is in the supplier's core supplier network. Past experience has been less than satisfactory with that company's products. Will using an approved sourcing for the component adversely affect your bottom line unit pricing? Can engineers work with the component supplier to ensure compatibility with the specifications? Is there an alternative supplier, a compromise, another way to defuse the cost difference? Plan all this ahead—while still at the office—and the impediments to any negotiation will be greatly reduced.

Practice sessions for a football team, an orchestra, or dancers are an expected and integral part of the activity and enjoyed by most as much as the game or performance itself. When it comes to rehearsing for a negotiation, however, people tend to back away, can't find time, don't think it's important. Just traveling to a foreign country should cause one to pause and ponder what will be encountered, let alone actually negotiating with someone from another culture. Role-playing prepared strategies over and over again will put a purchasing manager at ease for the real negotiations.

The well-known negotiation teacher Chester Karrass wrote a whole book entitled *The Negotiating Game*.[1] Others have likened the goings-on at a negotiating table as a war. One American buyer told me once after returning from three weeks in the Middle East, "It wasn't a negotiation, it was more like a war!" In any case, people who play games, as well as people who play war, practice, practice, practice.

Perseverance is like patience in the active sense. As already pointed out, foreigners have a longer sense of time and therefore tend to have more natural perseverance than Americans do. The purchasing manager

---

[1]Chester L. Karrass, *The Negotiating Game* (New York: Thomas Y. Crowell, 1970).

Case Study

While in Taipei negotiating for pricing on an industrial monitor, it became evident that the most expensive component in the assembly was the safety, nonreflective glass purchased in the U.S. and shipped to Taipei for assembly, subsequently to be shipped back to the U.S. for distribution. Anticipating this, our negotiation team was prepared to investigate alternative sources for the glass, namely Taiwan Glass or Asahi Glass in Japan. We never made our intentions known to the Taiwanese team.

During the negotiations we established the price of the glass then asked if it would be more cost-efficient to purchase the glass somewhere in the Far East. The Taiwanese team turned to their sourcing manager, who put his briefcase on the table. "We thought you might want to know that so we have prepared some samples and specification sheets for you to evaluate."

I do not know whether the Taiwanese team would have brought the issue to the table themselves. As it turned out, the cost of the glass finally used was substantially less than that of the U.S. glass and of better quality. However, a decimal of profit was lost by the Taiwanese company for not handling the more expensive glass. But they were prepared. And they were more than happy to oblige.

---

needs to match that by not giving in too early or agreeing too soon. The haggling that goes on in most of the Middle East and Asia is mostly habit. It's what's expected. Not to haggle is to not do business. Foreign merchants persevere. They like the interaction. Those who tend to be too quick to resolution usually miss the best deal.

Amiability is a necessity in any venue. It's even more important outside the U.S. if only to overcome the aforementioned perception of Americans. When T. Boone Pickens went to Japan and loudly demanded to have his way, he was summarily rejected by the company, the people, and the country (see the case study in Chapter 1). Asians, especially the Japanese, are outwardly humble, interested at all costs in saving face. While they may be boiling with rage inside, they will find some words, expressions or gestures to appear calm and amiable. Some of these signs were enumerated in Chapter 5.

Quick thinking is necessary for handling those gritty, unanticipated problems that most likely will come up during a negotiation. Quick thinking should not be confused with hastiness. Quick thinking is the ability to provide calm, thoughtful answers or have the knowledge to react appropriately to something one doesn't understand.

Competitiveness is a common trait in many of us. We just hate to lose. Competitiveness is not only winning, but being able to accept defeat—of certain points—graciously and counter with something else. A buyer might react to a missed first-delivery commitment by a supplier in the following way:

> "I'm disappointed in being unable to get the component by the required marketing date. Because the product is time-sensitive, that will surely have an effect on the total number that I will be ordering. Can my company help your people with the design, startup, manufacturing, or quality so that we might be able to bring the ship date in a little? Can we work with your suppliers to get materials sooner? Do you have any other suggestions?"

The buyer obviously had failed to get a delivery commitment date. However, she didn't give up. She went back into the fray with amiability and quick thinking. She was competitive.

Initiative is an important trait because in most countries people look up to a leader, one who takes the initiative. That is not to say that the buyer should be overbearing, dominant, or autocratic. One way a negotiator can take the initiative is to plan and prepare for the negotiation. Another way a buyer can show initiative is by asking his or her foreign counterpart about the other's country. The rewards from such an initiative will take you far in your acceptance in that country.

Reliability cannot be overstated. It is connected with honesty, trustworthiness, dedication, and more. No one wants to deal with someone who is unreliable, changes his or her mind at will, or doesn't follow through. A manager will find that infractions of reliability are looked on more harshly by the rest of the world than in the U.S.

Stamina goes along with perseverance and starts with the ability to fly halfway around the world and be bright and fresh at a 10 A.M. meeting in Tokyo, when one's body feels like the time is 10 P.M. Stamina is also

---

Case Study

You will probably leave the U.S. on an evening flight whether going east or west. If you are going west, you may arrive at 5 P.M. local time. If you are going east to Europe, you will probably arrive in the early morning. In either case, regardless of any sleep you got on the plane, you are ready for bed.

If you are in Tokyo, you will probably wake up at 3 A.M. the next morning, terribly hungry, with no restaurants open. To prepare for this, after you check into the hotel, find a bakery or convenience store close to the hotel and pick up some breakfast items (some travelers pack snacks for just such an occasion). Most international hotels in the Far East have hot water in the room for tea. Instant coffee is something to buy.

At 3 A.M., get up, eat something, do some planning, or go over your notes. In a couple of hours you will doze off. You can now awake again at 8 A.M. or so and be fresh for your meeting. And you can have another breakfast.

The problem is less frustrating when going to Europe because you will be arriving in the daytime and things will be available in the midafternoon when you awaken from your postarrival nap.

---

important when the manager must cover too much ground for the allotted time in country. This may cause the negotiations and meetings to go far into the night. The Japanese and Chinese think nothing of staying at the office until the last train out to the suburbs, which may be 11 P.M. And the manager must be prepared for some quick native takeout food; food that the manager will probably not be accustomed to or able to eat.

Flexibility allows the negotiator to excel in most of the other traits. One must be creative, able to change one's mind, and pick up on any change in the mood or tenor of the negotiation and reverse gears if necessary. Just as a football quarterback will, at the last second, change the play at the line of scrimmage when he sees a hole in the defense, the negotiator must be able to recognize an opportunity and seize that opportunity. The English word *opportunity* is derived from the Latin *ob portu* (before the port), which means waiting for the high tide so that the ship can breach the reefs and reach safe harbor.

PLANNING A STRATEGY

In addition to the preparation phase, there is more to be said for strategies. Probably the most important difference separating Americans from the rest of the world is that Americans are out there to do *business* while the rest of the world is looking for *relationships,* long-term relationships to be sure. That single fact is why Americans, more than anyone else, need to develop strategies. And those strategies must take into serious consideration the relationship factor.

Here is a simple checklist for planning from the buyer's side:

- What are the buyer's goals (e.g., price, quantity, delivery, and quality)?
- What will the buyer settle for (below which is your walkaway number)?
- Who is involved (both sides)?
- What are the buying needs?
- What are the hot buttons?
- What items may be conceded?
- Can the company walk away?

And here is a simple checklist for anticipating the supplier's side:

- What are the supplier's goals?
- What will the supplier settle for?
- Who is involved?
- What are the supplier's needs?
- What are the supplier's hot buttons?
- What items will the supplier concede?
- Can the supplier walk away?

Most probably, the list regarding the supplier will contain many assumed or perceived answers. That's all right. Americans tend to be more closemouthed when asked these types of questions. But overseas, it is sometimes amazing the answers that are quickly given to such questions as, What is most important to you in this quote, contract, relationship? or Is the possibility of this contract an important step for your company?

The strategy of location concerns the buyer's preferred location for the negotiations. If the buyer is going to negotiate with a foreign country it may be to his or her advantage to choose the supplier's venue. This allows easy access to interpreters, text translators, and the supplier's complete team, and gives the manager the opportunity to play the cultural student. It also greatly reduces the need to delay or defer the proceedings in the event the supplier needs to confer at length with other staff or executive individuals.

Within the area of strategy the buyer must plan for failure. Failure within each issue, failure of the entire negotiation. What will you do if you fail? What countermeasures will you have at your disposal, that have been preauthorized by management, should the occasion arise? Can you walk away? What if you can't get acceptable prices, terms, conditions, delivery, or warranty? Make a list of these and other items and work out what your fallback position will be. Never rely on the "everything will turn out all right" assumption. You will probably be far away from the office and the company, and last-minute adjustments may ultimately jeopardize the contract and the relationship.

DEVELOPING PRODUCT KNOWLEDGE

Nothing hurts a negotiation more than a buyer or negotiator who doesn't know the product, the industry or the technology. Naturally, there will be technical issues that should be handled by an engineer, but in the long run the buyer must be aware of the product and its function, and know how to pronounce the names of the parts.

When a new technology surfaces, such as surface-mount devices replacing pin-in-hole devices, there are usually marked differences in the manufacturing, assembly, and pricing of these components. Buyers need to be knowledgeable enough to be able to discuss such advancements.

Knowing a product's competition and its suppliers is important when discussing issues with a supplier during the negotiation. Much of that information can be gained from simple RFIs issued prior to or subsequent to

---

Case Study

During a routine negotiation with a supplier, a newly appointed electronics buyer was reading through the bill of materials to ascertain the sources of the parts. During the reading, several words were mispronounced, such as "kapa-sator" for capacitor and "DEE-o-deed" for diode. The supplier merely chuckled, but the expertise and negotiating position of the buyer was lost due to a perception of naiveté or incompetence.

---

the RFQ. It would be valuable to know, for instance, if the supplier's quote is in line with that of the competition, whether a quote has formally been made or not.

Other factors that must be researched are the components, their costs, their suppliers (single-source approval), component quantity, and availability. In other words, be knowledgeable about the parts that make up the product and where and how the supplier will be obtaining those parts.

RESEARCHING SUPPLIERS

Depending upon the nature and complexity of the quotation, one would hope that a pre-RFQ survey had been done to establish the qualifications of the suppliers on the RFQ list. That is a must-do first step. All parties to the RFQ should be able to supply the product in accordance with the specifications. If the purchasing manager is just feeling around for a supplier, he or she should use the RFI approach, which does not assume or state that a commitment will be made by the purchasing company subsequent to the receipt of information.

When a choice is made from an RFQ, however, it is time to get more details about the supplier. A suggested checklist includes:

- Financial status
- Mission or strategic goals
- Facility survey by the buyer (contingent on the value of the contract)

Case Study

While renegotiating an existing contract for a fairly expensive computer card assembly to be manufactured at a plant in Mexico, it became evident that the supplier was not going to budge on the price. Every reason was stated for the firm pricing, including increased costs of components, labor, engineering changes, and so on.

During a long break in the talks, the buyer sent an RFI to three other capable firms in Japan, California, and Alabama. All three RFIs came in at a lower price. Costs indicated on the one from California (a most-expensive manufacturing area) was a full 25 percent less than the Mexico plant had put forth.

Opening the next meeting, the buyer asked the current supplier, "Since I can get this product for less right here in the U.S., can you give me a good reason why I should be buying from Mexico, where the labor rates are only 10 percent of what they are here in the U.S.?"

Whereupon the supplier went back home and in a few days faxed a new quote, practically the same as the California supplier and just a few points above the buyer's wish price. The Mexico operation was sustained.

- Technology level of engineering and manufacturing
- Employee skills and training
- Supplier's purchasing abilities
- Supplier's component sources
- Manufacturing capacities
- Age and type of machinery
- Quality control (Statistical Process Control)
- Ramp-up ability (increases in orders)
- Internal supplier dependencies (names of personnel, i.e., in AP, quality, shipping)

- Shipping routings and component sourcing
- Procedures for nonconforming material, return material authorization, warranty, repairs

When forming strategies, the purchasing manager will want to do some research to establish what the supplier wants. What are the supplier's goals on this contract? What are his or her hot buttons of need? At what level are his or her negotiating skills? How does he or she react to problems, changes, new news?

FORMING A NEGOTIATING TEAM

The team approach is highly suggested to eliminate delaying tactics by departments or individuals involved with the product. Bringing the team together early will help facilitate the smooth outcome of any negotiation. This is most important when venturing outside the country, which in itself has built-in delays and unforeseen impediments. A typical team might include:

- Development engineer
- Manufacturing (process) engineer
- Quality engineer
- Packaging engineer
- Cost analyst
- Product manager
- Finance (AP, costing)
- Legal counsel (contracts)
- Intellectual property (patents) counsel
- Transportation
- Security (proprietary documentation)

Once a team has been identified, the purchasing manager needs to set the agenda for meetings, strategy and tactics sessions, and role-playing. Most important, time must be set aside for some cultural and language informational meetings for those who will be going overseas for the negotiations or communicating with the supplier via phone, fax or mail. Nothing is worse than a member of the team scuttling the deal through an innocent misstep in communication.

DEFINING A COST MODEL

With the help of engineering and a cost analyst, the purchasing manager should scrutinize the bill of materials and understand what is being purchased. Although the supplier may not have provided a costed quote (U.S. military contracts require this), the manager must be prepared to discuss the high-cost components of the purchase and where they are coming from, and negotiate for the reduction of those costs.

Also from the cost model, things like costs for direct labor (assembly and test), overhead, and profit can be anticipated. The uninformed and unpracticed buyer will, many times, make erroneous assumptions on his or her own in these areas. Details found in a cost model are food for negotiation. In addition, they will show the supplier that the buyer are serious about the deal and has done the homework. Overseas, this can do nothing but enhance the buyer's position, especially in the Far East and Europe, where attention to detail is demanded.

DOCUMENTING TACTICS

Based on strategies developed earlier, the purchasing manager should now know what he or she wants and have a pretty good idea of what the supplier wants. Now is the time to decide what plays, what ploys, what tactics to use to ensure that the negotiations end in a win–win situation for all. Make notes!

A first tactic is called deferral. The order in which discussions are scheduled is an important signal of the buyer's priorities. For example, if you lead with a discussion of the supplier's quoted price, that may be perceived to be your hot button. You would probably be in a better negotiation position if price did not come up until the second or third day. Again, Americans are perceived by most as being dollar-conscious above all. If the other side brings up the issue of price, it may be well to defer the discussion or change the subject. This can throw off the other side and confuse their own strategies.

Asian negotiators tend to offer a package deal rather than give in to small price changes, one issue at a time. In their minds, and rightly so, everything revolves around the price of the whole. Earlier delivery, better quality, changes in components, different shipping, and insurance will naturally affect the price. They will continually defer any commitment to an incremental change in price until all the issues are on the table. Therefore, an Asian negotiator will usually wish to defer the price issue until the last minute. Any insistence on your part to move price discussions forward will usually be to your detriment.

Another tactic is surprise. Well-prepared and practiced negotiators can use this tactic to great advantage. Again, it is designed to throw off the other side. Surprise usually comes in the form of new or significant information and could take the form, "Oh, by the way . . ." Some typical issues that seem to come from the supplier's side of the table include:

- New (later than quoted) delivery dates
- Changes in pricing from the quote (missed a component in the bill of materials or a clause in the terms and conditions)
- Use of outsourcing for a portion of the manufacture
- Striking clauses in the purchasing contract that are contradictory to the supplier's in-country laws

You can use surprise by withholding the actual quantity needed until the face-to-face meeting and renegotiating the price/quantity matrix in your favor. Remember, surprises should be calculated to reduce the price. The use of surprise is dependent on the flexibility of the other side, the anticipated time to resolve the issue, and lots of planning and practice related to the timing of the surprise.

What you want to avoid is springing a surprise and having the supplier withdraw temporarily (sometimes halting the negotiations for a lengthy time to study the issue) or walk away from the deal altogether. Don't get caught in the back-to-the-drawing-board pitfall. To prevent such a backfire, study the supplier and the culture. Areas like the Middle East frown upon major changes in the rules of the game after the game has begun. You may risk having to resource your needs.

Assuming the deal is done is a tactic based on the fact that ultimately you will be contracting with this supplier. This is a common tactic in a negotiation, but like surprise, there are risks. Most authors of negotiation

Case Study

A large computer manufacturer found itself in a bind when its own internal manufacturing facility withdrew its commitment from a year-long internal contract and could not provide the product by the publicly announced ship date. The buyer hastily formed and rehearsed a negotiating team of 14 experts, who flew to Japan to contract for the needed assemblies.

The purchasing manager opened the meeting with, "I have here [holding up a purchase order] a purchase order for our requirements as stated in the RFQ. I have signature authority to sign this order today. Our mission is to reach agreement on all the terms and conditions, specifically the delivery date, in the shortest period of time so that we may return to our work."

Now that's fait accompli. *But the risks. . . . The company was so interested in satisfying marketing needs that this approach certainly diminished any negotiating power it might have had.*

As it turned out, the Japanese had devised a plan (in the few short weeks since they'd received the RFQ) to reduce the manufacturing time of the assembly by upgrading some of the components and making a minor redesign of the circuit board. The cost savings was expected to be about 20% of the quoted cost. The buying company, in its haste to sign, rejected the offer in the belief that the Japanese could not pull off the changes in the required amount of time and that the first ship date would be delayed. Not making the changes affected the market price by nearly $200, and the product price competitiveness was soon criticized by the press as being too high—about $200 too high.

So a fait accompli *tactic, when stiffly adhered to, can have its risks.*

books categorize "assuming the deal" as *fait accompli,* or mission accomplished. Opposing sports teams would be well advised to both enter the field with the thought of winning—*fait accompli*—but there is more to it at the negotiating table.

Case Study

A buyer from a large department store found himself in Turkey negotiating for a year's supply of Oriental rugs. The quantities were in the thousands, and the sizes and descriptions were quite varied. Initially, the items were priced as a lump sum by the supplier. After arriving in the country to firm up the deal and leverage the pricing a little, the buyer was faced with an item-by-item haggling session as if he were down at the open market in Istanbul looking for one rug. The supplier appeared to have an individual love for each grade, style, size, and color of rug, and therefore each individual item held a special price, unknown to anyone until the necessary haggling had been performed. Three days later, the buyer had accumulated a modest discount from the quote, but the experience, according to him, was something he didn't ever want to repeat.

In the U.S. retail trade, a common tactic used by merchants is a combination of authority (marked or listed price) and take it or leave it. In negotiations, a listed price is merely a starting point. The take-it-or-leave-it tactic, however, can be dangerous, especially in Asia, and the purchasing manager is advised to proceed cautiously. If you reach this point, a strategy must have been established so that you can walk away at a certain point. Otherwise, you may be faced with: "Thank you, maybe we can do business another time."

Assuming that the buyer spent a considerable amount of time and money bringing this supplier to the negotiation table, such a failure reflects on the buyer who must have misread the supplier in his or her planning and research stages.

Buyers who negotiate in the Middle East and Southeast Asia will be confronted with the tactic of haggling. An American buyer who considers such activity appropriate only at the flea market could find him- or herself struggling when faced with this tactic.

Salami is a frequently used tactic by overseas negotiators. Salami refers to bringing up many little items one at a time and chipping away at the bottom line pricing, sort of like cutting a salami, one slice at a time. This is not, however, common in the Far East, where negotiators tend to save any commitment to pricing or a reduction thereof until all the issues are on the table.

> **Case Study**
>
> *It is a tradition in Mexico to pay a small fee, say $20, to assure a place in line for a truck trying to pass through customs at the border with the U.S. When this was brought forth at the negotiating table, the buyer explained that his company did not condone such payments and would not be a party to it. The buyer then asked the supplier that, since it was his truck carrying his goods (contract was FOB buyer's location), he should bear those costs. He did. Assuming that he did not increase his price, that's a nibble.*

Nibbling is another ploy that may be used effectively but usually is of little value on expensive items. It is of more importance to understand the supplier's concession posture. You might, for instance, in the early stages, ask the supplier to bear the cost of a slight modification or addition to the specifications, terms, or costs. Suppose you need an additional test performed such as a TUV (like UL certification but for European consumption). Could the supplier include that test in the quoted price?

The buyer close can be a very effective tactic. Usually we think of a salesperson making a close. A statement like, "Would you buy this car today if we can get it for you in green?" is a close. The buyer close goes like this: "If we increase the quantity of each shipment to 1,000 pieces per week, will you agree to price this contract at $3.85 per unit today?" Another: "If we concede the insurance clause, will that be all that is necessary to come to full agreement?" You are not conceding immediately, but you are attempting to break down that final bit of resistance from the other side. This tactic is seldom useful during the early stages of a negotiation, and the manager is advised to use it sparingly and only for a final push to agreement.

PLANNING FOR THE LONG HAUL

The purchasing manager should always assume that a negotiation will take longer than anticipated. Lots of time should be allotted for nonmeeting activities. Generally, generic subjects are discussed in the initial meeting. By the second meeting, the other side will caucus frequently with other members of their team. Caucuses and side meetings may take up to a day in the

Far East because so many individuals are on the team and a consensus of opinion must be reached before proceeding.

One way to reduce such delays is to refrain from negative or controversial surprises. Surprises should be limited to concession surprises that work in the supplier's favor.

If you are faced with long delays, take the time to learn more about the country you are dealing with. If you are in that country, take a trip to a museum, tourist spot, park, or cultural event. During off-record times, discuss your trip with someone on the other side. Doing so is a great way to smooth concerns and goes a long way toward building relationships— just what the other side is looking for.

Try to avoid purchasing a discount airline ticket or one that is not alterable for a small fee, say $50. Probably 50% of all negotiations do not go as planned. Many negotiators find that they are forced to return home empty-handed and wait for resolution of issues via fax and phone. There is no substitute for face-to-face communication. Be reasonable with your suppliers, make sure that all the cards are on the table before you depart your company, and be authorized to stay overseas a reasonable amount of time to resolve any issues.

REVIEW AND CRITIQUE

In professional sports, on the day after the game the tape or film is reviewed by the coach and players. What went wrong? What could we have done better? What went right? How did the other side react? What can we learn?

Such questions are not as easy to remember without a tape of the proceedings of negotiations. Therefore, try to hold a review session each evening after a day's negotiations. Ask your team the above questions. Regroup. Formulate revised strategies and tactics. List supplier reactions, concerns, issues, hot buttons, goals, strategies, and tactics. This information will be useful not only to you in future meetings but should be kept on file for others in your company who may have occasion to negotiate with that supplier.

THE PSYCHOLOGY OF NEGOTIATION

It is not the intention here to lump cultural areas of the world into little boxes; however, some general assumptions can be drawn that will start the negotiation team thinking about how the supplier is going to react, what tack he or she will take, and what he or she will be looking for.

In Exhibit 6–1, the arrows point to the psychological type of person a purchasing manager is most likely to find, related to the combined factors of behavior. For example, the analytical person will show a low assertion level but will reason only with a lot of facts—maybe an accounting manager. On the other hand, someone who exhibits a sloppy organization level and a quick decision level might be considered an extrovert—maybe Oscar Madison in the *Odd Couple* movie. Using these devices, Exhibit 6–2 represents what you might expect when negotiating in different parts of the world.

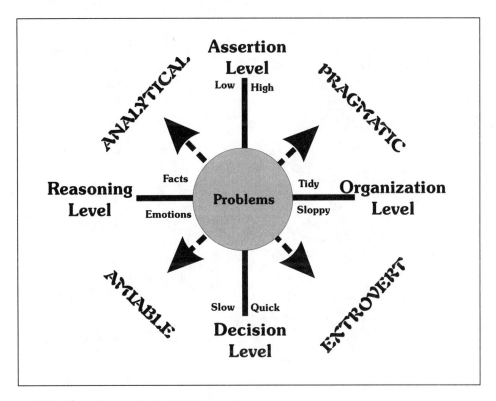

Exhibit 6–1. Psychological Makeup Chart

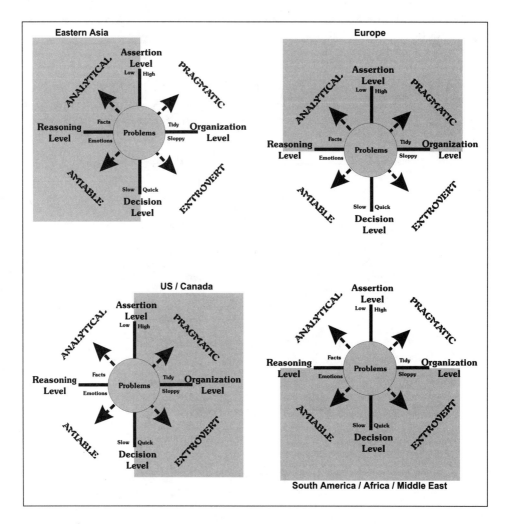

Exhibit 6–2. Psychological Makeup Cultural Division

CHAPTER 7

Contracting for the Goods

Just before the turn of the century, Henry Campbell Black compiled a plethora of legal terms into a book called *Black's Law Dictionary*. Since then, it has been revised and edited hundreds of times. In that dictionary, Mr. Black takes two-and-a-half pages to describe what a contract is. Basically, what he says is that a contract is an agreement between two or more persons which creates an obligation to do or not to do a particular thing.[1]

The essentials for a valid contract include the following:

- Competent parties
- Subject matter
- Legal consideration
- Mutuality of agreement
- Mutuality of obligation

Major American corporations—and their lawyers—tend to take the issue to extremes, producing contracts of 50 pages and more for material purchases. Most purchase orders contain terms and conditions (boilerplate)

---

[1] Henry Campbell Black, *Black's Law Dictionary* (St. Paul, MN: West, 1968).

on the reverse of the page so voluminous that they are set in four-point type and many times require a magnifying glass to read them.

On the other hand, I have seen a three-page, standard typewritten letter of agreement covering a commitment of over half a billion dollars between two major Japanese companies. It is not uncommon for individuals in many countries to contract with each other on mere trust, faith, and a handshake.

Why is it that Americans are so enamored of dozens and dozens of pages of legalize, which is not only difficult for the average American to understand but almost impossible to translate into other languages while retaining the intended legal meaning? An IBM corporate attorney once told me: "It's my job. That's what I get paid for—to produce words to protect the company." Needless to say, many foreigners look upon such contracts as mere piles of paper, to be dealt with as best they can and hope all will be well.

The level of fiduciary (a legal term for trust) relationships between individuals and companies in Asia, for instance, is much higher than in the U.S. This is partly due to a general unity of socioeconomic background, culture, religion, and ethnicity. The U.S. is referred to as the melting pot for the rest of the world, encompassing many origins, religions, cultures, and so on. As we know, this diversity has fostered a mistrust of others, and therefore we have the written contract to bridge those gaps and authenticate relationships, albeit through the legal system. Most foreign companies are used to the plethora of terms and conditions this places on their relationships, and proceed accordingly.

I like to think of a contract as a map or agenda defining the road the parties have agreed to follow in a specific business endeavor. Today, we can liken it, somewhat, to the documentation required for registration with the ISO 9000 standards. In any event, you will find yourself apologizing for the size of your contract in many parts of the world, which seems to defuse anxieties.

MAKING A CONTRACT

For those who are unfamiliar with the requirements of a contract and find themselves having to build one from scratch, the following sections review the necessities.

Agreement.   A contract generally starts out with the phrase "The parties hereto have agreed to . . ." To have a contract there must be mutuality of agreement. No agreement, no contract.

Competent.   The parties must necessarily be competent to agree. Wills (a form of contract), for instance, use the phrase "being of sound mind and body." We all know that minor children as well as ill and otherwise infirm individuals may not enter into a contract. If they do, the contract may be deemed null and void.

Writing.   A contract does not have to be in writing. If it is not, however, you would be advised to have several witnesses. When a contract is in writing, it can be changed only in writing, signed by the duly authorized representatives of the parties to the original contract. This may be called an amendment or addendum to the contract.

Mutual.   In addition to mutual agreement, there must be a mutual exchange. If John contracts to give you something for nothing it is not a contract. Items of value must be given and received. Contracts usually describe exchange of material goods or property in consideration of a sum of money. In many parts of the world, the barter system is still in practice, so it is not unusual to find contracts that exchange camels for rugs. Remember that items must be given and received in equal amounts; that is to say that the value of the camels must equal the value of the rugs in normal and customary terms.

Surprisingly enough, some U.S. contracts exchange goods in just that way. Due to the constraints on currency in areas like Eastern Europe and the former Soviet countries, it is not unusual to find that Levi's jeans may be exchanged for Pepsi-Cola. Countries exchange minerals for arms, chemicals for other chemicals, and electronics for food.

Performance.   There must be performance on both sides. One party must provide the required quantity and description of the goods and the other party must provide the required consideration (currency, goods, or service).

Consideration.   According to Black, consideration may be a right, an interest, a profit, or a benefit. This subject is quite lengthy and comes in many forms, details of which are not necessary to discuss here.

Obligation.   Each party is obligated to the other. The failure of a contract, called a breach, occurs when one of the parties does not perform his or her end of the bargain.

TYPES OF AGREEMENTS

There can be as many types of agreements as there are things to exchange. In the business of purchasing, there are 10 common agreements:

- Purchase order
- Letter of intent/interim aggreement
- Design agreement
- Production agreement
- Purchasing agreement
- Manufacturing rights agreement
- Consultant agreement
- Service agreement
- Confidential disclosure agreement
- Consignment agreement

Purchase Order

When accepted by a supplier, a purchase order becomes a contract, whether or not it is in writing. Acceptance may be either in writing or by performance, unless the purchase order requires acceptance in writing.

Letter of Intent/Interim Agreement

The purpose of the letter of intent is to bridge the gap between a verbal agreement of intent and a purchase order or formal written contract. This type of contract contains the most basic information (e.g., the names of the parties, a general description of the goods, and the consideration or price). It is designed to provide advance planning time in view of an impending contract.

Design Agreement

This is used to obtain the services of a vendor to design, modify, or produce prototypes of a product. The essence of this contract is for the supplier to provide work for hire and must include any intellectual property or patent rights of the contracting company. The protection of proprietary materials or documentation here can be difficult when dealing with many countries that do not agree wholly with international patents rights. This problem has been pretty well cleaned up in such countries as Hong Kong, Japan, and Taiwan but remains a thorny issue in China, where pirating of CDs, books, and computer software continues.

Production Agreement

Usually for the long term, this agreement identifies the purchase of certain quantities of a specific commodity to be manufactured by the supplier, for a stated price, and under specific terms and conditions. Products will generally be ordered on individual purchase orders or blanket releases from the supplier.

Purchasing Agreement

Sometimes referred to as a volume purchase agreement, this contract deals mainly with off-the-shelf items to be purchased from manufacturers, distributors, or retail outlets. It is used for such commodities as MRO, administrative and facilities supplies, and capital purchases. The pricing from the supplier can be based on a designated discount from published pricing, on a pricing/volume matrix, or sometimes on total dollar expenditures for a designated period.

Manufacturing Rights Agreement

The purchasing manager's company may decide to manufacture a product whose design or patent belongs to another. Conversely, it may decide to have another company manufacture a product it designed and patented. This type of agreement sets forth the terms and conditions, and rights and privileges of each company and is designed to protect the proprietary materials and intellectual property of each.

Consultant Agreement

This agreement is used to obtain the services of an outside expert.

Service Agreement

This contract may include both materials and services.

Confidential Disclosure Agreement

This standalone agreement is used to provide protection of a company's proprietary information such as documents, models, prototypes, and components.

Consignment Agreement

If a company furnishes or loans tools, machinery, parts, or materials to another, this agreement sets forth the terms of the loan and expectations of the care of the items by the other party. It may also list any fees, costs, obligations, or requirements that may be imposed or incurred by either party.

CHOOSING THE FORM OF CONTRACT

The manner in which consideration or payment is calculated will have an effect on how the contract is written and what clauses will be included. There are 10 basic ways to calculate the overall consideration issue:

- Firm fixed price
- Fixed price with escalation
- Fixed price incentive
- Fixed price with redetermination

- Cost plus fixed fee
- Cost plus incentive
- Cost sharing
- Cost without fee
- Time and material

Firm Fixed Price

Most purchasing contracts for goods contain a firm fixed price for the duration of the contract. Any changes to that price must be negotiated when the contract is renewed. A firm fixed price protects the buyer and allows the supplier to plan ahead for costs. That is not to say that under extenuating circumstances the supplier might not come back to the buyer in six months and plead for a change in the price. It happens all too often. Probably more often in construction and service contracting areas where low bidding is frequent and costs always seem to outrun the project.

The benefits of working with a firm-fixed-price contract include a minimum of administrative details. The buyer places the purchase order, referencing the contract price, and the supplier ships. The pressure here is on the supplier, who must contract for parts, materials, and supplies for the duration of the contract to protect the pricing and costs. The supplier also bears the risk of labor cost escalation due to strikes or the enactment of new laws.

The risks to the buyer include withdrawal of the product for whatever reason, sluggish sales, and technology changes forcing obsolescence. To protect the buyer, a termination clause allowing for cancellation of any future orders should be included. The supplier will undoubtedly ask for a contractual payment for such cancellation or reimbursement for parts, materials, and supplies on hand or un-cancellable.

Fixed Price with Escalation

This type of contract is used when economic or market conditions dictate that either the supplier or buyer, or both, may be in jeopardy of costs escalation during the term of the contract. Escalation computations must be linked to an impartial labor, material, or currency index.

This type of contract is used for large purchases and generally over a long period of time—two years or more. It may be affected by inflation, foreign currency exchange rates, or ongoing volatile technology changes. Many times in the early contracting stages, some costs are unknown, things like costs for labor, direct labor times for assembly and testing, certain material costs, insurance, customs duties, and sometimes even international shipping. It may take an unreasonable amount of time to identify these costs for a product not yet manufactured. In the area of foreign currency exchange rates, this type of contract allows for many different schemes to manage costs and protect the parties.

By the mid-1980s, currency escalation clauses were becoming common in contracts with Japan.

Case Study

From 1986 to 1992 the Japanese yen was on a free-fall. The exchange rate doubled in about five years. As far back as 1965, the yen stood at about 380 to the dollar. By 1985 it was in the low 200s. During 1986, in one three-month period, it dropped 50 points.

Hotels and restaurants were withholding their credit card charges for submission when the rate was more favorable. In one two-week hotel stay, the hotel could stand to gain several hundred dollars by such tactics, all to the grief of the business traveler, who was forced to reapply for reimbursement from his or her travel department.

Brazil and Argentina were another matter altogether. In Brazil from 1987 to 1990, the currency dropped six zeros and changed the name of the currency three times. A million crusados from 1987 was worth only one new cruzeiro by 1990. Today Brazil is using the real for its currency at yet another change in value. Even with escalation clauses there was pandemonium throughout contracting departments. The details of currency clauses are covered in Chapter 14. Although a fixed-price-with-escalation contract must include a lot more verbiage and detail, and requires more administration, it is designed to protect both the buyer and the seller from most liabilities.

Fixed Price Incentive

This contract benefits the supplier who wants to excel. It is used in highly competitive situations where a company will gain through aggressive pricing of the finished product and component cost reduction (see Exhibit 7–1). It is very useful in the consumer electronics, computer, and apparel markets. These areas all provide for a large amount of importing and incentive contracts. Purchasers set a target price and a ceiling price and include a variable profit formula. The supplier is on notice to be always conscious of his or her material and labor costs.

Fixed Price with Redetermination

This form of contract is most commonly found in the international marketplace to allow for foreign currency fluctuations. In the Far East, some currencies doubled in value against the U.S. dollar during the period 1987 to 1994. Some European currencies began to rise in value in the early 1990s. To protect both the buyer and seller from losses due to the value of money, the fixed-price-with-redetermination form of contract can be used.

The first thing to agree upon in such a contract is the source used to validate the currency exchange rate. U.S. contracts typically use the figures published in the *Wall Street Journal*. In the Far East, it is the *Asian Wall Street Journal*, published in Hong Kong. In Europe, it is the *European Wall Street Journal*.

	Example 1		Example 2 (Supplier loses)		Example 3 (Supplier wins)	
	Target Pricing		Profit Reduced 12%	Materials Costs Increased $10	Profit Increased 12%	Materials Costs Reduced $10
Purchased Material	60%	$48.74	72%	$58.74	48%	$38.74
Direct Labor	4%	$3.25	4%	$3.25	4%	$3.25
Factory Overhead	6%	$4.87	6%	$4.87	6%	$4.87
G & A / Selling	5%	$4.06	5%	$4.06	5%	$4.06
R & D	3%	$2.44	3%	$2.44	3%	$2.44
Misc.	2%	$1.62	2%	$1.62	2%	$1.62
Cost of Goods Sold		$64.98		$74.98		$54.98
Profit	20%	$16.25	8%	$6.25	32%	$26.25
Target and Contract Price	100%	$81.23	100%	$81.23	100%	$81.23
Price to Maintain 20% Profit				$89.98		
Ceiling Price		$85.00		$85.00		$85.00
			Supplier loses	($4.98)	Supplier gains	$10.00
			$85.98-$85.00		$26.25-$16.25	

Exhibit 7–1. Sample Fixed Price Incentive Comparison

The second point is to set the criteria for adjustment time. This defect criteria like action point is usually agreed upon when the currency exchange rate has moved a number of points against the dollar. Within the price/quantity matrix of a contract might be a unit price of, for example, $100. A typical clause can be found in Exhibit 7–2.

Another instance in which a fixed-price-with-redetermination contract is useful is when the manufacturing process is new and untried. The purchasing manager might anticipate learning curves as a significant factor with a particular supplier and thereby be unable to have a firm fixed analysis for direct labor hours. This might also be the case with a foreign firm that is entering into new technology areas and lacks the ability to project accurate manufacturing, assembly, and test times.

Unlike fixed-price-with-escalation contracts, the fixed price with redetermination does not require that information be available at contract time to make certain determinations. Other factors that might lead a purchaser to enter into a fixed price with redetermination are:

The parties agree that, over time, the exchange rate of their respective currencies will change. As of the date first mentioned above [date of contract] the exchange rate, as published in the *Asian Wall Street Journal* is ¥125 = US$1.00.

Each time the rate of exchange changes by at least 10 points (¥125 to ¥115) to the U.S. dollar, the parties will adjust this agreement by a 50% share of the percentage change. Accordingly, if the Japanese yen drops by 10 points (¥1,000), or 8%, the price paid by the Company for products described herein will increase by 4% or US$4.00. For example:

Contract unit price	= US$100.00
Previous exchange rate ¥125	= US$1.00
New exchange rate ¥115	= US$1.00
Difference	= ¥10, ¥125 or −8%
Agreed price increase (50% of 8%)	= +4%
New Company price	= US$104.00

Exhibit 7–2. Sample Currency Clause

Case Study

A supplier in Taiwan had just converted a portion of its computer card manufacturing facility to surface-mounted component technology. Since this process is significantly different from the former pin-in-hole technology, the supplier did not have a firm idea of the total hours needed to manufacture a particular card. The only information it had to go on was the equipment manufacturer's run rates and anticipated setup, maintenance, and repair times.

It was decided therefore to agree on an interim price that would cover the anticipated costs. The contract stated that after six months of manufacturing, the parties would reevaluate the data gathered and agree on a new price for the product. A fixed price with redetermination contract.

- Components used are leading edge and their pricing is not fixed.
- The price of a part of the component may be volatile (as with gold pricing in the early 1980s).
- Future volumes required are unknown.
- Production efficiency is unknown.
- Engineering changes are anticipated.

Within the scope of this type of contract the purchaser will want to protect his or her company by stating a maximum price redetermination, upward or downward. If you find that you have gone beyond the limits (dollars or percentage) set in the original contract, it is probably a good idea to negotiate a new contract or requote the item.

Cost Plus Fixed Fee

In this type of contract, the buyer assumes the risks, since the seller is guaranteed costs to be paid by the buyer up to some established level plus an additional fee. The buyer is responsible for auditing the seller's costs; however, so this contract is generally quite difficult to administer and agree on valid costs. All allowable costs must be included, as well as certain costs defined by the buyer. The amount of the fee is also preagreed to in this contract as a fixed cost or a fixed percentage of costs and does not increase.

This type of contract is typical when dealing with a supplier who will be totally responsible for sourcing all components and in absence of the buyer's approved source list. Auditing the supplier's records for sourcing and costing processes could be construed as a burden, but the purchasing company may not have the buyers necessary to provide all the sourcing information and the auditing is generally less time-consuming. In effect, under this contract a product is being made by another company and the supplier is reimbursed for its efforts.

Cost Plus Incentive

Here the incentive is totally for the supplier. This contract differs from the fixed price plus incentive in that the seller must charge only for the cost of the materials without profit; hence, the greater incentive for the supplier. An agreed-on fee is included for the supplier over and beyond the cost of materials and is based on estimated costs and a target price. If the seller's costs are reduced below the target price, both the seller and the buyer share in the reduction. Varying the percentages (50/50, 60/40, 25/75) gives the buyer a lot of negotiating room. The supplier can give up all or part of the incentive fee, but costs are still paid by the buyer.

Cost Sharing

In new technology as well as in new foreign venues, sometimes neither party is sure what the costs, risks, or exposure will be. This form of contract fits nicely in this case. Recently, so-called business partnerships have made wide use of this form of contract.

Here, both the buyer and the supplier agree to share costs. Generally, the supplier retains the rights to any possible products or patents that may result from the contract. Maximum limits of commitment must be firmly established.

Case Study

After over 50 years of dealing internationally, both buying and selling, a Fortune 100 company found itself deeply engrossed in learning the ins and outs of Korean law. As a point of negotiation, the Korean company decided that due to currency fluctuations between the U.S. and Korea, coupled with the wide variances in many areas of law, the production contract use Korean law and currency. The American negotiators initially looked at this as a "red herring" (not the real issue and one that would probably be conceded in the end). But this diversionary tactic lasted beyond the start date of manufacture, and the company was forced to provide letters of intent and interim contracts to ensure ship dates.

At the end, the Koreans did not concede. The contract was signed with the inclusion of Korean law as the governing clause and payments to be made in Korean won. A first for this company.

Cost without Fee

This form of contract is generally used for work for hire or research. The buyer pays only for what he or she gets, but unlike a fixed fee contract the buyer agrees to pay only for the product based on the documented costs of that product. Cost-without-fee contracts are awarded mostly to nonprofit organizations, universities, research labs, institutions, and foundations. Documentation is a must, and costs must be carefully monitored and audited. In the international venue this type of contract is used by a requisitioner from the buyer's marketing department to obtain ongoing market research, consumer trends, and per capita income analyses.

Time and Material

Typically, this form of contract is used to engage the services of an independent testing company or repair facility. Internationally, much of this sort of activity is ongoing. It requires accurate estimates of materials, and labor must be available up front. Penalties may be included for cost over-runs and late deliveries. Certainly, the buyer will want to choose suppliers carefully and understand their past performance through referrals or investigation.

ENFORCING A CONTRACT

Typically, a U.S. company's contract is governed by U.S. law; specifically, the law of the state where the company is located or where it is incorporated. Because the typical attorney usually knows little about the laws of Taiwan, Hong Kong, Singapore, or China, if the supplier wants an American firm's business, the supplier will have to comply with the buyer's law, or American law. Most companies agree.

Nonetheless, contracts have been written with the governing clause stating that the laws of the supplier's country prevail. Another protective ploy used by some suppliers is to have the contract written using the supplier's currency as the form of payment for all purchases.

Remember, though, that business between Far Eastern companies is usually performed under and governed by the most minimal of contracts. Trust in the relationship is what prevails.

ENVISIONING COST IN EVERY CONTRACT CLAUSE

Within a contract's every clause, every term, every condition, there is a potential cost; a cost to the buyer or a cost to the supplier. Exhibit 7–3 lists most of the probable items of interest that a purchasing manager might look for. When dealing in Europe, a purchaser will find that most costing terms and conditions will be accepted at face value and negotiated accordingly. In the Far East, however, where contract length tends toward the minimum, things like intellectual property, insurance, currency exchange, and quality will be looked on differently and may take a much longer time to negotiate.

Governing law.   If the parties agree to have the contract bound by the law of a country other than the U.S., say that of the seller, that is probably all right. However, American attorneys highly dislike having to

Exhibit 7–3. Costing of Terms

Engineering	Purchasing	Finance	Legal
Specifications	*Order Placement*	*Price/Quantity*	*Title & Loss*
Product description	Minimum lead time	EOQ decisions	Ownership
Approved vendors	Acknowledgment	Quantity	Liabilities
Packaging	Emergency PO	Redeterminable price	
Tooling & Test	*Shipping*	*Bill-back*	*Mfg. Rights*
Vendor owned	FOB Point	Date of cancellation	Supplier fails
Consigned material	Carrier	Review costs	Transfer of
Calibration	Title passage		liabilities
Hard/soft tools	Broker		
Engineering Changes	*Delivery Schedule*	*Order Cancellation*	*Termination*
Company initiated	JIT (just in time)	Timing	Exposures
Vendor initiated	Changes	Exposure to cost	Liabilities
Cost savings split	Expediting		Arbitration
Emergency handling	Replacements		
Quality	*Product Pricing*	*Consignment*	*Patent Rights*
MTBF	Price/quantity	Matrix	Ownership
Supplier certification	Long term contract	Depreciation	Patent search
Workmanship	Bill-back	Inventory control	Royalties
standards	Rejects		
Inspection			
Spare Parts	*Documentation*	*Payment Terms*	*Confidential Info*
Availability	Cost model	Date of receipt	Security
Warranty	Sourcing AVL	Authorizations	Storage
Duration of coverage			Management
Warranty		*Renewal Term Price*	*Public Disclosure*
Duration		Review of costs	Relationship
Failure analysis		Link to index	
Cost vs. MTBF			
Repairs		*Currency Exchange*	*Insurance*
In warranty		Rates	Liability
Post warranty		Formulas	Plant &
Repair warranty		Index	machinery

become even cursorily familiar with the laws of another country; they claim they can't even keep up with U.S. law. So the United Nations in 1980 devised a convention, called the Convention on Contracts for the International Sale of Goods (CSIG), for the administration and arbitration of contracts. A country who is a signatory to this convention agrees that its contracts with other members of CISG will be governed by CISG. (See details of CISG in Chapter 8.)

Arbitration and meditation.   When dealing in international law, the above CSIG provisions notwithstanding, a purchasing manager may find him- or herself in a dispute with the supplier. The terms *arbitration* and *mediation* are essentially the same. Both activities are conducted by neutral parties. However, a mediator is merely a suggester of alternatives between the parties, whereas an arbitrator will make a decision that will be binding upon the parties as per prearranged agreement. A whole group of organizations has cropped up to handle the communication between parties and is called alternative dispute resolution. Many disputes are professionally and ethically handled by the American Arbitration Association (AAA), whose web site is at www.ADR.org. The site AAA.org was already taken by some astronomers.

It is recommended that an arbitration clause be included in any contract. It might read something like the following:

> Any controversy or claim arising out of or relating to this contract shall be determined by arbitration in accordance with the International Arbitration Rules of the American Arbitration Association.

Should a dispute arise, the first step is to request a meeting with the AAA. This may be just a conference call, or you may arrange an in-person interview. During this interview, you will be asked to select an arbitrator or tribunal (more than three arbitrators) specializing in your area of dispute. This, of course may be preagreed on by extending the contract clause to include:

> For disputes covering an amount less than US$100,000.00, a single arbitrator will be selected. For disputes covering an amount greater than US$100,000.00, a tribunal of not less than three arbitrators shall be selected.

It is agreed that the place of arbitration shall be at the buyer's home office city. The language of the arbitration shall be English.

A complete text of the International Arbitration Rules of the American Arbitration Association may be printed from their web site at www.ADR.org.

Another similar arbitrating organization is the Global Arbitration Mediation Association (GAMA). GAMA's approach is unique in that it uses the Internet for communication. Forms are provided and fees disclosed so that the business of arriving at a resolution may be conducted without leaving your desk.

CHAPTER 8

Laws in International Business

Understanding international law, even as it relates specifically to importing, is a monumental task. Aside from the restrictions imposed by the U.S. Customs Service at American ports of entry, a virtual library full of laws, rules, regulations, treaties, and restrictions exists with which the purchasing manager must become at least vaguely familiar.

American companies must have a license to export from the U.S.—but not a license to import. However, a license is required for selling many products: firearms and pharmaceuticals, for example. The general rule is: if a company has a license to manufacture or sell the item, it probably has the necessary qualifications to import that item.

IMPORT QUOTAS

As a first issue, quotas have been placed on some imported goods. Many times American industry has screamed for protection against imports. Quotas are divided into two distinct categories: absolute quotas and tariff rate quotas.

Absolute quotas refer to the number of items that can be imported. These quotas may pertain to the number of items from a specific country or from the world as a whole. When that number is reached, no more. Tariff rate quotas are based on the tariff rate for certain quantities. For example, a buyer may be able to import tomatoes for $.02 per pound up to the quota amount (e.g., one million pounds nationally). After that point, the tomatoes may be assessed a $.10 per pound rate. This obviously makes the goods less attractive to the importer trying to compete. If the goods are in short supply at the market, however, a price hike that covers the additional tariff would be in order.

For information about the status of a quota or restriction on an item, check with the Department of Commerce on the Internet at www. DOC.gov, or write to:

Department of Commerce
14th Street NW
Washington, DC 20230

RESTRICTED ITEMS

In addition to restrictions protecting American industry, certain restrictions are placed on items that could pose a threat to the U.S. economy, security, personal health, or ecology (e.g., certain plants and animals). An interesting restriction is the one prohibiting bringing snakes of any kind onto the Hawaiian islands—even for a zoo. There are no snakes in Hawaii, and they don't want any.

Some general categories of restricted items are:

- Endangered species of wildlife or parts thereof
- Sexually explicit material
- Products manufactured by forced or child labor
- Counterfeit or knockoff items

ANTIDUMPING PROVISIONS

Importers have been known to be party to so-called dumping by exporters in certain countries. Dumping is the practice of the selling of goods in the U.S. below the producer's cost (or at least below the cost to produce the same items in the U.S.). The Trade Agreements Act of 1979 and subsequent amendments provide that antidumping duties be imposed when two conditions are met:

1. The Department of Commerce determines that the foreign subject merchandise is being, or is likely to be, sold in the U.S. at less than fair value.

2. The International Trade Commission determines that an industry in the U.S. is materially injured or threatened with material injury, or that the establishment of an industry is materially retarded by reason of imports of that merchandise.

COUNTERVAILING DUTY

The Tariff Act of 1930 and the Trade Agreements Act of 1979, subsequently amended, provide that countervailing duties be imposed when two conditions are met:

1. The U.S. Department of Commerce determines that the government of a country or any public entity within the territory of a country is providing, directly or indirectly, a countervailable subsidy with respect to the manufacture, production, or export of the subject merchandise that is imported into or sold (or likely to be sold) in the U.S.

2. In the case of merchandise imported from a subsidies agreement country, the U.S. International Trade Commission (ITC) determines that an industry in the United States is materially injured or threatened with material injury, or that the establishment of an industry is materially retarded by reason of imports of that merchandise.

If the U.S. Department of Commerce determines that a countervailable subsidy is being bestowed on merchandise imported from a country that is not a subsidies agreement country, a countervailing duty can be levied on the merchandise in the amount of the net countervailable subsidy without ITC determination of material injury.

INTELLECTUAL PROPERTY RIGHTS

You don't have to be an intellectual to understand intellectual property rights (IPR). But in many other parts of the world, something that has been designed, developed, or otherwise created may be subject to what is considered "the good of all." In North Korea, for instance, it is considered despicable that any one person or company should profit from a creation that ultimately is for the good of all. Therefore, inventions, patents, and such are not owned by the creator but become a universal gift for all to enjoy. Since our part of the Western world believes that creators and inventors should be compensated for their developments as an incentive to create more, the battle of intellectual property rights continues. An importer must make sure that the goods being imported are not already covered by a U.S. patent registered to another company or individual. That is considered counterfeiting and is prohibited.

There are five basic categories of intellectual property rights as defined by the U.S. Department of Commerce, Patent and Trademarks Office: a patent, a trademark, a copyright, a mask work, and a trade name.

A patent is issued to protect novel and useful inventions. Examples might be anything from a new type of kitchen gadget, to a machine to make semiconductors, to a new process for manufacturing spaghetti, to a new medicine, to a new type of hybrid vegetable that is the result of genetic engineering. Patents are issued by the U.S. Patent and Trademark Office of the Department of Commerce, usually for a term of 20 years, and are not renewable, except by special legislation.

A trademark is a design, slogan, or brand name used to identify products or services with a particular source. Some familiar examples include Coca-Cola, Xerox, Sony, IBM, and the Izod brand's alligator design. Once a trademark has been used in interstate commerce or other commerce regulated by Congress for the requisite time, it can be registered with the Patent and Trademark Office for a renewable term of 10 years and thus protected for as long as it remains in use. (If a bona fide intention to use the mark is shown, registration can be applied for, but the mark must be in use before registration is granted.)

A copyright protects original creations of "authorship" (e.g., books, music, original paintings, sound recordings, motion pictures, sculptures, and computer programs). Copyrights may be registered with the Copyright Office, Library of Congress, for a nonrenewable term consisting of the life of the author plus 50 years. Works made for hire (created for an employer) are copyrightable by the employer for a term of 75 years from publication or 100 years from their creation, whichever comes first.

A mask work is, in essence, the design of an electrical circuit, the pattern of which is transfered and fixed in a semiconductor chip during the manufacturing process. Mask works may be registered with the Copyright Office for a nonrenewable term of 10 years.

A trade name is a business name used by a manufacturer, merchant, or other party to identify its business or occupation. A trade name can be the name of a partnership, company, or other organization. While trademarks identify the source of a product and service marks identify the source of a service, trade names simply identify the producers themselves.

To register a claim to an intellectual property right, write to the appropriate agency for specific information. For patents and trademarks write to:

Patent and Trademarks Office
U.S. Department of Commerce
Washington, DC 20231
or
www.USPTO.gov

For copyrights and mask works, write to:

U.S. Copyright Office
Library of Congress
Washington, DC 20559
or
www.loc.gov/copyright

To obtain the help of the Customs Service in protecting any intellectual property for which the federal government provides registration and in which you have an interest, it is imperative that it first be registered with the proper agency.

PROTECTION AND ENFORCEMENT OF INTELLECTUAL PROPERY RIGHTS

How Customs Protects Intellectual Property

The action taken by the Customs Service to help protect intellectual property depends on the type of intellectual property involved. Customs has no authority to prevent the importation of goods that violate a patent unless directed to do so by an exclusion order issued by the U.S. International Trade Commission (ITC) under the provisions of section 337 of the Tariff Act of 1930, as amended. An exclusion order directs the secretary of the Treasury to deny entry to imports in violation of the order. The Customs Service acts for Treasury in enforcing these orders. The ITC can also issue exclusion orders against many other unfair trade practices, (e.g., violation of trademark, copyright, and mask work registrations as well as the violation of trade secrets, which are not otherwise protected by federal law).

The ITC can direct Customs to seize imports from repeat violators of an exclusion order. Details on the procedures for obtaining an exclusion order can be obtained by writing to:

U.S. International Trade Commission
500 E. Street SW
Washington, DC 20436
or
www.USITC.gov

Although Customs cannot enforce a patent on its own authority, it can assist patent owners in attempting to determine whether importation of certain infringing goods is taking place. Customs will survey imports and advise the patent owner of the names and addresses of importers whose goods appear to infringe the patent.

Customs charges a fee for this service, which may be of two, four, or six months' duration. Patent owners often use the results of Customs patent surveys as evidence for the ITC to begin exclusion order proceedings. The information may also be used in developing a patent infringement lawsuit.

Owners of registered trademarks, of registered copyrights, and of trade names can record these rights with the Customs Service. This is a relatively inexpensive procedure and subjects imports of items in violation of these rights to seizure and forfeiture as prescribed by the Customs regulations. Customs can protect a mask work only by means of an ITC exclusion order or court order directing denial of entry of infringing items.

The World Trade Organization

The WTO Agreement on Trade-Related Aspects of Intellectual Property Rights (TRIPS) recognizes that widely varying standards in the protection and enforcement of intellectual property rights and the lack of multilateral disciplines dealing with international trade in counterfeit goods have been a growing source of tension in international economic relations. This agreement addresses the applicability of basic GATT principles and those of relevant international intellectual property agreements, the provision of adequate intellectual property rights, the provision of effective enforcement measures for those rights, multilateral dispute settlement, and transitional implementation arrangements.

Part I of the agreement sets out general provisions and basic principles, notably a national treatment commitment under which nationals of other member countries must be given treatment no less favorable than that accorded to a member's own nationals with regard to the protection of intellectual property. It contains a most-favored-nation clause under which any advantage a member gives to the nationals of another member must normally be extended to the nationals of all other members, even if such treatment is more favorable than that which it gives to its own nationals.

Part II addresses different kinds of intellectual property rights. It seeks to ensure that adequate standards of intellectual property protection exist in all member countries, taking as a starting point the substantive obligations of the main preexisting conventions of the World Intellectual Property Organization (WIPO), namely, the Paris Convention for the Protection of Industrial Property and the Berne Convention for the Protection of Literary and Artistic Works. It adds a significant number of new or higher standards where the existing conventions were silent or thought inadequate. With respect to copyright, the agreement ensures that computer programs are protected as literary works under the Berne Convention and outlines how databases should be protected.

An important addition to existing international rules in the area of copyright and related rights is the provision on rental rights. Authors of computer programs and producers of sound recordings have the right to authorize or prohibit the commercial rental of their works to the public. A similar exclusive right applies to films, commercial rental of which has led to widespread copying. Performers are protected from unauthorized recording, reproduction, and broadcast of live performances (bootlegging) for no less than 50 years. Producers of sound recordings must have the right to prevent the reproduction of recordings for a period of 50 years.

The agreement defines the types of signs that must be eligible for protection as trademarks or service marks and the minimum rights that must be conferred on their owners. Marks that have become well known in a particular country enjoy additional protection. The agreement identifies a number of obligations for the use of trademarks and service marks, their terms of protection, and their licensing or assignment. For example, requirements that foreign marks be used in conjunction with local marks will, as a general rule, be prohibited.

Members must provide means to prevent the use of any indication that misleads the consumer regarding the origin of goods, and any use that would constitute an act of unfair competition. Higher levels of protection are provided for geographical identification of wines and spirits, which are protected even when there is no danger of the public's being misled about the product's true origin. Some exceptions are allowed, for example, for names that are generic terms, but any country using such an exception must be willing to negotiate to protect the geographical identification in question. Further negotiations are foreseen to establish a multilateral system of notification and registration of geographical identification for wines.

Industrial designs are protected under the agreement for a period of 10 years. Owners of protected designs are thus enabled to prevent the manufacture, sale, or importation of articles bearing or embodying a design that is a copy of the protected design.

The agreement requires that 20-year patent protection be available for all inventions, whether of products or processes, in almost all fields of technology. Inventions may be excluded from patentability if their commercial exploitation is prohibited for reasons of public order or morality; otherwise, the permitted exclusions are for diagnostic, therapeutic, and surgical methods and for plants and (other than microorganisms) animals and essentially biological processes for the production of plants or animals (other than microbiological processes). Plant varieties, however, must be protectible either by patents or by a sui generis system (such as the breeder's rights provided in the conventions of UPOV—the International Union for the Protection of New Varieties of Plants). Detailed conditions are set out for compulsory licensing or governmental use of patents without the authorization of the patent owner. Rights conferred in respect of patents for processes must extend to the products directly obtained by the process; under certain conditions alleged infringers may be ordered by a court to prove that they have not used the patented process.

Protection of layout designs of integrated circuits is undertaken on the basis of the Washington Treaty on Intellectual Property in Respect of Integrated Circuits opened for signature in May 1989, but with a number of additions: protection must be available for a minimum period of 10 years, the rights must extend to articles incorporating infringing layout designs, innocent infringers must be allowed to use or sell stock in hand or ordered before learning of the infringement against a suitable royalty, and compulsory licensing and government use is allowed only under a number of strict conditions.

Trade secrets and know-how that have commercial value must be protected against breach of confidence and other acts contrary to honest commercial practices. Test data submitted to governments to obtain marketing approval for pharmaceutical or agricultural chemicals must also be protected against unfair commercial use.

The final section in this part of the agreement concerns anticompetitive practices in contractual licenses. It recognizes the right of members to take measures in this area and provides for consultation between governments when there is reason to believe that licensing practices or conditions relating to intellectual property rights constitute an abuse of these rights and have an adverse effect on competition. Remedies against such abuses must be consistent with the other provisions of the agreement.

Part III of the agreement concerns enforcement. It sets out the obligations of member governments to provide procedures and remedies under their domestic law to ensure that intellectual property rights can be effectively enforced. Procedures must permit effective action against infringement of intellectual property rights and should be fair and equitable, not unnecessarily complicated or costly, and should not entail unreasonable time limits or unwarranted delays. They must allow for judicial review of final administrative decisions and, generally, of initial judicial decisions.

The civil and administrative procedures and remedies spelled out in the text include stipulations regarding evidence, provisional measures, injunctions, damages, and other remedies, including the right of judicial authorities to order the disposal or destruction of infringing goods. Members must also provide for criminal procedures and penalties at least in cases of willful trademark counterfeiting or copyright piracy on a commercial scale. Remedies must include imprisonment or fines sufficient to act as a deterrent. In addition, members must provide a mechanism whereby rightsholders can obtain the assistance of customs authorities to prevent the importation of counterfeit and pirated goods.

The agreement envisages a 1-year period for developed countries to bring their legislation and practices into conformity. Developing countries and, in general, transition economies must do so in 5 years, and least developed countries in 11 years. Developing countries that do not at present provide product patent protection in areas of technology have up to 10 years to introduce such protection. In the case of pharmaceutical and agricultural chemical products, however, they must accept the filing of patent applications from the beginning of the transitional period, though the patent need not be granted until the end of this period. If authorization for the marketing of the relevant pharmaceutical or agricultural chemical is obtained during the transition period, the developing country must, subject to certain conditions, provide an exclusive marketing right for the product for 5 years or until a product patent is granted, whichever is shorter.

Subject to certain exceptions, the general rule is that obligations in the agreement apply to existing intellectual property rights as well as to new ones. The Council for Trade-Related Aspects of Intellectual Property Rights monitors the operation of the agreement and governments' compliance with it.

World Intellectual Property Organization (WIPO)

The World Intellectual Property Organization—referred to in abbreviated form as "WIPO" in English and "OMPI" in French and Spanish—was established by a convention signed at Stockholm on July 14, 1967, and entitled Convention Establishing the World Intellectual Property Organization. The WIPO convention entered into force in 1970.

The origins of what is now WIPO go back to 1883, when the Paris Convention for the Protection of Industrial Property was adopted, and to 1886, when the Berne Convention for the Protection of Literary and Artistic Works was adopted. Each convention provided for the establishment of an international bureau, or secretariat. The two bureaus were united in 1893 and functioned under various names until 1970, when they were replaced by the International Bureau of Intellectual Property (commonly designated as "the International Bureau") by virtue of the WIPO convention.

WIPO became a specialized agency in the United Nations system of organizations in 1974. The objectives of WIPO are

- To promote the protection of intellectual property throughout the world through cooperation among states and, where appropriate, in collaboration with any other international organization.

- To ensure administrative cooperation among the intellectual property unions, that is, the "unions" created by the Paris and Berne conventions and several subtreaties concluded by members of the Paris union.

Intellectual property comprises two main branches: industrial property, chiefly inventions, trademarks, and industrial designs; and copyright, chiefly literary, musical, artistic, photographic, and audiovisual works.

In its role as protector *of intellectual property*, WIPO

- Encourages the conclusion of new international treaties and the modernization of national legislations.
- Gives technical assistance to developing countries.
- Assembles and disseminates information.
- Maintains services for facilitating the obtaining of protection of inventions, marks, and industrial designs for which protection in several countries is desired and promotes other administrative cooperation among member states.

Regarding the administrative cooperation, WIPO centralizes the administration of the unions in the International Bureau in Geneva and supervises such administration through its various organs. Centralization ensures economy for the member states and the private sector concerned with intellectual property.

TRADE ACT OF 1974

Section 301 Amendment

This section of the Trade Act of 1974 was designed to protect U.S. exporters from countries who are not complying with international trade laws or human rights issues, or are engaged in anti-competitive activity. Sometimes called the "presidential retaliation act," this section allows the U.S. president to deny non-compliant nations most-favored-nation status and thereby raise tariffs to double or more on all or selected commodities.

Super 301

The Omnibus Trade and Competitiveness Act of 1988 added an additional weapon to 301. Targeting "priority" unfair trade practices, and so-called trade-distorting measures of foreign countries, the Super 301 accelerated the investigation and implementation of constraints.

Case Study

In the early 1990s, Japan, India, and Brazil were notified that they were in violation of the Super 301 principles. Japan was cited for refusing to buy American-made commercial satellites, supercomputers, and forest products. India was cited for restrictions on foreign investment and for curbs on foreign-based insurance companies. Brazil was cited for extreme licensing requirements for all imports.

The cited countries were threatened with substantial tariff increases on their major exports to the U.S. and were given two years to "clean up their act."

Some journalists candidly referred to the Super 301 as the "trade version of the B-1 bomber." Others simply referred to it as "managed trade." The U.S. historically has placed minimal tariffs on imported goods even to the dislike of U.S. manufacturers, many of whom have since gone out of business. It seems that the language in former trade acts was not succinct enough to allow action within a reasonable time frame.

Special 301

Also created in the 1988 trade act, the Special 301 targets intellectual property rights. According to the provisions of Special 301, the U.S. trade representative must identify countries that:

- Have the most onerous and egregious acts, policies, and practices adversely affecting (actual or potential) the relevant U.S. products.
- Are not entering into good-faith negotiations or making significant progress in negotiations to address these problems.

Touted as the first really implementable trade bill in some time, the Super 301 was a shot heard around the world. GATT members and the Uruguay Round called for some additional kind of disciplined mechanism to manage such sweeping regulations. As of this writing, however, the

---

Case Study

In 1995, President Clinton, acting on information supplied by the U.S. trade representative and congressional investigations, notified the Japanese that they were in violation of Super 301. The Japanese, through their Ministry of International Trade and Industry (MITI), have historically placed extreme protectionist measures on Japanese automobile manufacturing. Few if any imports were allowed; practically none from the U.S. In addition, the Japanese had placed exclusionary restrictions on U.S.-made automobile parts, including those made in Japanese-owned and -managed plants in the U.S.

Accordingly, Clinton threatened implementation of Super 301 with a 100% tariff on all imported Japanese-made luxury model automobiles. Naturally, this created quite a stir among tens of thousands of American automobile dealers. The threat went down to the wire, and just hours before implementation the Japanese recanted and negotiated an agreement (some say a token agreement) to decrease their restrictions that were in noncompliance.

Super and Special 301 amendments stand as a monumental and enforceable deterrent to unfair trade practices.

UNITED NATIONS CONVENTION ON CONTRACTS FOR THE INTERNATIONAL SALE OF GOODS (CISG)

This law allows for an international set of laws to govern contracts by and between member nations. In a standard contract, usually near the end, a clause entitled "governing law" might read: "This contract shall be governed by the State of Florida, U.S.A." If the contract is with a CISG member, the governing of said contract reverts to CISG laws. There are other ways that CISG law may govern a contract, but the most common is for two companies that both reside in nonmember nations to elect to use CISG law for their contract.

Signatories to CISG as of 1997 are Argentina, Australia, Austria, Belarus, Bosnia–Herzegovina, Bulgaria, Canada, Chile, China (PRC), Cuba,

Czech Republic, Denmark, Ecuador, Egypt, Estonia, Finland, France, Georgia, Germany, Guinea, Hungary, Lesotho, Lithuania, Mexico, Moldova, the Netherlands, New Zealand, Norway, Poland, Romania, Russian Federation, Singapore, Slovakia, Slovenia, Spain, Sweden, Switzerland, Syria, Uganda, Ukraine, the U.S., Yugoslavia, and Zambia.

The preamble to the convention reads as follows:

THE STATES PARTIES TO THIS CONVENTION,

BEARING IN MIND the broad objectives in the resolutions adopted by the sixth special session of the General Assembly of the United Nations on the establishment of a New International Economic Order,

CONSIDERING that the development of international trade on the basis of equality and mutual benefit is an important element in promoting friendly relations among States,

BEING OF THE OPINION that the adoption of uniform rules which govern contracts for the international sale of goods and take into account the different social, economic and legal systems would contribute to the removal of legal barriers in international trade and promote the development of international trade,

HAVE DECREED as follows:

Should there be a contractual dispute between parties using CISG, the arbitration of disagreement or judgment on the breach will be handled by a CISG tribunal.

CHAPTER 9

International Agreements and Associations

Within the international community of trading nations, there are countless documents, laws, agreements, and quasi-contractual arrangements of methods to exchange goods. These usually take the form of a neverending assortment of acronyms that further complicate the business of understanding international trade. Listed are but a few of the most active terms.

GENERAL AGREEMENT ON TARIFFS AND TRADE (GATT)

The General Agreement on Tariffs and Trade (GATT) was established on a provisional basis after the Second World War in the wake of other new multilateral institutions dedicated to international economic cooperation—notably the Bretton Woods institutions, now known as the World Bank and the International Monetary Fund.

The original 23 GATT countries were among over 50 that agreed to a draft charter for the International Trade Organization (ITO), a new, specialized agency of the UN. The charter was intended to provide not only world trade disciplines but also contained rules relating to employment, commodity agreements, restrictive business practices, international investment, and services.

In an effort to give an early boost to trade liberalization after the Second World War—and to begin to correct the large number of protectionist measures that remained in place from the early 1930s—tariff negotiations were opened among the founding GATT contracting parties in 1946. This first round of negotiations resulted in 45,000 tariff concessions affecting $10 billion, or about one-fifth of total world trade value at that time. It was also agreed that the value of these concessions should be protected by early and largely "provisional" acceptance of some of the trade rules in the draft ITO charter. The tariff concessions and rules together became known as GATT and entered into force in January 1948. Although in its 47 years the basic legal text of GATT remained much as it was in 1948, there were additions in the form of "plurilateral," voluntary membership, agreements and continual efforts to reduce tariffs.

The ITO charter was finally agreed to at a UN conference on trade and employment in Havana in March 1948, but its ratification in national legislatures proved impossible in some cases. When the U.S. government announced in 1950 that it would not seek congressional ratification of the Havana Charter, the ITO was effectively dead. Thus, despite its provisional nature, GATT remained the only multilateral instrument governing international trade from 1948 until the establishment of the World Trade Organization.

WORLD TRADE ORGANIZATION (WTO)

The World Trade Organization (WTO), established on January 1, 1995, is now the legal and institutional foundation of the multilateral trading system. It provides the principal contractual obligations determining how governments frame and implement domestic trade legislation and regulations. It is also the platform on which trade relations among countries evolve through collective debate, negotiation, and adjudication.

The WTO is the embodiment of the results of the Uruguay Round trade negotiations and the successor to GATT.

How the WTO Differs from GATT

The WTO is not a simple extension of GATT. On the contrary, it completely replaces its predecessor and has a very different character. Among the principal differences are the following:

- GATT was a set of rules, a multilateral agreement, with no institutional foundation, only a small associated secretariat that had its origins in the attempt to establish an international trade organization in the 1940s. The WTO is a permanent institution with its own secretariat.

- GATT was applied on a provisional basis even if, after more than 40 years, governments chose to treat it as a permanent commitment. WTO commitments are full and permanent.

- GATT rules applied only to trade in merchandise goods. In addition to goods, the WTO covers trade in services and trade-related aspects of intellectual property.

- While GATT was a multilateral instrument, by the 1980s many new agreements had been added of a plurilateral, and therefore selective, nature. The agreements that constitute the WTO are almost all multilateral and thus involve commitments for the entire membership.

- The WTO dispute settlement system is faster, more automatic, and thus much less susceptible to blockages than the old GATT system was. The implementation of WTO findings regarding disputes is also more easily assured.

GATT 1947 continued to exist until the end of 1995, thereby allowing all GATT member countries to accede to the WTO and permitting an overlap of activity in areas like dispute settlement. Moreover, GATT lives on as GATT 1994, which is an integral part of the WTO agreement and which continues to provide the key disciplines affecting international trade in goods.

Objectives of the WTO

As a member of WTO you agree to grant to the products of other members no less favorable treatment than that accorded to the products of any other country. The provision on national treatment requires that once goods have entered a market, they must be treated no less favorably than the equivalent domestically produced goods. Three major precepts are

- **Providing predictable and growing access to markets.** While quotas are generally outlawed, tariffs or customs duties are legal according to the WTO. Tariff reductions made by over 120 countries at the Uruguay Round are contained in some 22,500 pages of national tariff schedules, considered an integral part of the WTO. Tariff reductions, for the most part phased in over five years, will result in a 40% cut in industrial countries' tariffs in industrial products from an average of 6.3% to 3.8%. The Round also increased the percentage of bound product lines to nearly 100% for developed nations and countries in transition and to 73% for developing countries. Members have also undertaken an initial set of commitments covering national regulations affecting various services activities. Like those for tariffs, these commitments are contained in binding national schedules.

- **Promoting fair competition.** The WTO extends and clarifies previous GATT rules that laid down the basis on which governments could impose compensating duties on two forms of "unfair" competition: dumping and subsidies. The WTO agreement on agriculture is designed to provide increased fairness in farm trade. That on intellectual property will improve conditions of competition where ideas and inventions are involved, and another will do the same thing for trade in services.

- **Encouraging development and economic reform.** GATT provisions intended to favor developing countries are maintained in the WTO, in particular those encouraging industrial countries to assist trade of developing nations. Developing countries are given transition periods to adjust to the more difficult WTO provisions. Least developed countries are given even more flexibility and benefit from accelerated implementation of market access concessions for their goods.

Countries seeking membership in WTO:

Albania	Jordan	Saudi Arabia
Algeria	Kazakhstan	Seychelles
Armenia	Latvia	Sudan
Belarus	Lithuania	Taiwan
Bulgaria	Macedonia	Tonga
Cambodia	Moldova	Ukraine
China	Mongolia	Uzbekistan
Croatia	Nepal	Vanuatu
Estonia	Panama	Viet Nam
	Russia	

WTO members include the following:

Antigua and Barbuda	Grenada	Norway
Argentina	Guatemala	Pakistan
Australia	Guinea	Paraguay
Austria	Guinea Bissau	Peru
Bahrain	Rep. of Guyana	Philippines
Bangladesh	Haiti	Poland
Barbados	Honduras	Portugal
Belgium	Hong Kong	Qatar
Belize	Hungary	Romania
Benin	Iceland	St. Kitts and Nevis
Bolivia	India	St. Lucia
Botswana	Indonesia	St. Vincent and the Grenadines
Brazil	Ireland	Senegal
Brunei Darussalam	Israel	Sierra Leone
Burkina Faso	Italy	Singapore
Burundi	Jamaica	Slovak Republic
Cameroon	Japan	Slovena
Canada	Kenya	South Africa
Central African Republic	Korea	Spain
Chile	Kuwait	Sri Lanka
Colombia	Lesotho	Suriname
Costa Rica	Liechtenstein	Swaziland
Cote d'Ivoire	Luxembourg	Sweden
Cuba	Macau	Switzerland
Cyprus	Madagascar	Tanzania
Czech Republic	Malawi	Thailand
Denmark	Malaysia	Togo
Djibouti	Maldives	Trinidad and Tobago
Dominica	Mali	Tunisia
Dominican Republic	Malta	Turkey
Ecuador	Mauritania	United Kingdom
El Salvador	Mauritius	United States
European Community	Morocco	Uruguay
Fiji	Mozambique	Venezuela
Finland	Myanmar	Zambia
France	Namibia	Zimbabwe
Gabon	Netherlands	
Germany	New Zealand	
Ghana	Nicaragua	
Greece	Nigeria	

Case Study

One of the first major flaps that surfaced in opposition to NAFTA was in the area of vegetables, namely, tomatoes. U.S. growers claimed that they were drowning in a flood of cheap Mexican tomatoes. From Florida to California, cries of foul went to the state and federal offices, the ITC, and others—to anyone who would listen.

As a diversionary tactic, growers asked officials to increase the inspections of vegetables coming in from Mexico to ensure their freedom from contaminates such as fertilizers and pesticides as well as the use of child labor for picking and sorting, activities that are banned in the U.S., resulting in a more expensive and lower-yielding product.

As of this writing, lobbying is going on from the Florida Tomato Exchange and the Florida Farmers and Suppliers Coalition.

NORTH AMERICAN FREE TRADE AGREEMENT (NAFTA)

On August 12, 1992, Canadian Minister of Industry, Science and Technology and Minister for International Trade Michael Wilson, Mexican Secretary of Trade and Industrial Development Jaime Serra, and U.S. Trade Representative Carla Hills completed negotiations on the proposed North American Free Trade Agreement (NAFTA). During the next two years, opposing factions complained, demonstrated, and otherwise expressed their displeasure with this agreement. Most took the stand that it would significantly affect American producers and that many of them would go out of business. By January 1994, however, the agreement had been ratified and signed by the member countries. Chile was admitted to the agreement in December of that year.

The objectives of this agreement, as elaborated more specifically through its principles and rules, including national treatment, most-favored-nation treatment and transparency, are to:

- eliminate barriers to trade in, and facilitate the cross-border movement of, goods and services between the territories of the parties;
- promote conditions of fair competition in the free-trade area;

- increase substantially investment opportunities in the territories of the parties;
- provide adequate and effective protection and enforcement of intellectual property rights in each party's territory;
- create effective procedures for the implementation and application of this agreement, for its joint administration and for the resolution of disputes; and
- establish a framework for further trilateral, regional, and multilateral cooperation to expand and enhance the benefits of this Agreement.

Taking a look at the progress of trade with Mexico and Canada specifically we find certain increases.

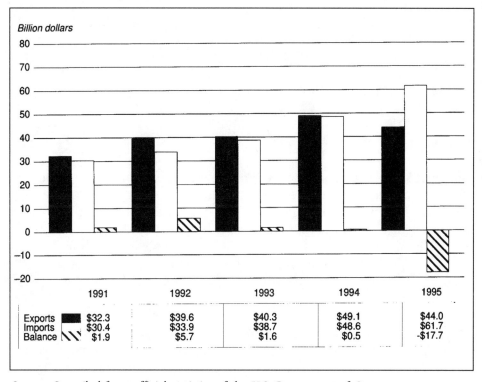

	1991	1992	1993	1994	1995
Exports	$32.3	$39.6	$40.3	$49.1	$44.0
Imports	$30.4	$33.9	$38.7	$48.6	$61.7
Balance	$1.9	$5.7	$1.6	$0.5	-$17.7

Source: Compiled from official statistics of the U.S. Department of Commerce.

Exhibit 9–1. U.S. Trade with Mexico: Exports, Imports, and Trade Balance, 1991–95

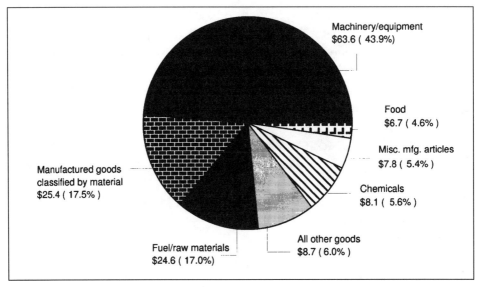

Machinery/equipment
$63.6 (43.9%)

Food
$6.7 (4.6%)

Misc. mfg. articles
$7.8 (5.4%)

Chemicals
$8.1 (5.6%)

All other goods
$8.7 (6.0%)

Manufactured goods
classified by material
$25.4 (17.5%)

Fuel/raw materials
$24.6 (17.0%)

Note: Because of rounding, figures may not add up to totals shown.
Source: Compiled from official statistics of the U.S. Department of Commerce.

Exhibit 9–2. U.S. Imports from Mexico

ASSOCIATION OF SOUTHEAST ASIAN NATIONS (ASEAN)

The world's longest running economic partnership is the Association of Southeast Asian Nations (ASEAN). Comprised of Brunei, Indonesia, Malaysia, the Philippines, Singapore, Thailand, and Viet Nam, these countries are dedicated to becoming a part of the global trading miracle. These nations comprise about 300 million people and have a combined gross national product (GNP) approaching $300 billion. That's about a $1,000 per capita GNP today, compared with less than $400 just 20 years ago. A quantum leap for these newly industrializing nations.

A large part of ASEAN trade is naturally with the Americas, but an increasing amount is being sought from Europe. The first ASEAN-EU (European Union) summit was held in 1996. Currently, the EU is a goods and services trading partner, but ASEAN members are more interested in the intangible areas of investment and technology-transfer relationships.

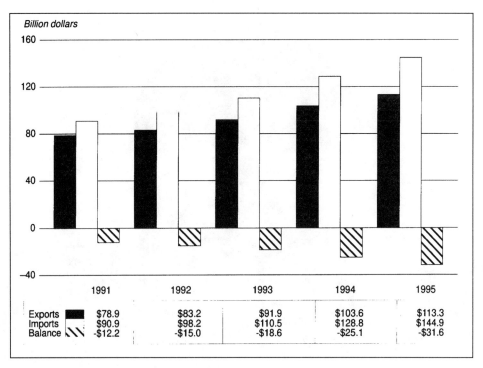

Billion dollars	1991	1992	1993	1994	1995
Exports	$78.9	$83.2	$91.9	$103.6	$113.3
Imports	$90.9	$98.2	$110.5	$128.8	$144.9
Balance	-$12.2	-$15.0	-$18.6	-$25.1	-$31.6

Source: Compiled from official statistics of the U.S. Department of Commerce.

Exhibit 9–3. U.S. Trade with Canada: Exports, Imports, and Trade Balance, 1991–95

ASEAN unity is likely to allow a degree of independence for these developing countries within a world that is increasingly interdependent. Southeast Asia may protest against possible dominance in seeking greater autonomy, yet the region also largely praises the results of economic order and cooperation. ASEAN can become every bit as prosperous and integrated as the European Union, but only with the security umbrella provided by the U.S. and global markets supported by agreements such as APEC.

See more about ASEAN countries in Chapter 5, in the section "Southeast Asia: The New Frontier."

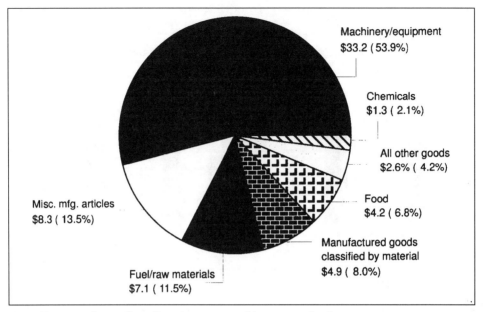

Machinery/equipment
$33.2 (53.9%)

Chemicals
$1.3 (2.1%)

All other goods
$2.6% (4.2%)

Food
$4.2 (6.8%)

Manufactured goods
classified by material
$4.9 (8.0%)

Fuel/raw materials
$7.1 (11.5%)

Misc. mfg. articles
$8.3 (13.5%)

Note: Because of rounding, figures may not add up to totals shown.
Source: Compiled from official statistics of the U.S. Department of Commerce.

Exhibit 9–4. U.S. Imports from Canada

ASIA PACIFIC ECONOMIC COOPERATION (APEC)

The Asia Pacific Economic Cooperation (APEC) group was formed in the face of potential trade conflicts in areas around the Pacific Rim. Formed in 1990, APEC economies account for about 40% of the world's population and one-half of its economic output. It also constitutes about 30% of the world's area, 40% of trade, and 50% of the energy consumption.

As of January 1, 1997, APEC comprised 18 nations:

Australia	Indonesia	Papua New Guinea
Brunei	Japan	Philippines
Canada	Korea	Singapore
Chile	Malaysia	Taipei
China	Mexico	Thailand
Hong Kong	New Zealand	United States

Although APEC is more of a talking organization than a law-forming body, several cooperative measures are being addressed such as the reduction of tariffs, installation of a dispute mediation board, harmonization of product standards and testing procedures, and interactive emergency financial mechanisms.

These and other undertakings are designed to deepen and broaden the outcome of the Uruguay Round. APEC meetings and summits give credence to discussions on such abusive trade practices as dumping, copyright infringement, and antitrust actions by the members.

ASIAN FREE TRADE AGREEMENT (AFTA)

In 1994, ASEAN gave rise to yet another entity—the Asian Free Trade Agreement (AFTA), which seeks intra-ASEAN tariff reductions by the year 2000. What this means to the importer is a potential reduction of intra-ASEAN materials and suppliers as well as subcontract ventures, which are common within the area.

ANDEAN TRADE PREFERENCES ACT (ATPA)

In 1991, the U.S. signed the Andean Trade Preferences Act (ATPA) with Bolivia, Colombia, Ecuador, and Peru. It was primarily designed to combat the production and export of illegal drugs by assisting farmers in converting their coca crops to other worthwhile commodities that would be purchased by the U.S. duty-free. Duties are generally reduced on a sliding scale over a five-year period. Listed imports from Colombia and Bolivia have been eligible for duty-free entry under ATPA since 1992. Modeled after Caribbean Basin Economic Recovery Act, it excludes certain commodities such as rum, wearing apparel, accessories, and many leather goods. It is primarily aimed toward farmers, but is not without its controversy in certain industries here at home.

Imports to the U.S. from ATPA countries have been brisk and have more than doubled in three years.

Country	1993	1994	1995
Colombia	$323,369	$411,642	$499,261
Peru	11,594	107,430	207,568
Ecuador	34,335	72,905	147,859
Bolivia	32,124	91,840	84,099
Total	$401,421	$683,817	$938,789

Note: Figures in thousands.

Case Study

ATPA allows member countries to sell flowers—duty-free—in the U.S. The hidden agenda in getting this act through Congress was to encourage the named countries to substitute flowers for coca, the plant used to produce cocaine.

Within five years, these countries accounted for nearly 75% of the $8 billion flower trade in the U.S. American flower growers complained. In July 1996, growers began lobbying for a reinstitution of tariffs or a tax on imported flowers. The Colombia Flower Council, while anxious, stated that the institution of such sanctions was only a remote possibility. Since most of the flowers imported by the Andean countries flow through Miami, Florida, many firms in that city would oppose sanctions. As of this writing, the battle goes on.

ORGANIZATION FOR ECONOMIC COOPERATION AND DEVELOPMENT (OECD)

The Organization for Economic Cooperation and Development (OECD) was patterned after the OEED (Organization for European Economic Cooperation) which was formed to administer aid to European countries under the Marshall Plan after World War II. Canada and the U.S. joined the OECD in 1961 and thereby formed the OECD.

The basic missions of the OECD are to:

- achieve the highest sustainable economic growth and employment and a rising standard of living in member countries while maintaining financial stability and thus contribute to the development of the world economy;

- contribute to sound economic expansion in member as well as non-member countries in the process of economic development; and
- contribute to the expansion of world trade on a multilateral, nondiscriminatory basis in accordance with international obligations.

The OECD is also, importantly, a forum for policy analysis and debate among practitioners from senior levels of government. Its working methods, based largely on a very close interaction between the secretariat and the intergovernmental committees, give participants access to an extensive network of professional contacts. The "OECD approach," including its normative role of multilateral surveillance through "peer review," fosters analysis and evaluation by members of their respective situations and policy perspectives and encourages the search for convergent solutions through dialogue.

The OECD differs from other intergovernmental organizations in three respects:

- As it has neither supranational legal powers, nor financial resources for loans or subsidies, its sole function is direct cooperation among the governments of its member countries.

- At the OECD, international collaboration means cooperation among nations essentially on domestic policies where these interact with those of other countries, in particular through trade and investment. Cooperation usually means that member countries seek to adapt their domestic policies to minimize conflict with other countries. Governments frequently seek to learn from each others' experience with specific domestic policies before they adopt their own courses of action, whether legislative or administrative.

- By focusing the expertise of various OECD directorates and of various member government departments on specific issues, the OECD approach benefits in particular from a multidisciplinary dimension. The organization deals both with general macroeconomic and with more specific or sectorial issues.

Experience shows that the fields in which the OECD serves as a vehicle for international discussion and cooperation are becoming increasingly numerous because of the rapid growth of international interdependence.

Through globalization of the world economy, national borders are, in part, losing their economic meaning. The policies of individual countries are more and more affected and constrained by the interaction of domestic policies of one nation with those of another. Many policies that previously had little international impact now have consequences for trade and investment and may generate friction with other countries. The OECD offers a forum for its members to discuss and study such developments and to develop collaborative and cooperative approaches to the management of their economies.

CENTRE FOR COOPERATION WITH THE ECONOMIES IN TRANSITION (CCET)

In March 1990, the OECD council decided to create the appropriate infrastructure for making its experience and expertise readily available to countries with reforming economies, to assist their progress toward pluralist democracy and a market economy. To this end, the council established the Centre for Cooperation with the Economies in Transition (CCET) and appointed Salvatore Zecchini, deputy secretary-general of the OECD, as director. The centre is entrusted with the tasks of channeling advice and assistance over a wide range of key issues and of organizing an economic policy dialogue between the organization and these economies.

The centre is mainly responsible for:

- designing and managing the OECD's integrated program of activities, carried out by the organization's specialized directorates, in support of economic reform in the transition economies;

- providing the focal point for all the OECD's contacts with these countries and access to OECD expertise, involving experts from member countries, the business sector, and the labor unions in the OECD's assistance activities;

- maintaining contacts with other international organizations working in the same field to ensure effective collaboration and coordination;

- offering a certain amount of training in some specialized fields to officials from the reforming countries.

CARIBBEAN BASIN ECONOMIC RECOVERY ACT (CBERA)

The Caribbean Basin Economic Recovery Act (CBERA), operative since January 1, 1984, authorizes the U.S. president to proclaim duty-free treatment or reduce duties on eligible products of designated Caribbean, Central American, and South American countries. The primary goal of CBERA is to promote export-oriented growth in the Caribbean Basin countries and to diversify their economies away from such traditional agricultural products and raw materials as aluminum, bananas, coffee, petroleum, and sugar.

CBERA requires the U.S. International Trade Commission to report annually on the actual and probable future effects of CBERA on the U.S. economy in general, on U.S. industries, and on U.S. consumers. The effects of duty reductions are measured by estimating

- the extent to which consumers benefit from duty reductions through lower prices (consumer surplus);
- the loss of tariff revenues to the government; and
- the potential displacement of domestic production.

Net welfare effects are measured by subtracting estimated tariff revenue losses from estimated gains in consumer surplus. The potential displacement in domestic production is measured based on the change in demand for competing domestic products. Probable future effects are estimated based on an analysis of recent investment data.

The U.S. has had a collective trade surplus with the countries designated for CBERA benefits since 1987; that surplus was $2.3 billion in 1995. U.S. merchandise imports from the 24 CBERA beneficiaries totaled $12.6 billion in 1995, or 1.7% of U.S. imports worldwide, while U.S. exports were just under $14.8 billion.

Welfare effects include changes in consumer surplus and producer surplus that result from price changes. To produce maximum potential welfare and displacement estimates, the analysis used in this report does not consider changes in producer surplus because it assumes that production in each market faces no constraints in meeting demand over the relevant range. That means the supply of U.S. domestic production is assumed to be perfectly elastic (the supply curves in all of the markets are horizontal) and, consequently, U.S. domestic prices are assumed not to fall in response to CBERA imports.

More than two-thirds of total U.S. shipments from CBERA beneficiaries enter free of duty under one of several U.S. provisions. Imports entering duty-free under CBERA provisions totaled a record high $2.2 billion in 1995, or 17.7% of imports from the CBERA beneficiaries; imports valued at $37 million paid duties that were reduced, but not eliminated, under other CBERA provisions. In comparison, imports from CBERA beneficiaries that entered duty-free under the generalized system of preferences (GSP), which was not operative from August 1 through December 31, 1995, were $260 million. Articles eligible for GSP duty-free entry (when that program was operative) are also eligible for duty-free entry under CBERA and can enter under either program.

Two countries, the Dominican Republic and Costa Rica, supply the bulk of the shipments entered under CBERA provisions. These two countries combined have accounted for more than one-half of total annual CBERA entries since 1989. In 1995, the Dominican Republic was the top supplier of leather footwear uppers and jewelry of precious metal, the leading items entered under CBERA. The top CBERA entries from Costa Rica were jewelry of precious metal and electrothermic hair dryers.

Effects of CBERA on U.S. Industries and Consumers

Of the $2.2 billion worth of U.S. imports that entered under CBERA provisions in 1995, $1.4 billion of those imports could not have received tariff preferences under any other program. The commission used a partial-equilibrium analysis of the 25 leading items benefiting exclusively from CBERA tariff preferences in 1995 to produce estimates of the maximum potential effects of CBERA.

All of the items analyzed for which data were available produced net welfare gains for U.S. consumers. Ethyl alcohol yielded the largest such gains (valued at $7.6 million); followed by frozen concentrated orange juice ($1.8 million); medical instruments ($824,000); fresh cantaloupes, entering from September 16 through July 31 ($672,000); frozen vegetables ($656,000); trunks, suitcases, and briefcases with outer surface of other textiles ($577,000); and jewelry and parts of precious metal except silver, and except necklaces and clasps ($568,000).

Industries estimated to experience maximum displacement of more than 5% of the value of U.S. production were electrical variable resistors

(10.6% displacement, valued at $781,000), frozen vegetables (9.1% displacement, valued at $498,000), ethyl alcohol (5.9% displacement, valued at $84.3 million), and pineapples (5.5% displacement, valued at $3.2 million).

UN OFFICES

The International Trade Centre UNCTAD/WTO (ITC) is the focal point in the UN system for technical cooperation with developing countries in trade promotion. Not to be confused with the USITC (U.S. International Trade Commission discussed in the next section) the UNITC was created by GATT in 1964 and since 1968 has been operated jointly by GATT (now by the WTO) and the UN, the latter acting through the UN Conference on Trade and Development (UNCTAD). As an executing agency of the UN Development Program (UNDP), the ITC is directly responsible for implementing UNDP-financed projects in developing countries and economies in transition related to trade promotion.

Main Program Areas

The ITC works with developing countries and economies in transition to set up effective trade promotion programs for expanding their exports and improving their import operations. This covers six key areas:

1. Product and market development. Direct export-marketing support to the business community through advice on product development, product adaptation, and international marketing for commodities, manufactures, and services. The aim is to develop and market internationally competitive products and services to expand and diversify these countries' exports.

2. Development of trade support services. Creation and enhancement of foreign trade support services for the business community are provided by public and private institutions at the national and regional levels. The objective is to ensure that enterprises have the facilities to export and import effectively.

3. Trade information. Establishment of sustainable national trade information services and dissemination of information on products, ser-

vices, markets, and functions to enterprises and trade organizations. The purpose is to lay a foundation for sound international business decisions and for appropriate trade promotion programs.

4. Human resource development. Strengthening of national institutional capacities for foreign trade training and organization of direct training for enterprises in importing and exporting. The goal is to achieve efficient foreign trade operations based on relevant knowledge and skills.

5. International purchasing and supply management. Application of cost-effective import systems and practices in enterprises and public trading entities by strengthening the advisory services provided by national purchasing organizations, both public and private. The aim is to optimize foreign exchange resources expended on imports.

6. Needs assessment and program design for trade promotion. Conception of effective national and regional trade promotion programs based on an analysis of supply potential and constraints, and identification of related technical cooperation requirements. The objective is to reinforce the link between trade policy and the implementation of trade promotion activities.

In all of these services, the ITC gives particular attention to activities with the least developed countries (LDCs).

Trade Promotion Projects

The ITC's technical cooperation projects are carried out in all developing areas, at the national, subregional, regional, and interregional levels. They are undertaken at the request of governments of the countries concerned. Projects are administered from ITC headquarters in Geneva and are implemented by ITC specialists who work in close liaison with local officials. A project may last from a few weeks to several years depending on the number and types of activities involved.

National projects often take the form of a broad-based integrated country project, which includes a package of services to expand the country's exports or improve its import operations. In some cases, national projects cover only one type of activity. Subregional, regional, and interregional projects may also deal with either one or a combination of

ITC services, depending on the trade promotion and export development requirements of the group of countries concerned.

All of the ITC's technical cooperation projects are systematically monitored and evaluated to ensure that the objectives initially agreed to between the government and the ITC are being achieved.

Headquarters Services

In addition to specific technical cooperation projects with individual developing countries and economies in transition or groups of these countries, the ITC provides services that are available to all such countries. These include publications on trade promotion, export development, international marketing, international purchasing, supply management, and foreign trade training, as well as trade information and trade statistics services of various types.

Purchasing Help

Within the ITC is an organization called the International Purchasing and Supply Management Section (IPSMS). This organization, in conjunction with public and private institutions, provides training and consulting on cost-effective import systems to trading companies. One of their goals is to facilitate the processes and reduce costs and time redundancies.

FEDERAL TRADE-RELATED ORGANIZATIONS

International Trade Commission

The U.S. International Trade Commission (USITC), not to be confused with the United Nations ITC above) is an independent, nonpartisan, quasi-judicial federal agency. Established by Congress in 1916 as the U.S. Tariff Commission (the Trade Act of 1974 changed the name to the U.S. International Trade Commission), the agency has broad investigative powers on matters of trade. The USITC is a national resource for the gathering and analysis of trade data. The data are provided to the president and Congress as part of the information on which U.S. trade policy is based.

The USITC is *not* a policy-making body. It is *not* a court of law. It does *not* negotiate trade agreements. USITC activities include:

- determining whether U.S. industries are materially injured by reason of imports that benefit from pricing at less than fair value or from subsidization;
- directing actions, subject to presidential disapproval, against unfair trade practices such as patent, trademark, or copyright infringement;
- making recommendations to the president regarding relief for industries seriously injured by increasing imports;
- advising the president whether agricultural imports interfere with price support programs of the U.S. Department of Agriculture;
- conducting studies on trade and tariff issues and monitoring import levels; and,
- participating in the development of uniform statistical data on imports, exports, and domestic production and in the establishment of an international harmonized commodity code.

In countervailing duty and antidumping investigations, which involve either subsidies provided to foreign companies through government programs or the selling of foreign products in the U.S. at less than fair value, the USITC works in concert with the U.S. Department of Commerce. The Commerce Department determines whether the alleged subsidies or dumping are actually occurring and, if so, at what levels (called the subsidy or dumping margin). The USITC determines whether the U.S. industry is materially injured by reason of the dumped or subsidized imports. If the Commerce Department's final subsidy or dumping determination and the USITC's final injury determination are both affirmative, the Commerce Department issues an order to the U.S. Customs Service to impose duties.

Another function is to assess whether U.S. industries are being seriously injured by fairly traded imports, and it can recommend to the president that relief be provided to those industries to facilitate positive adjustment to import competition. Relief could take the form of increased tariffs or quotas on imports or adjustment assistance for the domestic industry.

The USITC is the government's think tank on international trade, conducting objective studies on many international trade matters, including nearly every commodity imported into or exported from the U.S. as well as any topic requested by the president, the Senate Committee on Finance, or the House Committee on Ways and Means.

The USITC frequently holds hearings as part of its investigations and studies; the hearings are generally open to the public and the media. Although the USITC cannot function as a judicial body, it makes determinations in investigations involving unfair trade practices, mainly involving allegations of infringement of U.S. patents and trademarks by imported goods. If it finds a violation of the law, the USITC may order the exclusion of the imported product from the U.S.

The Harmonized Tariff Schedule of the U.S. (HTS) is a list of all the specific items that are imported into and exported from the U.S. The USITC is responsible for continually reviewing this document. (See Chapter 13 for examples of the HTS.)

The USITC maintains one of the most extensive libraries specializing in international trade in the U.S. The National Library of International Trade houses over 100,000 volumes and approximately 2,000 periodical titles related to U.S. industry and international trade laws and practices as well as several CD-ROM and on-line information data bases. The library is located on the third floor of the USITC building. It is open during agency hours.

If you are not planning to travel to Washington soon, the USITC maintains a web site at www.USITC.gov. This extensive site allows you to print or download volumes of information including the Harmonized Tariff Schedules (abbreviated) and all correspondence and speeches made by or in relation to the USITC.

U.S. International Trade Commission

500 E Street, SW

Washington, DC 20436

(202) 205-1819

or

www.USITC.gov

International Trade Administration

The International Trade Administration is an arm of the U.S. Department of Commerce and as such provides assistance mostly to exporters. It also monitors unfair trade practices, however. The mission of the ITA is stated as follows:

- To encourage, assist, and advocate U.S. exports by implementing a national export strategy, by focusing on the big emerging markets, by providing industry and country analysis for U.S. business, and by supporting new-to-export and new-to-market businesses through strategically located U.S. export assistance centers, 83 domestic commercial service offices, and 134 overseas offices and commercial centers in 69 countries.

- To ensure that U.S. business has equal access to foreign markets by advocating on behalf of U.S. exporters who are competing for major overseas contracts, and by implementing major trade agreements, such as GATT and NAFTA.

- To enable U.S. businesses to compete against unfairly traded imports and to safeguard jobs and the competitive strength of American industry by enforcing antidumping and countervailing duty laws and agreements that provide remedies for unfair trade practices.

The ITA may be reached at:

U.S. Department of Commerce

International Trade Administration

14th and Constitution Ave. NW

Washington, DC 20230

(202) 482-2112

or

Trade Information: (800) USA-TRAD(E)

or

www.ita.doc.gov

International Bureau of Chambers of Commerce (IBCC)

The International Bureau of Chambers of Commerce (IBCC) is a world forum of chambers of commerce. It is a unique international meeting place for exchange of experience and expertise on policy and technical issues. Participants in the IBCC's work are executives of chambers from developed and developing countries as well as economies in transition.

The IBCC also represents chambers of commerce from all over the world in contacts with intergovernmental organizations and other international bodies. The IBCC's mission is as follows:

- To promote chambers of commerce, help them to support the private sector, and contribute to world economic growth and development.

- To strengthen the chamber of commerce movement worldwide; improve cooperation with chambers in developed and developing countries, in economies in transition, and with their regional associations.

- To administer the ATA Carnet System and its international guarantee chain functioning under the World Customs Organization (WCO—formerly the Customs Co-operation Council [CCC]) conventions on temporary admission of goods; promote expansion of the system throughout the world.

- To manage the IBCC-Net system, a new IBCC service designed to provide electronic facilities for the exchange of business opportunities and similar trade information between chambers of commerce worldwide.

- To promote greater involvement of chambers of commerce in electronic commerce and EDI issues.

- To expand technical assistance and training programs for executives of chambers in developing countries, in central and eastern Europe and other transition economies. This task is carried out with the help of well-established chambers and intergovernmental organizations such as the International Trade Centre UNCTAD/WTO, the UN Development Program/Private Sector Development Program (UNDP/PSDP), and the European Commission.

The IBCC may be reached at:
International Bureau of Chambers of Commerce
of the
International Chamber of Commerce
38, Cours Albert 1 er,
75008 Paris, France
Voice: 33 (1) 49.53.28.28
Fax: 33 (1) 49.53.29.42
www.icc.ibcc.org

WHAT TO DO WITH THIS INFORMATION

By now you're probably drowning in alphabet soup. Not to worry. Within all this are sources of help for you in your importing endeavors and help for your suppliers in their quest for quality and increased sales. Through the programs of many of these organizations you will be able to access assistance, technical know-how, funding, and more.

CHAPTER 10
Ensuring Quality

When searching for quality in the global marketplace the purchasing manager must consider both the quality of the *product* and, many times forgotten, the quality of the *infrastructure*. Most books on importing and international business do not even include an index listing for *quality*. This seems strange, given the multitude of problems associated with quality and its negotiation and maintenance. The best contract price is of little value if the product is delivered late, doesn't conform to quality standards, or is unsalable.

In the area of quality of the infrastructure, it might be appropriate to start with some obvious questions:

- Can the supplier get the product to the port (transportation, roads, fuel, etc.)?
- Can the supplier be communicated with effectively and continually (phone, fax, air express)?
- Are there prohibitive laws or regulations that will delay shipments?
- What is the ability of the workforce (education, training, experience) in providing quality administrative support?
- Are in-country technical services sufficient to calibrate and maintain machinery and gauges?

When product-quality issues come up, the purchasing manager will have other concerns:

- Does the supplier have a *documented* quality plan?
- Is the supplier certified to ISO 9000? What section? Which sites?
- To what instrumentation standard are measurements taken?
- What is the level of education and training of operators, inspectors, and maintenance and repair technicians?

In preparing to investigate such quality issues there are a few considerations. First, don't assume. The workers and managers in Malaysia may look, think, and act like those in Japan, but invariably they will be playing with an entirely different set of rules. This is not necessarily because they live in a different country, but because of their different socioeconomic and cultural background. Conversely, just because a major computer firm is manufacturing high-quality components in Singapore does not necessarily mean that the communications equipment made in Singapore will be of comparable quality. For these determinations, the buyer must delve deeply into the culture and management objectives of the company.

Another common assumption stems from the physical location of a company. Just because a company is located in Germany (renowned for high quality standards) does not mean that it will turn out a high-quality product. The company may not be owned or managed by Germans—it could very will be a foreign subsidiary of a Brazilian firm. Proceed carefully and knowledgeably.

IN SEARCH OF THE TIGER

To assess the quality factor of foreign suppliers, a little history is in order. Following World War II, most of the world's industrial base was in a state of mass disarray. In the U.S. and the U.K., factories were in pretty good shape except for the fact that the byword in manufacturing was "get the product out, worry about the quality later—we have a war to win and a tank that needs fixing is better than no tank at all."

The industrial base of most of the rest of the world was in shambles, however. Prewar industrial giants Japan and Germany found their factories leveled. France, Italy, Russia, and most of the rest of Europe were devastated as well. That's the bad news. The good news for the "fabulous fifties" was that American factories were pumping out most of the world's manufactured goods. Whatever mankind needed, the U.S. produced. But again, due to the so-called bull market in products, quality took a backseat.

Meanwhile, Japan and Germany were rebuilding, with the latest technology, the latest machinery, the latest manufacturing process controls. Germany was able to capture the market for consumer electronics and scientific products early on. Such names as Blaupunkt and Grundig became household words around the world.

But Japan had different plans. Japan's culture steered it toward long-term strategies and objectives that began with a 20-year plan and visions that strung out for the next hundred years. With this mindset, the Japanese engaged the services of an American statistician, Dr. W. Edwards Deming. Deming was sent to Japan to assist the occupation forces with studies on such things as nutrition, agricultural production, housing, fisheries, etc. Always interested in manufacturing statistics as well, it was not long before Japanese engineers sought him out to see just what new ideas they could learn about quality and statistics from their former enemy. But let's back up just a bit.

Dr. Deming was well received by engineers and statisticians in the U.S., but totally rejected by management. It was management's view that scrap, waste, and rejects were due to the human factor alone, and that if enough good workers were trained properly, quality would be 100%. They did not understand, as engineers did, that processes have variation, statistical variation, and that in order to improve a process you must have a *stable process,* another statistical measurement. Management just did not understand.

It was partly due to this frustrating situation with American businesses that Dr. Deming was so enthusiastic when he found a ready, willing, and able management ear in Japan. Most of the early meetings were informal affairs, of chats around the dinner table. In late 1949, the founder of the Japan Union of Scientists and Engineers (JUSE), Mr. Ken-ichi Koyanagi, invited Dr. Deming to teach statistical methods. Thus began a long and fruitful relationship for Japanese industry. Dr. Deming not only taught statistics, he made management aware of the most important factor in manufacturing, the customer and customer service. The Japanese agreed. The Japanese believed. The Japanese followed the "customer" path. The fervor with which the Japanese accepted and practiced. Dr. Deming's principles was almost like a religion. Looking at it another way, Dr. Deming motivated the entire industrial base with the fervor of a Tony Robbins motivational seminar. In 1951, the JUSE established the Deming Prize to be awarded to corporations that have demonstrated outstanding results in improvement of quality. The tiger had been born.

It was this customer awareness and high level of quality conscious-ness that led Japan to capture the world market in a variety of products. Starting small, in the 1950s, it was cameras. In the 1960s, the products ranged from stereo equipment to televisions and tape and video recorders. In the 1970s the Japanese improved their automobile industry and cap-tured the gasoline-starved market with their four-cylinder small cars while Detroit held steadfastly to its perception of the customer as one desiring V-8 engines and lots of steel. The 1980s saw a massive increase in Japanese computers, heavy equipment, and hand power tools; and in the 1990s, it was robotic equipment and industrial machines. Japan and its 20-plus-year visions had become the U.S.'s largest trading partner (in 1992 $533 billion in imports), with more than twice the imports from any other region or country. All this because of quality and customer awareness.

FROM ONE TIGER TO A WHOLE CIRCUS

All this activity was not to be limited to Japan alone. The entire Pacific Rim was to become a whole pack of tigers. Other Asian countries saw what was happening in Japan and wanted a piece of the pie. First to surface as quality producers were Taiwan and Hong Kong. Both were noted formerly as suppliers of cheap paper, plastic, and bamboo articles. They too began to pick up speed in the search for the customer.

Then it was Singapore, noted for its computer parts (specifically hard-disk drives), and Thailand who joined the circus. The Philippines, Malaysia, China, and most recently even Viet Nam have moved into high-tech pro-duction.

Meanwhile, back in the U.S., American goods were becoming harder to get. Suppliers quoted costs of production, costs of labor, and other excuses as reasons why prices were high. Buyers just naturally began to go elsewhere for their needs.

QUALITY HAS MANY LANGUAGES

Now when you venture abroad, you become instantly aware of differences in the quality language. For example, take the metric system that most of the world uses. What system is used in your specifications: ASA, SME, ANSI? But that's just the tip of the iceberg.

In most other industrialized countries today, the ISO 9000 quality standards prevail. More and more imported products bear the CE mark. What does that mean to a purchasing manager? It means that if the supplier is certified to ISO 9000 or one of its subsets, the buyer can be assured that that supplier has a detailed quality plan in place and that an independent agency has verified that the plan is being implemented. (More about that later in this chapter.)

The other side of the quality language is language itself. A purchasing manager cannot be too careful in providing specifications to the foreign supplier. The best method is to provide the documentation in the native language of the supplier. But that is not always true. In Brazil, for example, the manager is likely to find the design department staffed by second- and third-generation Germans and the quality or process control departments staffed by Japanese. (Incidentally, the largest Japanese community outside of Japan can be found in São Paulo, Brazil) Ask the supplier regarding the language used for the documentation.

To be double sure that the message is getting across, the purchasing manager should ask for a reverse translation. Have the documentation translated into the foreign language, then have another company or individual not connected with the first translator translate the documentation back into English.

That brings us to the term *interpreter,* as opposed to *translator.* It is the job of the interpreter to understand a language's idioms, clichés, dialects, vernacular, jargon, acronyms, and slang and provide the listener (reader) with the proper *meaning* of the words, not just the translation.

WHAT TO EXPECT AND WHERE

Quality tends to be relevant to a particular product set. Where there is a concentration of suppliers of similar products, there is a larger and more diverse pool of experts in that field. Silicon Valley, just south of San Francisco, is known for its computer manufacturing. Over a hundred companies there make similar products. Central North Carolina, around Highpoint, is noted for its furniture manufacturing. Omaha, Nebraska, is noted for its diversity of insurance companies, and New York City for its publishing houses.

Case Study

While on a personal shopping trip on the Ginza in downtown Tokyo, Japan, I learned that there were some marked differences in quality. The product was a Nikon camera. Having priced the particular camera before going abroad, I had arrived at an average price of US $500. I thought that by buying the camera in the country of manufacture I could save a few dollars.

Naturally, I was aghast when I saw a sticker price of ¥135,000, or about US $730 at the current exchange rate. I asked the clerk how this could be. She replied that the gold-stickered "passed" items in the U.S. were those that qualified for export and were of a lower grade than the platinum-stickered items that were for sale in Japan. She explained that the Japanese were much more demanding about quality and that only the best products were retained for sale in-country. The lesser quality was for export, which is why they were cheaper in the U.S. This decision, I found out, was made by MITI (Ministry of International Trade and Industry).

So goes it with countries. Michael Porter, in his *Competitive Advantage of Nations*,[1] talks of the clustering of competitive industries. Here are some international examples:

Denmark	Household products, pharmaceuticals
Sweden	Pulp, paper, and related machinery
Germany	Chemicals, printed and related machinery
Italy	Ceramic tiles

For the buyer who is sourcing with an eye to quality, it would probably be prudent to start within an area or country that specializes or has a lot of local competition in a particular product. Another factor related to the centralization of similar industries is the job-hopping that goes on in that area. Centralization draws experts and craftspeople who know that there is more than one place where they can find employment and job satisfaction.

---

[1] Michael E. Porter, *The Competitive Advantage of Nations* (The Free Press, NY, 1990).

The first place to start looking for information on industry clusters by country is the import statistics in an almanac. Follow that up with a search on the Internet under the country name. Country profiles may also be obtained from the Department of Commerce through the Internet (www.doc.gov).

MANAGING SUPPLIERS

The procedures used to ensure quality overseas are not radically different from those used here in the U.S. However, many companies do not have a documented and implemented supplier management program at all. Differences may depend on the product type or the supplier's national regulations. Be aware that outside the U.S., the government and its agencies generally play a greater role in the regulation and management of industries as well as the exporting of goods and services. And that includes the quality of those goods and services.

THE FIRST STEP IN MANAGING QUALITY

Early on in potential supplier contacts the purchasing manager needs to start talking about quality. Some of the items of discussion:

- Supplier's quality control plan documentation
- Quality organization chart (names of individuals)
- Engineering change procedures
- Inspection procedures
- No-defect-found (NDF) procedures
- Nonconforming material procedures (NCM)
- Mean time before failure (MTBF)
- Failure analysis
- Statistical process controls (SPC)
- Calibration standards (gauges, tools)

Through such a discussion, it will be obvious to the supplier that the manager is knowledgeable and serious about quality. In effect, the manager is putting the supplier on notice that the manager's company will be watching quality and will be demanding nothing but the best. By the way, a discussion of acceptable quality level (AQL) of, say, 98% when talking to the Japanese will cause snickers at the conference table.

Case Study

During the early days of personal computer manufacturing at IBM, suppliers were informed that they would do business only with firms that maintained a 98% quality level and would therefore only accept 2% per lot as rejects.

One day, a buyer at IBM received a special package at his desk from a Japanese supplier of hard-disk drives. The letter attached read something like this: "Enclosed are the 2% rejected and nonconforming disk drives from lot #12345. Only perfect product was shipped to your assembly facility. We hope this pleases."

Don't limit your discussions of quality to the product. Remember to include such things as on-time delivery, just-in-time delivery, engineering change lead time, quantity ramp-up lead time, production capacity, material acquisitions, warranty, and repair. All that is really attributable to the overall quality of the supplier. That brings us to the five-step quest for quality.

1. Business as usual. Just keep doing what you're doing

2. Identify and notify. The tasks needed to identify all the quality issues and let the supplier know that those issues are going to be watched have already been discussed.

3. Qualify. A qualified supplier is primarily one who maintains a 93% on-time delivery and a less than 5% reject rate (Use any number you can live with.)

4. Certify. A certified supplier is one who can maintain a 98% on-time delivery schedule and for one year and a reject rate of less than 2%. (Again, use any number).

5. Business Partnering. When you have established a long-term relationship at or above the certified level.

Exhibit 10–1.

IDENTIFYING AND NOTIFYING A SUPPLIER

This procedure can be as simple as sending a letter of notification to each supplier on the list. The letter might include the supplier's current delivery and quality ratings, dollar value of the buyer's company's commitments to the supplier over the past year, the buyer's plans for tracking or monitoring the suppliers future performance, and what the buyer expects.

Suppliers who currently do not have any status-monitoring systems might become intimidated by such an announcement. The buyer has to make the decision whether or not to do business with these companies in the first place (see the survey and evaluation forms later in this chapter). These could be the very suppliers that are currently causing problems for the company, and a resourcing decision may have to be made.

It has been my experience, however, especially in the Far East, that suppliers thrive on data, and the very fact of implementing a tracking system, and furnishing them more data and demanding more data from them will appeal greatly to them. Additionally, it will indicate that you are making a sterling attempt to fulfill the requirements of ISO 9000, with which they are probably already registered. (More about ISO 9000 in Chapter 11.) The notification letter should be neutral in nature and not a demand or a mandate. The following is a sample:

Dear Supplier,

The ABC Company is striving to become a world-class provider of widgets. To attain that goal, we will be selecting world-class suppliers for our components.

Your company has been a supplier to the ABC Company for over five years, and we value that relationship. In addition to our normal and customary communications, our buyers will be closely monitoring your performance and sending you status reports as it relates to the following items:

— On-time delivery
— Product quality
— Accuracy of paperwork (invoices, packing slips, RMAs, etc.)
— Response to engineering changes
— Warranty replacement shipping times
— Costs, pricing, and competitiveness

Please note the enclosed Supplier Qualification and Certification Plan for suppliers to the ABC Company. Your firm will be eligible to compete with other suppliers for continued and/or additional business from our purchasing department.

If you have any questions or concerns related to our new directions, do not hesitate to contact myself or our purchasing manager at any time.

Yours truly,

ABC Buyer

By all means, don't send this letter until you have formulated and documented your plans and have systems in place to provide the data necessary to carry out your strategy.

QUALIFYING A SUPPLIER

When dealing with suppliers outside the country, even Canada and Mexico, it is imperative that nothing be taken for granted. Expectations learned from dealing with American suppliers will most probably not hold water in another country. It is best to proceed step by step, with caution.

First, establish a system for measuring and tracking compliance with those qualities of the buyer/supplier relationship that are important to purchasing:

- Product specification compliance—acceptance level, nonconforming material, rejects, scrap, rework
- On-time-delivery compliance—a reasonable delivery window
- Paperwork compliance—sales order acknowledgment variances to purchase order, packing list errors, invoice errors, change-order discrepancies
- Communication compliance—phone tag with supplier personnel, lost or missing faxes, E-mail response time.
- Contract compliance—noncompliance with specific clauses in contract with the supplier

Having decided on what is to be measured, let's look at how it will be measured. Many manufacturing-specific software programs for computers allow for historical tracking of this type of information. Without the benefit of these, however, you can provide the required statistical control with a simple spreadsheet application on a PC. The problem usually arises, not in the designing and development of such a spreadsheet, but in finding the time to enter the data.

You can start with a simple checklist. After all, you are not going to provide this high level of tracking for all of your suppliers, just the ones that you are trying to qualify. You might start with your top five "dollar-committed" suppliers. Make a single-page check sheet for each supplier similar to Exhibit 10–2. Hang it on a clipboard next to your desk and use it daily.

XYZ Supplier						
	MONDAY	TUESDAY	WEDNESDAY	THURSDAY	FRIDAY	TOTAL
Phone calls no connect	xxxx	xx	xxx	xxxxx	x	15
Pricing Error	x					1
Quantity Error	xx		xxx			5
Quality Error		xx	x			3
Packaging Error	x					1
Packing list error	x	x		x		3
					GRAND TOTAL	28

Exhibit 10–2 Check List

Product Specification Compliance

Establish communication with your quality inspection team. Have them provide some sort of tracking system for product specification compliance. You should be aware of variances and returned material activity (RMA) developed at incoming inspection. In addition, you should monitor products rejected during the manufacturing process as well as the defective products or components discovered during rework, repair, and replacement. To accomplish this, your process must include some form of failure analysis.

On-Time Delivery Compliance

Set a delivery window, for example, 3 days early/2 days late. If the delivery falls within the window, it can be considered on time. For overseas shipments, this window may be a little unrealistic. Try starting with weeks instead of days. For production parts that have regular shipments, delivery compliance could be tracked one week a month or one month a quarter.

Of course, all this requires the supplier to become highly conversant in the realities of overseas shipments, times, delays, pitfalls, and so on. That's a lot of work. But those suppliers who can provide that knowledge and service are naturally the ones with which to do business.

In the absence of a computerized system to accomplish this task, try using the check sheet approach. In one column, put the actual agreed-upon delivery date. In the next column, enter the window dates. In the third column, put the actual delivery date. With a little bit of computation and observance, you will quickly see whether or not the supplier has per-

Case Study
How *not* to perform failure analysis

The automotive repair industry is probably the most guilty in this area. When faced with a system that does not perform, typically a mechanic will replace ALL components in that system rather than attempt to diagnose the "root cause." While the cost of labor in some cases to discover the root cause component may be higher than the cost of all the components in the system, this is not always the case. Mechanics, however, persist in using the same approach to practically every problem.

Take the passive restraint (safety belt) system in some automobiles. The components are the track assembly, the motor, the controller, and the actuator (underseat switch). Total cost of all the components may be as high as $500. Service mechanics claim that they have no way of testing each component, so they replace all. Labor cost, 2 hours at $75, bringing the consumer's total to nearly $700 to fix a safety belt.

The same tends to hold true for the cooling system, which consists of an electric fan, a controller, a relay, and two sensing units. Answer? Replace all for a cost of over $200. There was a time when the problem of "no fan" could be remedied by replacing the fan belt for under $5.

Under the present system of "replace all" the manufacturer (original or aftermarket) does not get feedback regarding the true MTBF of a component and therefore has no way to correct the problem in future models.

formed to the terms of the contract. A simple graph using the zero line as on-time will show the supplier's variance in detail. (See Exhibit 10-3.)

Paperwork Compliance

Sales order acknowledgment discrepancies must be noted at the earliest moment. Set aside time for reviewing and comparing the acknowledgment

Promised Delivery	Early Window	Late Window	Actual Delivery	Variance In Days
01/10	01/05	01/20	01/09	0
01/23	01/18	02/02	01/30	0
02/14	02/09	02/24	02/05	-4
02/28	02/23	03/09	02/20	-3
03/14	03/09	03/24	03/10	0
03/30	03/25	04/09	04/11	2
04/09	04/04	04/19	04/20	1
04/23	04/18	05/03	05/06	3
05/01	04/26	05/11	05/13	2
05/14	05/09	05/24	05/30	6
05/30	05/25	06/09	06/13	4

Exhibit 10–3. Delivery Performance

to the purchase order. Remember that these products are not coming from a few hundred miles away. By the time the wrong product has gone through the international maze, you will undoubtedly incur extra charges to get it returned.

Packing list errors are generally referred to the buyer for resolution. The variance is usually a quantity difference or no packing list, but can be a "wrong product received."

When dealing internationally, you might find the packing list in a language or format that is unintelligible to the receiving department. You can correct the latter by communicating with the supplier. Don't try to keep these problems in your head. Make a checklist.

Invoice errors (referrals from accounts payable) can be a real headache in the global accounting world. If you have not negotiated all transactions to be made in U.S. dollars, the accounts payable department will be quite upset. In addition to currency issues, however, international invoices will invariably contain numerous charges for a multitude of activities such as insurance, port charges, demurrage, carting, handling, forms management, and so on. An arrangement with the supplier's accounts receivable or billing department will be invaluable in ensuring that there are no surprises.

Nevertheless you will need to track these variances, not just assist in putting out the fires.

Change order discrepancies can be a problem for the buyer who does not appreciate the lead time for certain products. International shipping schedules coupled with the supplier's ability to react to a change order can add weeks, maybe months to the exercise. Changes in quantity, delivery, specification, and such may take much longer than anticipated.

The buyer's job is to communicate these caveats to all company personnel that may be involved in a change order. This includes production control, engineering, design and development, marketing—all must be made aware that you are not purchasing these products from a shop down the street. Failure to accomplish this may result in expensive air shipments, returns or unusable product for which you have paid.

Communication Compliance

An example is the "phone tag with supplier personnel." Use a check sheet. Every time you call the supplier and can't get through, put an "X" on the date. When you do get through, put a checkmark. At the end of the week, add up the marks and get a percentage of first-time contacts.

Much international business today depends on overnight express, faxes, and E-mail. If these means of communication are not possible, problems will arise. Try to limit the number of possibilities of loss in this area.

Overnight mail may arrive before 10:00 A.M., but not reach your desk until the next day or so. Establish a notification system with your mail facility to get this mail on a timely basis. Faxes (continuous paper) can get tagged on the end of someone else's mail. Plain-paper sheets can be miss-sorted. E-mail can be inadvertently erased before reading or printing by you or someone else. Be aware of these pitfalls and implement systems to counter their happening.

Contract Compliance

In addition to the above considerations, a contract may contain other requirements. Noncompliance with any term or condition of the contract is a quality problem. (See more about contracts in Chapter 7.)

CERTIFYING A SUPPLIER

After going through the necessary steps to qualify a supplier, you are now ready for the next logical step in the progression, certification. To become certified in anything naturally requires more of something. A certified public accountant (CPA), for example, is required to maintain certain standards, pass a rigorous examination, and provide proof of continuing education in his or her field. So it is with suppliers. Meeting the minimum standards to become a qualified supplier does not mean that you are a favored supplier or that you meet anything other than the minimum requirements. Some requirements that you might want to consider in your certification program include:

- Maintain 98% or better on-time delivery
- Become a reliable just-in-time supplier
- Maintain a 98% or better acceptance rate
- Undergo a complete on-site inspection by buyer's company

Overseas companies are just as appreciative of awards as American companies are, if not more so. Provide a memento or wall plaque for your certified suppliers. Your plaque proclaiming a company's superior performance will hang proudly in the supplier's lobby. Employees will see it every day, and it can encourage them to maintain that superior relationship. By maintaining a combination of on-time delivery and the high level of acceptance and product reliability, you must recognize the supplier in such a manner that it will continue to provide this service.

Outside of the customary requirements listed above, when you reach the certification stage with a supplier, you will want to understand its financial condition. You will want first to know that the supplier will be around for a few years if you are going to depend on it for the long haul. Second, you will want to understand the percentage of dollar commitments that you will be placing with the supplier relative to its gross sales. You will not want to be caught in a situation in which your cancellation of business (for whatever reason) will put that supplier out of business. Reasons may range from product end-of-life, to supplier's future nonconformance, to a marketing or product shift within your company. During the early days of computers, it was not unusual for a component or assembly supplier to be 75% or more dependent on just one large company for its gross sales. In the early 1980s, this was due to the lack of suppliers for certain parts coupled with the huge manufacturing requirements for those parts from just a few manufacturers like IBM, Apple, and Compaq.

Other points to investigate are:

- How long has the supplier been in business?
- Is the supplier a wholly owned company or a subsidiary or division?
- What is the stability of the supplier's suppliers?

SETTING UP A JUST-IN-TIME (JIT) SUPPLIER OVERSEAS

I'm not going to go into the detailed ramifications of how to accomplish this task here. Dozens of books are available to help you through this. However, most assume that you are doing business with an American company in an American location. Other countries may not be as familiar with the requirements and will need additional coaching and training.

The first and foremost qualification that the foreign supplier must possess is a detailed and practiced knowledge of the ins and outs of overseas shipments and documentation. The supplier must also have several sets of shipping plans and the inventory to back them up. It is not unusual for totally unforeseen circumstances to interrupt JIT shipments in the international shipping lanes. The supplier must be ready and able to duplicate lost, delayed, or damaged shipments via air freight at any possible moment.

Irrespective of "force majeure" (acts of war, God, nature), the JIT arrangement will be just what it says—no parts, no production. Some common experiences are unreasonable and unexplained delays at the border for customs, your country or theirs; rerouting delays due to storms or military action; goods damaged or destroyed on ship; mislabeled and misrouted goods; lost and stolen goods; and so on. There is virtually no way that you can depend on "no surprises" in the business of international freight.

You might remember that it was the Japanese who pioneered the JIT strategies with their suppliers. The Japanese are noted for working very closely with suppliers. In most cases, their long-term relationships began with the buying company setting up a supplier from scratch, with some financial and engineering help from the buying company. That's being close. To accomplish JIT, there must be real-time, not hypothetical production requirements and a close monitoring of the supplier's suppliers as well. ISO 9000 documentation speaks to this from a quality standpoint, but it is the marketing forecasting by the buying company that must be communicated to the suppliers so that they may anticipate an increase or decrease in requirements. Current data is insufficient in this regard.

SURVEYING A SUPPLIER

Qualifying a supplier may not require performing a detailed survey in person. You can devise a self-administered audit/survey form and send it

---

Supplier Survey

Company

_____

Address

_____

City _____ State/Prov. _____ Zip_____

Country _____ Phone _____ Fax _____

Contact Person _____ Position _____

Describe location and condition of the facility _____

_____

_____

Type of business _____

Approximate size of facility _____ ft/mtr

Office area _____ %/ft/mtr _____ Mfg. ____ %/ft/mtr Whse ____ %/ft/mtr

General interior appearance/comments _____

_____

Total employees _____ Direct _____ Indirect _____

Documentation of Operating Procedures (explain) _____

_____

_____

Exhibit 10–4. Sample Survey Form

to the appropriate individual (salesperson, quality, security) for completion. The term *audit,* after translation, might be a little intimidating to certain suppliers, so you might prefer to call the document a survey instead. The information gathered from the survey will undoubtedly give you greater insight into the operations of the supplier and let you know more about the controls that are in place.

For the certification stage, it is highly recommended that you travel to the supplier's location and perform a survey. There is no substitute for firsthand knowledge and observation. You can, however, delegate this responsibility to an in-country firm. Third-party inspections and surveys are covered shortly. If you do the survey yourself or hire a third party,

> **Case Study**
>
> *A large American computer manufacturer contracted for several hundred thousand computer displays from a very well known and reputable firm in Taiwan. The relationship grew over the years as a sole-source supplier, and literally hundreds of engineers, buyers, managers, and others visited the manufacturing facility. The facility evolved within the confines of a factory used prior to World War II to manufacture clothing. Several floors had been lined with sewing machines of the old belt-driven type. This mechanical situation required lots of lubrication, and the floors, which were made of six-inch-thick planking were soaked with lubricants, lint, and dust. Prior to installing the necessary machinery, the firm leveled the flooring with plywood and installed vinyl tile.*
>
> *You guessed it. Eventually there was a fire in the factory, and the entire building became engulfed in a terrifically hot inferno in less than 20 minutes. It burned to the ground along with millions of dollars worth of machinery, proprietary molds for injection equipment, blueprints, data, files, and all.*
>
> *But there was a disaster plan. Duplicate molds and much of the specification data were stored in another facility. New equipment was installed in short order in the other facility. The no-ship, line-down situation was remedied within six weeks, and the impact on sales was minimal. All this in absence of a completed and detailed disaster recovery plan—something you would be wise to check for if you rely heavily on any supplier.*

here are some of the required members you should look for on the survey team:

- Design/development engineer (mechanical, electrical, chemical)
- Process engineer (process control, robotics, machinery)
- Quality assurance engineer (inspection, nonconforming material, rework)
- Packaging engineer (international shipping experience)

- Procurement representative (buyer, manager)
- Legal representative (insurance, law, governmental)
- Security (proprietary and intellectual property)

In reference to the case study on the previous page, remember that in other countries, construction laws, liability statutes, zoning regulations, building specifications, and other safety concerns may be different or nonexistent.

In the Taiwan instance, the condition and age of the factory were never noted by any of the surveyors during the course of the relationship with the company. The disaster recovery plan for a sole-source supplier must take into account all possibilities for disaster.

Third-Party Surveys

Not every company can provide a weeklong trip for the type and number of individuals necessary for a complete and valid survey. International engineering firms and third-party inspection or consulting firms in the U.S. as well as overseas may be able to perform the service for you instead. In addition, a survey team native to or familiar with the foreign territory may be able to perform a more valid survey than your own people.

Many countries have yellow pages directories that contain listings for inspection organizations. The *Japan Yellow Pages* lists several dozen such organizations, many of whom are specialized in various commodities such as food, electric meters, bearings, knitting, chemicals, and such. Latin American countries are included in *The Directory for the Americas* and list engineering firms that may be contacted for inspection purposes. You also may be able to obtain a listing of such firms from the chamber of commerce in the country in question.

As time goes on, ISO 9000 is emerging as *the* international standard for quality, operations, and inspections and is quickly leveling the playing field for many manufacturing disciplines. At best, a potential supplier who has passed the rigors of ISO 9000 registration may require only a detailed survey of one particular area such as security, shop floor technology, or administrative function. This will greatly reduce the buyer's expenses and provide an all-round satisfactory result. Needless to say that that supplier will have most or all of the required documentation. (ISO 9000 is covered in detail in Chapter 11.)

Supplier Evaluation Form

SUPPLIER _____ DATE _____

ADDRESS _____

PRODUCTS _____

	Always 6	5	Usually 4	3	Seldom 2	1	Never 0
Is experienced in our standards							
Delivers quality materials..................							
Is sincere in desire to serve.............							
Has competitive prices							
Delivers at quoted prices.................							
Has technical ability.........................							
Anticipates our requirements							
Will stock special items							
Supplies catalogs & technical data ...							
Is helpful in emergencies							
Regularly solicits our business..........							
Supplies quotations promptly...........							
Has 24-hour availability....................							
Handles rejections promptly.............							
Keeps promises...............................							
Delivers on schedule							
Delivers per instructions							
Has adequate delivery service							
Maintains good records.....................							
Ships order quantities accurately......							
Packages properly							
Invoices correctly							
Total number of checks.....................							
No. checks × point value....................							

Total score _____

Instructions
1. Evaluate the supplier on each question and check appropriate box.
2. Count up the number of checks in each column by the column value.
3. Multiply the number of checks in each column by the column value.
4. Add together the point values to arrive at the total score.

Exhibit 10–5

CHAPTER 11

ISO 9000 and Quality Standards

ISO is the International Organization for Standardization. This worldwide federation of standardization bodies coordinates the efforts of over a hundred countries. In the U.S., the American National Standards Institute (ANSI) and the American Society for Quality Control (ASQC), manage standards and publish sister documents to ISO 9000 called ANSI/ISO/ASQC Q9000 series.

The first question that is usually asked about ISO 9000 and international quality issues is, "If a company is registered with an ISO 9000 standard, does that mean that it produces high-quality product?" The answer is, "Not necessarily so." Nevertheless, the ISO series of standard regulations make a buyer's job, especially that of an international buyer, much easier.

In general terms, the ISO, headquartered in Geneva, Switzerland, has promulgated a set of specifications that when followed to the letter will inform the world that a registered company has the necessary documentation that will assist in maintaining a quality system. That documentation governs the statistical management of products and processes.

As a sidelight, the acronym for International Standardization Organization (ISO) might be likened to the Greek word *iso*, meaning "equal" as in *iso*bars (lines of equal pressure) on a weather map or *iso*metric (equal-sided) triangles.

An ISO 9000 certified auditor once further simplified the requirements of ISO 9000 for me thusly:

Say what you do,
Do what you say,
Measure the process,
Act on the results

To "say what you do" is to possess and maintain thorough documentation that will provide detailed step-by-step directions for every process within a company. It must be a so-called SOP, or standard operating procedure. That documentation must include administrative processes as well as manufacturing and testing processes, for example, the operation of the mail room as well as the quality test lab.

Secondly, to "do what you say" means that the importing company's training program has ensured that every employee is following the written documentation to the letter. ISO auditors will match the documentation with interviews of employees.

The third statement, "measure the process," requires some form of statistical process control (SPC) using proven standard statistical methods that will provide the company with information on each process, such as machine-run rates, defect rates, process times, scrap, setup, and rework. In an administrative area such as purchasing, SPC can be the supplier management program (as defined in Chapter 9), or tracking the number in invoice referrals, defective packing slips, or returned (RMA) material.

"Acting on the results" requires the importing company to have preset defect criteria for each process. An example could be the defect point of three invoice referrals per month per supplier. If that point is reached, the predetermined plan is to notify the supplier, ask for a reason for the defective invoices, request a "get-well" plan from the responsible department, and then track the progress toward improvement. But the buyer's quest for price, delivery, and quality does not always end on a happy note for all. The following is a true story providing not only an insight into the variances in interpretations of international regulations but into the wide cultural diversity that prevails in different parts of the world.

Case Study

Meeting the developing regulations of the ISO 9000 and the EC marketplace may be bothersome, but the alternative offered by the government of China is much more than an inconvenience. According to a 1997 report, 18 factory managers in Beijing were executed for producing poor-quality refrigerators at a factory outside the Chinese capital.

Charged with ignoring quality controls, the managers were shot before the factory's 500 workers. Those executed included the plant manager, quality manager, engineering managers, and other key personnel.

Although refrigerators are one of the most-sought-after items in China, the factory was notorious for producing units with a reputation for failure. Consumers frequently wait up to five years for a refrigerator. For years, the management ignored workers' complaints that component parts did not meet specifications and that the finished products did not function properly. The managers were quoted as saying "Ship it" to meet deadlines and quotas, regardless of product quality.

According to minister of economic reform spokesman Xi-Ten Haun, the soldiers were justified in their response because the managers' careless attitude showed ill regard for their countrymen.

WHAT EXACTLY IS ISO 9000?

ISO 9000 is a set of standards for both quality management and quality assurance that has been assembled and adopted by over 90 countries worldwide. These standards can be applied to a large multinational manufacturing company or a small business with fewer than 10 employees.

Although most think that the language contained therein is highly generalized in nature, one must look to the fact that an independent registrar certified by the Registrar Accreditation Board (RAB) will decide whether or not a company is in compliance with the stated requirements.

The standards are contained in a series of booklets, each between 10 and 20 pages in length, and can be described as follows:

- ISO 9000—explains fundamental quality concepts and provides guidelines for the selection and application of each standard.
- ISO 9001—model for quality assurance in design, development, production, installation, and servicing.
- ISO 9002—model for quality assurance in the production and installation of manufacturing systems.
- ISO 9003—quality assurance in final inspection and testing.
- ISO 9004—guidelines for the applications of standards in quality management and quality systems.

A close reading of the contents will reveal that ISO 9000 and 9004 are merely guidance manuals. Standard 9001 is the so-called mother standard in that it includes the entire scope of requirements for any industry from the design and development of a product to the servicing of that product.

Since not every company designs or develops what it makes (it may perform work for others), standard 9002 was developed. It covers only the production, installation, and servicing aspects.

Standard 9003 covers only the disciplines of final inspection and testing. The interesting part of standards 9001 to 9003 is that in the more abbreviated standards of 9002 and 9003, those applicable paragraphs are identical to those contained in ISO 9001.

The ISO has set itself a goal of updating and revising these standards every five years.

WHAT ISO 9000 MEANS TO THE IMPORTER

First and foremost, understand that ISO 9000 is fast becoming the de facto standard throughout the world. The time for a "wait-and-see" attitude is past. If you are importing, your customers will soon, if not already, be looking for the "CE" logo stamped on your company's products.

Aside from that, suppose your company is manufacturing a product for a customer that requires you to be ISO 9000 registered. The customer may require that all the components of your product be purchased from ISO 9000 registered suppliers. ISO 9001 states the following:[1]

---

[1] ANSI/ISO/ASQC Q9001-1994, American Society for Quality Control, Milwaukee, 1994.

4.6.4   Verification of purchased product.

4.6.4.1 Supplier verification at subcontractor's premises. Where the supplier proposes to verify purchased product at the subcontractor's premises, the supplier shall specify verification arrangements and the method of product release in the purchasing documents.

4.6.4.2 Customer verification of subcontracted product. Where specified in the contract, the supplier's customer or the customer's representative shall be afforded the right to verify at the subcontractor's premises and the supplier's premises that subcontracted product conforms to specified requirements. Such verification shall not be used by the supplier as evidence of effective control of quality by the subcontractor.

Verification by the customer shall not absolve the supplier of the responsibility to provide acceptable product, nor shall it preclude subsequent rejection by the customer.

Because ISO 9000 was developed in Europe, many European commodities have already followed the EEC requirement to conform to the standards. As of 1996, the following products must contain the CE marking to be sold in the EEC (See exhibit 11-1).

- Medical devices
- Telecommunications equipment
- Industrial safety equipment
- Industrial laboratory equipment
- Commercial scales
- Gas appliances

Exhibit 11-1

Some feel that such requirements make the buyer's job more difficult. Others believe the opposite. Buyers are interested in the quality and performance of their suppliers. Right? To have quality and performance, a company must have an organized system. Organized systems must be documented. And ISO 9000 requires documentation, lots of it. If a company is already registered with ISO 9000, it will make sourcing and qualifying of suppliers easier.

The ISO series of quality documents includes other valuable references. One other international standard that you might want to be aware of is ISO 14000. This sets rules for environmental management. Another ISO/ANSI/ASQC document that will prove valuable is A80402-1994. This document provides a detailed glossary of vocabulary for the international business of quality terms. The purchasing manager will be able to determine the difference between quality management, quality control, and quality assurance. In brief:

- Quality management is that function that determines quality policy, objectives, and responsibilities through planning and implementation.
- Quality control includes the operational techniques and activities of monitoring a process and eliminating causes of defects.
- Quality assurance melds the requirements of internal and external (customer) requirements and objectives and includes all the available functions necessary to provide confidence that a company will fulfill its quality goals.
- Quality system is the organizational structure and the resources involved in all phases of the quality functions.

If one's purchasing department finds itself performing audits on its own, for example, for non-ISO companies, it might be helpful to get a copy of ISO 10011, "Guidelines for Auditing Quality Systems." This document outlines the various procedures in planning, forming an audit team, and quantifying results.

Additionally, if the manager's team includes a quality engineer or equivalent, series 9004 can provide information on quality system elements for services, processed materials, and general quality improvement.

IS ALL THIS ISO BUSINESS WORTH IT?

In 1991, the British government commissioned a survey of the status of businesses registered with ISO 9000. The results in many cases were astonishing:

- 89% reported greater operational efficiency.
- 48% reported increased profitability.
- 76% reported improvement in marketing.
- 26% reported increased export sales.

What all this means for a purchasing department or company is really up to management. Not everyone succeeds in the ISO or quality management reengineering task. But if nothing else happens during the quest, it will provide time to take a microscopic look at how the company buys things and where the defects in the organization are.

CHAPTER 12

International Shipping

As long as people have gone to sea in ships, sea trade has opened new frontiers, supported wars, and built economies. The past 50 years or so have seen a massive expansion of trade and along with that a massive resurgence of seaport activity. By weight, more than 90% of all U.S. imports and exports travel by sea. In 1995, $573 billion worth of cargo traveled by sea between U.S. ports and 230 foreign countries.

Virtually every U.S. port is pouring hundreds of millions of dollars into expanded facilities and equipment. Competition is fierce for the business. Former fishing-only ports are expanding to handle containers, larger-draft ships, and international facilities.

PACKAGING FOR SHIPMENT

Some say that the packaging for international shipment is a science; others that it is an art. Freight forwarders pride themselves on their knowledge of the myriad of alternatives in their business. They know that what works domestically will never work on a two-week jaunt across the Pacific Ocean.

Four major points must be taken into consideration:

- Moisture-proofing (shrink or stretch wrap)
- Maximum weight (pounds per container)
- Breakage (padding, strapping, bracing)
- Theft (marking, securing)

Modern ocean vessels are quite seaworthy compared with the caravels Columbus used to cross the Atlantic in 1492. The seas, however, are just as treacherous as they were back then. Don't assume that every crossing is as calm and serene as the pictures you see of a cruise ship plying the placid Caribbean waters in a travel video. Cargo will be banged around, sprayed with water, bumped, dropped, shifted, and otherwise insulted during its voyage.

In that regard, packaging overkill, with some attention to weight, is the rule. In any event, a good sealed shrink wrap of individual customer packages that are inside the box, that are inside the crate, that are inside the container, that may or not be inside the ship is best. Envision the ancient Chinese box-in-a-box-in-a-box.

CONTAINERIZATION OF SHIPMENTS

A shipping container is like the semitrailer seen on the road every day. Actually, many of those semis are containers lashed to flatbed trailers. This concept was started in the 1950s and popularized by the Sea-Land corporation in 1956. The advantages of containers over individual pallets is obvious: one hoist moves up to 3,000 cubic feet of cargo. Unloading of a container ship may take as little as 12 hours in a full-service port as opposed to several days for smaller units. Additionally, the cargo receives greater protection from moisture, theft, and internal ship movements. Accordingly, insurance costs are lower and dock costs are a quarter of those for other types of cargo.

A logical extension of the container-loading technique is the container on a barge on a ship. Also called lighters, or lighter-aboard ship (LASH), these barges can be tendered to ports too shallow to allow a full-sized container ship into the harbor. A large LASH vessel may carry up to 38 barges or 1600 containers.

As with all things there are caveats. Planning is essential. Is the shipment a full container load? What sizes of containers does the shipping vessel carry? If a container is fully loaded, what is its weight? Some of these problems can be solved by a combination of superb marking of shipment packages and a reliable forwarder at the port of embarkation with great attention to detail.

In reference to weight, you may have to calculate your container load if your items are fairly heavy. A common container is about 40-by-8-by-8 feet, holding about 2,300 total cubic feet and up to 48,000 pounds.

Securing the Shipment

In spite of of 30-foot waves breaking over the bow of a container ship and the slamming of the hull into the waves, beveled glass and crystal lighting fixtures seem to survive the crossing from China. Porcelains and crash-sensitive computer parts arrive safely. But leave nothing to chance. Ensure sufficient packaging of the goods both internal and external by running the specifications by a knowledgeable shipper or forwarder with similar experience. You want a clean bill of lading.

Marking the Shipment

First and foremost, don't emblazon a shipment with the company logo. Imagine a few hundred pallets of computers with foot-high logos proclaiming "IBM." This could set up the shipment for the greatest computer robbery.

International traders use what are called "blind marks." These may be any mark, recognizable at a distance, and reproduced on the bill of lading and commercial invoice for identification. Neither the shipper's name nor the importer's name should appear on external packaging. (Don't confuse this external crate marking suggestion with the external "customer/end-user" packaging marking requirements.) Every external package is, however, required to show the country of origin. It would also be prudent to include the international marks for handling such as "Use no hooks" or "Fragile, handle with care."

Container Consolidations

It is very possible that your shipment may not fill even the smallest container (about 1,200 cubic feet [about 33 cubic meters]). The term here is "less-than-container-load," or LCL. A trans-Pacific shipment may cost $250 per cubic meter. Half a container, or 16 cubic meters, thusly costs about $4,000; whereas a full container may cost only $1,500. Just as with truck and rail shipments a small shipment becomes a candidate for consolidation by an ocean freight forwarder.

Simply stated, it is the forwarder's job to consolidate several shipments at the port of embarkation and sort them out again at the port of debarkation. Generally, the fee for this service is substantially less than consigning a full container for a few pallets of goods.

Many international forwarders advertise the business as a nonvessel operating common carrier (NVOCC). They transport overland, consign space in containers, negotiate with shipping lines, handle all the paperwork. The technical term for this multicarrier operation is *intermodal*. The advantage is that the NVOCC will eventually create a huge volume of goods, thereby allowing it to negotiate very favorable rates with the steamship line. Accordingly, since NVOCC is buying space at wholesale and selling at retail, it can set up its own rate schedule. This schedule can, at times, be less than for a direct shipment with a particular line.

Furthermore, if space is guaranteed on a particular vessel and that vessel is detained or damaged or quarantined, the importer must wait. With an NVOCC, the shipment is merely transferred to another line or vessel. It is the agent who is being paid, not the line.

The disadvantage is that these carriers tend to operate only on heavily traveled routes, and if the supplier is out of the way you may not save much. Additionally, if you are going to use a NVOCC agent, your letter of credit and other documentation must reflect that.

Since these NVOCC firms focus on the transportation of goods, a freight forwarder to prepare insurance and the documentation may still be needed.

INSURING THE GOODS

The most important thing to remember in the area of transportation is that the carrier is not responsible for loss or damage unless you can prove negligence, a difficult task in today's courts. Therefore, it is imperative that you have a working knowledge of the various insurance laws and regulations as they relate to shipping by sea and air.

The insurance business is regulated by the Carriage of Goods by Sea Act (COGSA). This act limits the carrier's liability to the terms of the bill of lading only and up to a limit of $500 per package (customary freight unit). It is the shipper's responsibility, or through the importer, to declare a higher value for the shipment and insure it accordingly. Just as the U.S. Postal Service or UPS vendor might ask if the shipper wants to declare a higher than minimum value for a parcel, the carrier or his agent must, by law, give the shipper the opportunity to do so.

If you do a great deal of shipping, you can obtain a blanket policy with prescribed limits for all your shipping. This might be the wisest decision because you then have total control over the terms and conditions, limitations, and restrictions of *your* policy. Your shipping terms with the shipper then might be CFR (cost and freight) only.

Also, be aware that insurance provided by an air carrier in conjunction with the air bill does not qualify as an insurance certificate with most banks. Apply for your own insurance if this is the case so that you will have a certificate of insurance to present to the bank with your documentation.

A DEFINITION OF TERMS

If no cargo was shipped on a particular vessel, the vessel would be safe in port. Right? The shipper and the shipper's insurance company bear a portion of the ship's liabilities. Therefore, when you purchase marine insurance, you will find protection against "general average agreement." The words do not really describe the problems you can encounter with this clause. What it means is that if the vessel is damaged by fire, collision, or storm, the ship owner has the option of collecting on a portion of *your* insurance claim before you can take possession of your goods. In some instances, such a claim has become a lien against the goods, holding them at the port for periods of time for which the importer also incurs costs. The following other terms are important to note:

- Perils of the sea. In marine insurance terms, perils of the sea is stranding, heavy weather, collision, sinking, or seawater damage. Not included are fire, explosion, or cross-container contamination such as leaking chemicals or fuels.

- Inland coverage. Because standard marine insurance policies cover only the main carrier, it is advisable to also purchase inland coverage if you will be transshipping to another location.
- Free of particular average. This means that partial loss or damage is not insured, only total loss.
- With particular average. This term includes partial loss and damage (minimums may apply).
- Average irrespective of percentage (named perils). This term indicates total coverage including theft, water, steam, loading equipment, and fuels damage.
- Free of capture and seizure (FC&S). This term indicates a denial of claims for pirating or confiscation by governments or persons during civil war, rebellion, or civic disturbance et al.
- Strikes, riots, and civil commotions (SR&CC). This term indicates a denial of claims due to labor disputes and other civil disobediences.

Note that while you may receive an advantage in premium, especially when dealing with certain countries for accepting some of these exclusions, an all-risk policy is preferable and may not cost substantially more. You don't even have to prove what caused the loss.

After all of that, you can obtain an open policy that covers 110% (advisable) of all perils, all carriers, wharfage, demurrage, and more.

UNDERSTANDING THE ACRONYMS OF SHIPPING

The International Chamber of Commerce has provided a worldwide standard for shipping terms called International Contract Terms or INCOTERMS. A copy of the entire glossary of terms may be obtained from

ICC Publishing
156 Fifth Avenue
New York, NY 10010
(212) 206-1150
or
www.iccwbo.org

Some of the more common designations include the following:

- Ex-works (EXW) [name of plant]. A somewhat archaic term that simply means "from the supplier's factory." You pay freight and take title of the goods at the supplier's dock. You may incur the costs of loading the truck there as well.

- Free on board (FOB) [name of port]. *Free* means that it is free to you (included in quoted price), up to and including the named port. Some people say "freight on board," which is wrong. If it is the port of export, you pay and take title as soon as the goods are *on board* the vessel. If it is the port of debarkation or entry (for example, FOB New York), you take title in New York and pay charges, including unloading the vessel, from there.

- Free carrier (FCA) [name of place]. A fairly recent designation that replaces FOB an inland port/point or ex-works. The supplier loads the goods to a carrier at its dock and they are yours. It's a common designation for air shipments. Generally the supplier will pay to load a truck at its dock, but you may be charged for loading fees at an airport or a container consolidation point.

- Free alongside ship (FAS) [name of vessel, port of export]. Supplier delivers the goods to the closest point to a ship (a steamship warehouse) and they are yours.

- Cost and freight (CFR) or (CF) [name of port]. Supplier pays freight and insurance to a named port of entry. You take over from there. This term is for ocean only. Inland shipments usually take the form CPT, or carriage paid to [name of point].

- Cost, insurance, and freight (CIF) [name of port]. Same as CFR with the addition of supplier paying insurance and ancillary charges to a named point. Again, the insurance added to inland shipments (CPT) is called CIP, or carriage and insurance paid to [name of point].

- Ex-dock (EXD) [name of entry port]. Supplier pays all fees, insurance, and freight as well as customs duties. You take title when you sign for the goods at your import dock.

These designations are intended to determine who pays whom, what charges go to whom, and the point at which title passes.

DETERMINING SHIPPING RATES

The tariff on a shipment of goods is the rate charged from a predetermined schedule of rates. Every so often a product comes along that defies categorization and the shipper lists NOS or NES as the rate. Beware. Check the bill of lading as soon as it arrives. Chances are you will be paying too much under those rates. Cargo not otherwise specified (NOS) and cargo not elsewhere specified (NES) are usually found on steamship tariffs or rates and mean that there is no tariff precedent for the particular goods. No one has shipped them before, or if so, they did so under a different product name. These terms are a catchall. A bit of planning on your part, in conjunction with your supplier, should eliminate any misclassification of your goods. Check the rate schedules with a reliable shipper, forwarder, or agent.

CHAPTER 13
Understanding Customs and Tariffs

U.S. CUSTOMS

The U.S. Customs Service, a bureau of the U.S. Treasury, is responsible for ensuring that all goods and persons entering the U.S. comply with U.S. laws and regulations. In addition, the Customs Service is responsible for monitoring all land, sea, and air border crossings of people.

Over 100 million vehicles, 55 million commercial airline travelers, and 40 million pedestrians pass through U.S. land border ports-of-entry every year. Customs is responsible for collecting duties, taxes, and fees; intercepting contraband; and enforcing the laws and regulations of other U.S. government agencies. In 1994, the Customs Service handled shipments for over 318,000 importers, 350 of which accounted for over half that volume. Today, Customs provides a major source of revenue for the federal government, returning over $16 to the taxpayer for every dollar appropriated by Congress for its operation.

The duties and responsibilities of the U.S. Customs Service are mandated by acts of Congress. They are as follows:

- Assessing and collecting customs duties, excise taxes, fees, and penalties due on imported merchandise

---

Historical Note

Few people know that the Customs Service is one of the oldest institutions in the country. Created in 1789 by the First Congress, the duties charged by this agency constituted the major source of income for the fledgling country for nearly 130 years. It was not until the income tax became a viable source of income in the early 1900s that the Customs Service lost this prestigious position.

- Interdicting and seizing contraband, including narcotics and illegal drugs

- Processing persons, baggage, cargo, and mail, and administering certain navigation laws

- Detecting and apprehending persons engaged in fraudulent practices designed to circumvent customs and related laws

- Protecting American business and labor and intellectual property rights by enforcing U.S. laws intended to prevent illegal trade practices, including provisions regarding quotas and the marking of imported merchandise; the Anti-Dumping Act; and, by providing records of copyrights, patents, and trademarks

- Protecting the general welfare and security of the U.S. by enforcing import and export restrictions and prohibitions, including the export of critical technology used to develop weapons of mass destruction and money laundering

- Collecting accurate import and export data for compilation of international trade statistics

In addition to its own laws, Customs enforces well over 400 other provisions of law for at least 40 agencies. A number of these statutes are quality-of-life issues that relate to the environment, such as motor vehicle emission controls, water pollution standards, pesticide controls, freon smuggling, and the protection of endangered wildlife. Other laws safeguard American agriculture, business, public health, and consumer safety.

THE TRADE ENFORCEMENT PLAN

U.S. Customs, in concert with interagency policies, laws, and regulations, manages the massive flow of goods across U.S. borders. This plan has five major components: compliance measurement, compliance assessment, trade intervention, sustained customer interactions, and investigations.

Compliance Measurement

The statistically valid compliance measurement (CM) system was brought to full utilization in fiscal year 1995 and produced a full one-year baseline compliance level for each of the 1,249 four-digit harmonized tariff numbers. The data derived from this CM application is proving essential in developing sophisticated trade compliance approaches, including the stratification of commodities for informed compliance purposes.

Compliance Assessment

A compliance assessment is the first phase of a Customs audit. During this phase, Customs officers, including auditors and import specialists, review, examine, and test samples of an account's documentation, internal controls, operations, and procedures to determine whether information submitted or required is accurate, complete, and in accordance with the laws and regulations administered by the Customs Service. Whether or not Customs decides to expand a compliance assessment into a complete audit, compliance assessments are useful trade compliance tools in that they may identify for Customs the specific areas requiring improvement by companies who have demonstrated either clear instances of noncompliance or inadequate internal controls.

Trade Intervention

The Office of Strategic Trade, along with the Offices of Field Operations and Investigations, develops, executes, and evaluates what has been termed "trade interventions." The intervention or "problem-solving" process applies targeting and analysis methodologies to emerging trade issues. This process is primarily designed to raise the level of compliance within the "primary-focus" industries. Furthermore, trade intervention involves analyzing and evaluating compliance measurement and compliance assessment results and remeasures areas of noncompliance to ensure that performance has improved.

Sustained Customer Interactions

Customs plans to improve trade compliance by assuring that all significant information sources are effectively available to its "customers" in the trade. By working more closely with members of the trade to establish a better exchange of information, Customs hopes to maximize trade compliance and to establish this informed-compliance component of its annual enforcement plan.

Investigations

Defining the scope of the investigations portion of its annual plan presents some difficulties for Customs, inasmuch as the investigative function generally begins subsequent to the detection or suspicion of a violation. There-

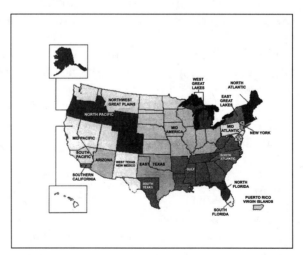

Exhibit 13–1. Customs Regional Service Locations

fore, a normal time lag exists between the actions of other Customs functions such as examinations, intervention, or audits and the beginning of an investigation. Nonetheless, as part of every annual Trade Enforcement Plan, Customs plans on dedicating investigative resources to critical areas of concern, as determined by the findings of earlier trade compliance initiatives.

ASSESSING DUTIES

Duties or tariffs are listed in the Harmonized Tariff Schedules (HTS) of the U.S. This voluminous document lists virtually every commodity in the world. Some commodities may be listed in dozens of forms making identification of products highly difficult (a compelling reason to hire an expert). Exhibit 13-2 includes some examples of listings for wool in the HST:

SPECIAL PROGRAMS WITH SPECIAL TARIFFS

Within the HTS, several special rates have been developed to comply with various treaties, associations, or agreements. These are as follows:

- Generalized System of Preferences (GSP)
- Automotive Products Trade Act (APTA)
- Agreement on Trade in Civil Aircraft
- Canada NAFTA
- Caribbean Basin Initiative (CBI)
- Israel Special Rate
- Andean Trade Preference Act (ATPA)
- Agreement on Trade in Pharmaceutical Products
- Uruguay Round Concessions on International Chemicals for Dyes
- Mexico NAFTA

To find out more about the basis of these and other agreements, see Chapter 9.

Unimproved wool and other wool not finer than 46s, greasy, shorn, not carded or combed, for special uses

Unimproved wool and other wool not finer than 40s, greasy, shorn, not carded or combed, not for special uses

Wool, excluding unimproved, finer than 40s but not 44s, greasy, shorn, not carded or combed, not for special uses

Wool, excluding unimproved, finer than 44s but not 46s, greasy, shorn, not carded or combed, not for special uses

Wool, excluding unimproved, finer than 46s, greasy, shorn, not carded or combed

Unimproved wool and other wool not finer than 46s, greasy, not shorn, not carded or combed, for special uses

Unimproved wool and other wool not finer than 40s, greasy, not shorn, not carded or combed, not for special uses

Wool, excl. unimproved, finer than 40s, but not 44s, greasy, not shorn, not carded or combed, not for special uses

Wool, excluding unimproved, finer than 44s but not 46s, greasy, not shorn, not carded or combed, not for special uses

Wool, excluding unimproved, finer than 46s, greasy, incl. fleece-washed, not shorn, not carded or combed

Unimproved wool and other wool not finer than 46s, degreased, not further processed, shorn, not carded or combed, for special uses

Unimproved wool and other wool not finer than 40s, degreased, not further processed, shorn, not carded or combed, not for special uses

Wool, excl. unimproved, finer than 40s but not 44s, degreased, not further processed, shorn, not carded or combed, not for special uses

Wool, excl. unimproved, finer than 44s but not 46s, degreased, not further processed, shorn, not carded or combed, not for special uses

Wool, excl. unimproved, finer than 46s, degreased, not further processed, shorn, not carded or combed, not for special

Unimproved wool and other wool, not finer than 46s, degreased, shorn, not carbonized, not carded or combed

Unimproved wool and other wool, finer than 46s, degreased, shorn, not carbonized, not carded or combed

Unimproved wool and other wool not finer than 46s, degreased, not further processed, not shorn, not carded or combed, for special uses

Unimproved wool and other wool not finer than 40s, degreased, not further processed, not shorn, not carded or combed, not for special uses

Wool, excl. unimproved, finer than 40s but not 44s, degreased, not further processed, not shorn, not carded or combed, not for special uses

Wool, excl. unimproved, finer than 44s but not 46s, degreased, not further processed, not shorn, not carded or combed, not for special uses

Wool, excl. unimproved, finer than 46s, degreased, not further processed, not shorn, not carded or combed, not for special uses

Unimproved wool and other wool, not finer than 46s, not shorn, not carbonized, degreased and further processed, not carded or combed

Wool, finer than 46s, not carded or combed, not carbonized, not shorn, degreased and processed to remove grease

Wool, finer than 46s, not carded or combed, not carbonized, not shorn, degreased and processed to remove grease

Unimproved wool and other wool, not finer than 40s, carbonized, not further processed, not carded or combed

Wool, excluding unimproved, finer than 40s but not finer than 44s, carbonized, not further processed, not carded or combed

Wool, excluding unimproved, finer than 44s but not finer than 46s, carbonized, not further processed, not carded or combed

Wool, excluding unimproved, finer than 46s, carbonized, not further processed, not carded or combed

Unimproved wool and other wool, not finer than 46s, carbonized and further processed, not carded or combed

Unimproved wool and other wool, finer than 46s, carbonized and further processed, not carded or combed

Exhibit 13–2

REMEDIES FOR THE IMPORTER

Although the U.S. Customs Service may seem to throw endless confusion into the process of importing and managing the record keeping and classification of goods, there are ways to recoup some or all of customs duties. But again, this requires more paperwork.

Duty Drawback

Simply stated, a duty drawback is a refund or rebate of prior duty paid when the importer exports the goods or finished product containing imported goods out of the U.S. Variables fall into four major categories:

1. Manufacturing drawback. Imported components are used to produce a final product that is exported from the U.S.
2. Manufacturing drawback. Domestic components are substituted for imported components of like kind and quality in the manufacture of goods that are then exported from the U.S.
3. Same-condition direct identification drawback. Imported goods are reexported in condition identical to that in which they were imported. Some modifications to the goods are now allowed since 1993 under the Customs Modernization and Informed Compliance Act (part of NAFTA).
4. Same-condition substitution drawback. Domestic goods are exported in place of fungible imported products when both are in the possession of the same person.

To clarify the reexport condition, the imported good must materially accompany the exported item on exit. That is, you cannot claim a drawback for tools, machinery, fuels, expendables, and so on, because they do not customarily travel with the product. Typical inclusions are imported computer components, wiring and wiring assemblies, and included software. Excluded items would include equipment used to test the machine prior to export and washing and cleaning supplies. An interesting case evolved in which imported grains were allowed a drawback as a portion of exported meat grown from the ingestion of that grain.

Substituted U.S. goods categories are limited to three years from the date of entry to qualify for a drawback.

Filing a Ruling Letter

It is in the interest of the sound administration of the Customs Service and related laws that persons engaging in any transaction affected by those laws fully understand the consequences of that transaction prior to its consummation. For this reason, the Customs Service will give full and careful consideration to written requests from importers and other interested parties for rulings or information setting forth, with respect to a specifically described transaction, a definitive interpretation of applicable law or other appropriate information.

A ruling may be requested under Part 177 of the Customs Regulations (19 C.F.R. Part 177) by any person who, as an importer or exporter of merchandise, or otherwise, has a direct and demonstrable interest in the question or questions presented in the ruling request, or by the authorized agent of such person. A "person" in this context includes an individual, corporation, partnership, association, or other entity or group.

A request for a ruling should be in the form of a letter. Requests for valuation and carrier rulings should be addressed to:

Commissioner of Customs
Attention: Office of Regulations and Rulings
Washington, DC 20229

The division and branch in the Office of Regulations and Rulings to which the request should be directed may also be indicated, if known. Requests for tariff classification rulings should be addressed to:

Director
National Commodity Specialist Division
U.S. Customs
New York, NY 10048
Attn.: Classification Ruling Requests

These requests may also be sent to any service port office of the Customs Service.

WHAT IS A BONDED WAREHOUSE?

A bonded warehouse is defined by U.S. Customs as a building or other secured area in which dutiable goods may be stored, manipulated, or undergo manufacturing operations without payment of duty. Authority for establishing bonded storage warehouses is set forth in Title 19 of the U.S. Code, section 1555.

Upon entry of goods into the warehouse, the importer and warehouse proprietor incur liability under a bond. This liability is canceled when the goods are

- exported;
- withdrawn for supplies to a vessel or aircraft in international traffic;
- destroyed under Customs supervision; or
- withdrawn for consumption within the U.S. after payment of duty.

Nine different types or classes of Customs bonded warehouses are authorized under Customs regulations.

1. Premises owned or leased by the government and used for the storage of merchandise that is undergoing Customs examination, is under seizure, or is pending final release from Customs custody. Unclaimed merchandise stored in such premises shall be held under "general order." When such premises are not sufficient or available for the storage of seized or unclaimed goods, such goods may be stored in a warehouse of class 3, 4, or 5.

2. Importers' private bonded warehouses used exclusively for the storage of merchandise belonging or consigned to the proprietor thereof. A class 4 or 5 warehouse may be bonded exclusively for the storage of goods imported by the proprietor thereof, in which case it should be known as a private bonded warehouse.

3. A public bonded warehouse used exclusively for the storage of imported merchandise.

4. Bonded yards or sheds for the storage of heavy and bulky imported merchandise; stables, feeding pens, corrals, or other similar buildings

or limited enclosures for the storage of imported animals; and tanks for storage of imported liquid merchandise in bulk.

5. Bonded bins or parts of buildings or elevators to be used for the storage of grain.

6. Warehouses for the manufacture in bond, solely for exportation, of articles made in whole or in part of imported materials or of materials subject to internal revenue tax; and for the manufacture for home consumption or exportation of cigars made in whole of tobacco imported from one country.

7. Warehouses bonded for smelting and refining imported metal-bearing materials for exportation or domestic consumption.

8. Bonded warehouses established for the cleaning, sorting, repacking, or otherwise changing the condition of, but not the manufacturing of, imported merchandise, under Customs supervision, and at the expense of the proprietor.

9. Bonded warehouses, known as "duty-free stores," used for selling conditionally duty-free merchandise for use outside the Customs territory. Merchandise in this class must be owned or sold by the proprietor and delivered from the warehouse to an airport or other exit point for exportation by, or on behalf of, individuals departing from the customs territory for foreign destinations.

Advantages of Using a Bonded Warehouse

When using a bonded warehouse, the importer is not liable for payment of duty until merchandise is withdrawn for sale or consumption. An importer, therefore, has control over use of money until that time. If no domestic buyer is found for the imported articles, the importer can reexport the goods, thereby canceling his or her obligation to pay duty.

Many items subject to quota or other restrictions may be stored in a bonded warehouse. Check with the nearest Customs office before assuming that such merchandise will be placed in a bonded warehouse.

Full accountability for all merchandise entered into a Customs bonded warehouse must be maintained; that merchandise will be inventoried and the proprietor's records will be audited on a regular basis. Bonded merchandise may not be commingled with domestic merchandise and must be kept separate from unbonded merchandise.

Merchandise in a Customs bonded warehouse may, with certain exceptions, be transferred from one bonded warehouse to another in accordance with the provisions of Customs regulations. Basically, merchandise placed in a Customs bonded warehouse, other than class 6 or 7, may be stored, cleaned, sorted, repacked, or otherwise changed in condition, but not manufactured.

Articles manufactured in a Class 6 warehouse must be exported in accordance with Customs Regulations. Waste or byproducts from a class 6 warehouse may be withdrawn for consumption upon payment of applicable duties. Imported merchandise may be stored in a Customs bonded warehouse for a period of five years.

ESTABLISHING A BONDED WAREHOUSE

An owner or lessee seeking to establish a bonded warehouse must make written application to his or her local Customs port director describing the premises, giving the location, and stating the class of warehouse to be established.

Except in the case of a class 2 or 7 warehouse, the application must state whether the warehouse is to be operated for the storage or treatment of merchandise belonging to the applicant or whether it is to be operated as a public bonded warehouse.

If the warehouse is to be operated as a private bonded warehouse, the application must also state the general character of the merchandise to be stored therein, with an estimate of the maximum duties and taxes that will be due on the merchandise at any one time.

The application must be accompanied by the following:

- A certificate signed by the president or a secretary of a board of fire underwriters that the building is a suitable warehouse and acceptable for fire insurance purposes. At ports where there is no board of fire underwriters, certificates should be obtained and signed by officers or agents of two or more insurance companies.
- A blueprint showing measurements to be bonded. If the warehouse to be bonded is a tank, the blueprint shall show all outlets, inlets, and pipelines and shall be certified as correct by the proprietor of the tank. A gauge table showing the capacity of the tank in U.S. gallons per inch or fraction of an inch of height shall be included and certified by the proprietor as correct.

When a part or parts of the building are to be used as a warehouse, a detailed description of the materials and construction of all partitions shall be included.

Bonds for each class of warehouse shall be executed on Customs form 301.

Duty-free shops (class 9) have specific requirements governing their establishment. These requirements include location, exit points, record-keeping systems, and the approval of local governments.

To find your local customs office, consult your local telephone directory under federal government listings. You will find your local port director under "U.S. Treasury Department, Customs Service."

FOREIGN TRADE ZONES

A foreign trade zone is something like a bonded warehouse, only larger in scope and purpose. The object of such zones is to bring in foreign goods, combine them with domestic goods, repack, sort, assemble, exhibit or otherwise manipulate the goods, and then reexport them to another country (without the foreign goods actually entering the U.S), all duty-free. The entire port of Singapore set itself up as a foreign trade zone to be able to bring goods in from one country, perform what is called "value-add," and reship the goods to another country. This one fact alone may account for the tremendous growth of Singapore in the late 1970s and 1980s.

The mission of foreign trade zones is to:

- help facilitate and expedite international trade;
- provide special customs procedures as a public service to help firms conduct international trade–related operations in competition with foreign plants;
- encourage and facilitate exports;
- help attract offshore activity and encourage retention of domestic activity;
- assist state/local economic development efforts;
- help create employment opportunities.

Foreign trade zones are established in accordance with the provisions of 19 U.S.C. §81 based on the Foreign Trade Zones Act of 1934. Currently, there are over 200 such installations handling in excess of $100 billion in transfers of goods. They must be located at or adjacent to a port of entry and are authorized and managed by the U.S. Department of Commerce. A list of current zones may be found in Appendix C of this book. For new listings, look in your phone book under "U.S. Government."

One advantage of these zones is that product may be brought onto U.S. shores without paying any duty. Only when the goods leave the confines of the foreign trade zone for a domestic U.S. destination must they go through the normal customs procedure and pay duty. This provides a definite delivery advantage coupled with a cash flow benefit. Furthermore, there is no set time limit for storage within a zone, as long as storage fees are paid.

A quick look at the differences between a bonded warehouse and a foreign trade zone will reveal that the goods in a foreign trade zone require no bond for future duty. Therefore, in the case of large volumes of goods, storage in a foreign trade zone means a cost savings and cash flow advantage.

WHAT HAPPENS IF GOODS ARE SEIZED BY U.S. CUSTOMS?

U.S. Customs seizes merchandise that a traveler or importer attempts to import in violation of U.S. law on behalf of over 40 agencies of the U.S. government. These include the Food and Drug Administration (FDA), the Departments of Commerce, State, Defense, and Treasury, the Environmental Protection Agency (EPA), the Consumer Product Safety Commission (CPSC), the Drug Enforcement Administration (DEA), and many others, for whom Customs acts as enforcement arm at the U.S. borders, ports of entry, and mail locations.

Some merchandise seized is prohibited (narcotics, hazardous materials) and some is merely restricted (subject to trade embargoes such as those against Iran, North Korea, Cuba, etc.). Some merchandise is seized due to violation of entry requirements (failure to declare, false valuation to reduce duty, etc.). Some is seized to secure payment of a penalty.

What happens next? Due process. All seizures, forfeitures, mitigation, and property dispositions are strictly governed by laws designed to afford the greatest possible due process. The process goes as follows:

1. Seizure notice. The importer is provided with a Notice of Seizure listing the items seized, the law(s) violated, the violator's options (rights

and time to petition, elect judicial or administrative processing, etc.) and the Customs contact location and telephone number. The seizing officers also look for information on other possible claimants to the property. Customs sends identical seizures notices to all other known persons with a valid interest in the property, who have the same rights as the violator.

2. Adjudication. The Fines, Penalties and Forfeitures Officer (FPFO) for the Customs Service port takes custody of the property and assigns the case to a specialist. If the importer files a petition for administrative relief, the mitigating facts and circumstances the importer provides, together with the report and findings of the seizing and investigating of ricers, are evaluated and weighed by the specialist. The specialist makes a recommendation to forfeit some or all of the property to the government; remit (give back) some or all of the property to the violator or claimant; remit the property and issue a penalty; release the property for immediate reexportation; or return some or all of the property upon payment of a sum of money based on the property's value in lieu of forfeiture. In this last type of resolution, the money paid is then forfeited to the government.

3. Forfeiture Notice. Forfeiture proceedings are instituted when the violator/claimant fails to petition or comply with the FPFO decision within the specified time. Forfeiture proceedings consist of public announcement, or advertisement, of Customs intent to forfeit. This provides claimants with additional notice and time in which to make claims on the property. The form used depends on the value of the merchandise. Intent to forfeit low-value merchandise is posted in the customhouse of the service port area controlling the seizure. Customs advertises forfeiture of higher-value merchandise in a newspaper of general circulation in the appropriate area on three successive occasions, seven days apart. A previously unknown claimant, or one with new facts, may seek to interrupt the forfeiture proceedings by contacting Customs. If the petition is accepted but fails again, Customs must reinstitute forfeiture proceedings (the advertisement process) from the beginning. On completion, title to the property is transferred to the government.

What happens to forfeited property? Depending on the character of the forfeited property, it may be destroyed, shared with other government agencies, retained for Customs use, or sold at auction. (Note: None of the property rights or procedures described pertain to seizure of prohibited substances (Schedule I drugs, etc.), which are forfeited to the government immediately after seizure and destroyed as soon as possible thereafter according to federal and local environmental laws.)

Overview of Customs Modernization Act

On December 8, 1993, the U.S. Congress enacted Customs modernization provisions under Title VI of the North American Free Trade Agreement Implementation Act (Public Law 103-082). These provisions are commonly called the Customs Modernization Act (Mod Act). The Mod Act is based on two basic tenets: shared responsibility and informed compliance. Shared responsibility means that importers and Customs have a mutual responsibility to ensure compliance with trade and Customs laws. The purpose of informed compliance is to maximize voluntary compliance. The informed compliance concept imposed many publication, consultation and notice obligations on Customs.

The Mod Act fundamentally alters the relationship between importers and the Customs Service. The act shifts the legal responsibility for declaring the value, classification, and rate of duty applicable to entered merchandise to the importer and requires importers to use reasonable care to assure that Customs is provided accurate and timely data. Customs retains the ultimate responsibility to "fix" the value, classification, and rate of duty. Informed compliance is based on the premise that to meet their responsibilities, importers need to be clearly and completely informed of their legal obligations. Under the Mod Act, Customs will spend more time and use more effective methods to inform the public, with the goal to maximize voluntary compliance and reduce the number of instances in which forced compliance is necessary.

THE CUSTOMS MODERNIZATION ACT

A lot of trust has been levied upon the importer by the U.S. Customs Service since 1993. That was the year the Customs Modernization Act (Mod Act) was passed, allowing *shared* responsibility for compliance with trade laws and regulations. Under this law the importer is responsible for:

- declaring the value of the import
- classification of the goods
- rate of duty applicable to entered goods

U.S. Customs is responsible for informing the importer of his or her rights and duties and responsibilities under the law. In other words, don't make mistakes and don't cheat.

All the necessary information for this responsibility is contained in what the Customs service calls a "CATKIT." The CAT refers to "compliance assessment-team," and the contents of this kit are available on the Internet (TREAS.GOV, choose Bureaus, then the U.S. Customs Service and search for CATKIT). It is downloadable in Wordperfect and other formats. The results provide you with a complete handbook in 30 sections that you can print as needed.

As stated by the U.S. Customs Service, the purpose of this handbook is to provide audit procedures and steps to be used by regulatory auditors in conducting compliance assessments and audits of importers' customs systems. Compliance assessments and audits are conducted to assure that importers' systems provide accurate and complete Customs entry data at an acceptable level of compliance with Customs regulations and laws.

This handbook, *Importer Audit Program,* incorporates Customs Modernization Act concepts. Implementation of the *Importer Audit Program* will ensure importer compliance with laws and regulations and encourage the improvement of importers' record keeping systems.

What all this means is that the U.S. Customs Service will be spending less time on searching for classification of goods and rate making and leave that business up to the importer on the honor system. However, the Compliance Assessment Team, the CATs, will be auditing regularly, looking for errors, omissions, and flagrant violations of the law. The word to the wise is beware, be as honest as you can, and have the necessary documentation to back up your claims.

CHAPTER 14

Managing Repair and Warranty

Books on importing contain little information on the subject of warranty. What happens when you receive inferior goods from the supplier in the form of nonconforming material (NCM)? What happens when material is returned from your distributor or retail outlet—return material/goods authorization (RMA)? Or worse yet, what happens when an end-user returns an imported product for repair or replacement? Do you send the product back to China?

Before addressing such specifics, let's take a look at warranty as a definition and the types of warranties likely to be encountered in the international marketplace.

DEFINITION OF WARRANTY

Under the law of sales, a warranty is a guarantee or promise made by a seller that the product conforms to certain or specific qualities. Warranties may be express or implied.

Express Warranty

An express warranty relates to the comparison of actual delivered goods with certain facts or writings and may be created in three different ways:

1. An affirmation of fact or a promise put forth by the seller (even if that statement appears only in the seller's advertising labeling or packaging)
2. A description or specification of the goods
3. A sample or model of the goods

It is not necessary to put an express warranty in a contract; courts will uphold an express warranty based on the above three determinations. Therefore, an express warranty is virtually impossible to disclaim by any contractual clause.

Implied Warranty

The implied warranty falls into different categories as well:

1. Warranty of merchantability
2. Warranty of fitness
3. Warranty of title
4. Warranty against patent infringement

A warranty of merchantability implies a minimum quality guarantee: that the goods are manufactured to ordinary standards of care and that they are of average grade, quality, and value as similar goods sold under similar circumstances.

The warranty of fitness implies that the goods are fit for the ordinary purposes for which such goods are used. Simply stated, the goods will perform the advertised task and are suitable for the buyer's particular needs.

Warranty of title, as one would assume, is a guarantee that the seller holds title of ownership of the goods that he or she intends to sell. The warranty against patent infringement is a little more complicated. In essence, a seller who manufactures a product to the exact specifications of the buyer cannot be held liable for patent infringement. On the other hand, should the specifications be those of the seller, and they infringe upon another existing international patent, the seller would be liable. There is a tremendous amount of litigation and consternation on this point due to the fact that several inventors, in several different countries, may come up with the same idea practically simultaneously. In a case of this type, the buyer as well as the seller may become defendants.

It is the practice of practically every seller to deny any and all of the above in a written contract. This is perfectly legal to do. (See "Typical Contractor Protection Clause" later in this chapter.) Again, it is nearly impossible to disclaim an express warranty (unless both parties agree in writing), but all the other warranties may be denied.

BUYER'S CONTRACTUAL RESPONSIBILITIES

With the exception of incoming NCM, which will most probably be returned to the supplier, the purchasing company is responsible for the service and repair of goods after they leave its facility. That brings up such subjects of spare parts, technical manuals, assembly, repair and test tools, and training. Will the supplier furnish these? This will be part of the contract and early negotiations with the supplier (see Chapter 7). Within the contract, a standard spare parts list, the duration of availability of those spare parts, third-party and aftermarket sourcing of spare parts, equivalents, or substitutions must be addressed.

The contract must be spelled out in detail, for example, such terms as NCM and mean time before failure (MTBF), so that your company can calculate the necessary stock levels of spare parts and number of service personnel based upon the expected sales numbers. Such figures furnished by suppliers are never accurate and are skewed toward the lowest possible number to enhance their claims of product reliability. In that light, find out what the lead time for spares is. Also find out whether they sourced from a third party or manufactured by the supplier. What happens at end-of-life? Who will be supplying spares and for how long? An unwritten industry standard seems to be seven years' availability for most parts from most suppliers, but certain products and certain suppliers have been known to pull the plug on parts as soon as orders for new products cease. Be careful in the wording of your contract to ensure supplies.

This brings up the subject of quality already covered in Chapter 10. Even if you have provided clauses within the contract to cover quality, and those terms and conditions are being followed, oversights occur; engineering specifications, tests, and such can never anticipate the inevitable. Below are some additional clauses that, when included whole or in part in a contract, will assist in managing such eventualities.

Case Study

A large computer company contracted with a supplier in Korea for color monitors. The negotiations were lengthy and competitive; cost-cutting was brutal from the supplier's side based on the supplier's unfounded assumption that it had to be the low price leader. Many corners were cut in the sourcing of parts, assembly, and testing of the product.

As a result, an unusually large percentage of the monitors failed during the first six months of use. Lacking a repair facility in the U.S., the Korean company decided early on to scrap the defective monitors in the U.S. and replace them with new units. This created a major financial burden for the supplier and a marked loss of confidence for the U.S. company. Over 100,000 failed units were scrapped, leaving the supplier in a deficit situation on that particular contract.

INSPECTION AND ACCEPTANCE CLAUSES

Contractor will provide and maintain an inspection procedure and quality assurance program as described in Attachment 1 to this contract for products and their production processes. This procedure and program will be sufficient to permit Contractor to meet the quality standards described in Attachment 1.

Contractor will inspect and test all products prior to delivery, pursuant to the Acceptance Test Procedure set forth in Attachment 1. The ABC Company may, subject to mutual agreement and at the ABC Company's cost, update or modify the Acceptance Test Procedure during any term of this Agreement.

The ABC Company will have the right to observe Contractor's performance and Contractor's compliance with provisions of this Agreement through periodic process reviews at Contractor's locations at mutually agreeable times. Records of all inspection work done by Contractor, including gauge inspection and equipment calibration, will be made available to the ABC Company at reasonable times upon request.

The ABC Company may inspect and test all products prior to acceptance or rejection and may refuse to accept products or lots of products which do not conform to the specifications in this Agreement. The act of payment for products will not be construed as the ABC Company's acceptance of same.

The ABC Company reserves the right to assign an employee of the ABC Company or an independent contractor(s) in residency at Contractor's facility for the purpose of source inspection (inspection of items before export). In the event that the ABC Company assigns an independent contractor(s) in residency, Contractor shall have the right to review each such applicant and express approval or disapproval, but Contractor shall not withhold such approval unreasonably. Contractor shall provide adequate office space, equipment, and facilities for use by the ABC Company or its representatives sufficient enough to allow the ABC Company to carry out any of the provisions of this Agreement.

If the ABC Company rejects products, the ABC Company will return rejected products as Nonconforming Material and debit Contractor for the purchase price originally paid by the ABC Company. Return Material Authorization for such products will not be unreasonably withheld by Contractor. Contractor will, at its own option, either repair, adjust, or replace such rejected products within thirty (30) days from the date of receipt at Contractor's facility.

Contractor will be liable for all expenses and duties occasioned by the return to Contractor for return shipping, repair, refund, adjustment or replacement and the subsequent return to the ABC Company of all products which did not meet the specifications set forth in this Agreement.

Product Warranty Clauses

Contractor warrants that products delivered to the ABC Company by Contractor hereunder conform in every respect to all specifications which are part of this Agreement and will be free from defects in material and workmanship under normal use and operation for a period of sixteen (16) months from date of manufacture or twelve (12) months from date of purchase by end-user, whichever comes later.

Contractor will either repair or replace all products found to be defective during this warranty period with products which conform to the specifications which are part of this Agreement and in force at the time the defective products were delivered. Contractor will deliver replacement or repaired products within thirty (30) days from the date Contractor receives the defective products.

All products repaired by Contractor will exhibit an identifying mark to indicate that the product has been reworked or repaired and the latest date of delivery.

Typical Contractor Protection Clause

Contractor hereby disclaims all other warranties as to materials and workmanship, either express or implied, including without limitation, any implied warranty of merchantability or fitness for a particular purpose. Contractor will not be liable to the company for special, indirect, incidental, or consequential damages which may arise from breach of this section.

Product Repair Clauses

Contractor agrees to provide product repair service to the ABC Company at a reasonable price and lead time until the end of five (5) years after the last term of this Agreement expires or is terminated, pursuant to terms and conditions substantially similar to those set forth in the Product Repair Service Agreement, Attachment 3. Such repair service shall be made available in the Continental United States or contractor will make available to the ABC Company the necessary spare parts, tools, manuals, and training such as to enable the ABC Company to duplicate such facilities in required locations. The foregoing notwithstanding, the ABC Company will have no obligation to have any products repaired by Contractor.

Spare Parts Clause

Contractor agrees to provide spare parts internal to the product. Such spare parts will be made available for sale to the ABC Company and carry Contractor's part number only. Those parts, components, or subassemblies determined by Contractor to be required as spare parts will be identified by part number, description and location in the ABC Company Service Manual described in Section 12 and Attachment 4. A listing of such spare parts will be made a part of this Agreement as Attachment 8.

Having addressed all of the above, the purchasing manager must still decide, before the contract is signed, what happens to defective products. In summary, you must contract for:

- Life of the product
- Spare parts inventory before and after end-of-life
- A repair facility (you, the supplier, third party)
- Procedure for repair versus replace decisions
- Returned-material specifications, authorizations
- Who bears the costs of return or repair

CHAPTER 15

Managing Accounts Payable

One of the most important resources for any business is its bank. If its business leads a company to international relationships, it must have an intranational bank. If one's current bank is a novice in the international marketplace, go shopping. Features to look for include:

- Does the bank have current relationships with overseas banks, especially in the countries where you are going to do business?

- Does it have experience in dealing with overseas letters of credit and wire transfers?

- Does it maintain a strong international desk?

- Is it knowledgeable and expeditious in handling of paperwork?

- What is its credit policy, collateral, receivables, and terms?

When it comes to paying for goods, you and your bank will become very familiar. Traditionally, the method of payment in international trade has been the letter of credit. Historically and still in some circles a letter of credit is called *documentary credit*. This more accurately describes the piece of paper in that the bank has documented that the purchasing company has the credit for the funds, these funds have probably been frozen by the bank, and it is holding the funds until valid paperwork is submitted

Sample letter of credit

2 July 1996

Issuing Bank: Applicant:
Number One Bank   ABC Company
123 Main Street   11 Union Street
Anytown, USA   New Town, USA
Issuing Bank Reference: 54321

Advising Bank: Beneficiary:
Merchantile Export Bank   Hansmueller Mfg.
23 Vertistrasse   3000 Rhinestrasse
Hamburg, Germany   Hamburg, Germany

By order of the ABC Company, we issue in favor of ___Hansmueller Mfg.___ this documentary letter of credit, which is available ___on sight___ against your drafts for US
$101,000.00 (one hundred one thousand United States dollars) against presentation of the
following documents:

X	Commercial invoice plus 3 copies
X	Packing list
	Certificate of origin issued by Chamber of Commerce
X	Customs invoice
X	Marine/air insurance policy covering [X] all risks [ ] war risks
X	Full set of clean on board bills of lading issued to order of shipper, marked freight prepaid

Evidencing shipment of: 15,000 sets of silver plated flatware as per pro
                                       forma invoice 98765 dated 1 January 1996
Shipped from Beneficiary: Hamburg, Germany
Shipped to Applicant: New Town, USA
Terms: CIF, Hamburg
Date of expiry: September 23, 1996
Partial shipments: Prohibited
Transshipments: Prohibited
Special conditions: None

All documents aforementioned to be presented within 10 (ten) days of arrival at port.

In confirmation of this letter of credit

_____
For the Number One Bank
Authorized Signature

Exhibit 15–1

that proves the goods were delivered as prescribed by the order and in good condition. (Refer back to the discussion of documents in Chapter 3.)

Letters of credit are managed under the Uniform Commercial Code and the Uniform Customs and Practice for Documentary Credits (UCP), as established by the International Chamber of Commerce. Typically, both are referenced in the opening paragraphs of such documents.

Using a bank to protect both the importer and the exporter is common practice except in some long-term relationships between larger companies who have set up computerized wire transfer arrangements (discussed later).

The three requirements for issuing a letter of credit follow:

1. The rule of independence. A letter of credit is considered independent from the sales contract or any other agreement between the parties.

2. The rule of strict construction. Terms and conditions of the letter of credit are strictly adhered to.

3. The documents-only rule. Banks deal in documents only—no documents, no payment.

The biggest caveat in using such prearranged payment schemes is that the payment is wholly dependent upon the printed word, not on actu-

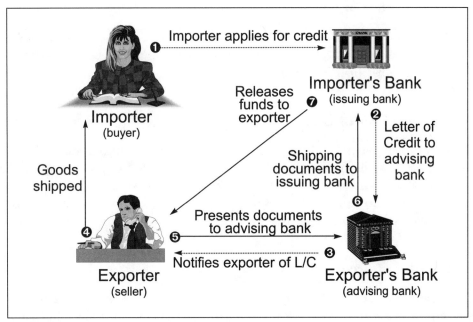

Exhibit 15–2. Typical Importing Flow

ality. In other words, the supplier can ship the wrong goods, but if the paperwork states that it shipped the right goods, it will be paid. If the buyer doesn't catch the error in time and negotiate a delay or fix, the goods are his or hers. The supplier has been paid.

TYPES OF PAYMENT DOCUMENTS

Over the years, many ways to pay suppliers have been used, and the international market seems to have devised the most complicated. Letters of credit are the most common. They shift responsibility for payment from the buyer's accounts payable department to its bank.

Normal Letter of Credit

This form is probably only used in a new relationship between buyer and seller when little time is available for investigating the other. It is a one-time, one-shipment document that provides for payment of the goods upon satisfactory receipt.

Revolving Letter of Credit

This is sort of like a revolving charge. A credit limit is established for blanket shipments or for a variety of products over a specified period of time, such as one year from one supplier to one buyer.

Assignable Letter of Credit

This type of letter of credit is to be assigned to one or more suppliers to your supplier. This may be used when a large order for goods is placed and the supplier has limited capital resources to procure the parts or materials necessary to begin manufacture. In short, the buyer is guaranteeing payment to the supplier's suppliers and subcontractors.

Time Letter of Credit

Time simply means the delayed payment terms that the buyer has agreed to with the exporter. Instead of a sight draft or check, in which the bank pays the exporter upon "sight" (and completeness) of the documents, the bank sets up payment for a certain number of days (30, 60, 90, etc.). The check is then called a "time draft." A "date draft" is commensurate with a postdated check and allows for payment to the exporter on a specified date. A supplier will probably not extend these types of credit to a buyer until the relationship has been active for some time.

Revocable versus Irrevocable Letter of Credit

As the terms imply, the former may be canceled (revocable) and the latter may not under any circumstances. Banks, in their typical manner, have the option to amend the terms of an irrevocable letter of credit to read "revocable," and then revoke them. Because of this fact, revocable letters of credit are rarely used except perhaps between branches of the same company in different countries.

Standby Letter of Credit

Used as a remedy for nonpayment, this form is used when the buyer has failed in some way to perform or to pay for the goods. To comply with the standby letter of credit, the necessary documents must certify the nonperformance. This type of form is not used in the normal course of international business in the exchange of goods. More appropriately, it acts as a guarantee of performance whereby the beneficiary receives compensation for damages (sometimes incidental and consequential) in the event of nonperformance.

A standby letter could be used for compensation for costs due to delays in a subcontractor's performance. Another use is to guarantee payment for replacement of substandard goods over and above the original contract language.

Banker's Acceptances

A more secure way of handling credit is for the exporter to extend credit to the bank, which in turn must validate the importer's credit. This requires a letter of credit with an accompanying check (draft) to the exporter for the amount of the purchase. The exporter submits the check with the documents upon delivery and gets his or her money. If the payment schedule is longer than sight, the exporter may negotiate with the bank to be paid a lesser amount (a discount) if he or she wishes the funds sooner.

Naturally, as a long-term relationship evolves, such payment terms as direct payment (by mail with cashier's check, wire transfer, or other means) are an option. Incidentally, wire transfers are usually conducted by the buyer's bank by means of the Society for Worldwide Interbank Financial Transactions (SWIFT) system and are becoming more prevalent today than drafts. Open accounts with delayed terms are also used. Some uneasy exporters may ask for prepayment or cash with order terms. In this regard the purchasing agent is advised to do some homework on the exporter to establish its stability and ability to ship the goods.

Detailed information on the intricacy of letters of credit may be obtained in *Publication 500, Documentary Credits* from:

International Chamber of Commerce
156 Fifth Avenue
New York, NY 10010
(212) 206-1150

MANAGING EXCHANGE RATES

In the international marketplace, a dollar is not necessarily a dollar. The relationships between world currencies are forever changing on a daily, sometimes hourly, basis.

Chapter 7 covered clauses that would account for the variables in currency exchange rates. The most important thing to remember when dealing with this issue is to lock in the rate at the time of shipment. A bank is not going to be interested in haggling between the importer and exporter after the paperwork has been completed.

Many times the terms of payment are not in U.S. dollars. This, of course, is negotiable with the supplier. Most countries welcome payment in U.S. dollars because they need the dollars in their country for other pursuits. It is not unusual, however, to have terms of currency required in the designated currency of the country in which one is doing business. In such a case, the purchasing manager will want to lock in currency conversion terms in the contract or the acceptance of the quotation. Regardless of contract terms, the customs duty (if applicable) levied upon the goods will be factored at the value of the currency on the day of export from the supplier.

The conversion rate of U.S. dollars to foreign currencies is managed by the Federal Reserve Bank of New York. Common international currencies are computed daily and are published in major newspapers such as the *New York Times* and the *Wall Street Journal.* Specific quotes on unusual exchanges may be obtained from the Federal Reserve Bank.

The U.S. Department of Commerce can be consulted on the Internet at www.DOC.gov. The DOC Office of Import Administration publishes a historical tracing of daily exchange rates using either the Federal Reserve quotes or the Dow Jones Business Information Services.

The stated value of the goods is important because U.S. Customs will assess duties according to that value. Accordingly, there is a lot of communication going on between U.S. Customs and the Federal Reserve Bank.

There are two prices for currency, one for buying and one for selling it. U.S. Customs traditionally uses the "buying rate" published on the day of export for factoring dutiable charges, even though the importer may have different contract payment terms with the supplier. When dealing with countries with soaring inflation rates, prices quoted in terms of their domestic currency may have startling effects on your charges.

Many Asian suppliers, wary of the fluctuations of currencies over time, like to press for contract clauses addressing the issue of payment. These issues generally involve quite a bit of mathematics and usually refer to the *Asian Wall Street Journal* for quotes on exchange rates. See Chapter 7, the section on contracts, currency fluctuation clause.

OBTAINING IMPORT FINANCING

American trade organizations are focused upon supporting the export business because of the trade deficit. An importer may receive a cold shoulder when looking for financing or information from such organizations as the Export-Import (EXIM) Bank or the Small Business Administration.

Your first avenue will probably be your own (internationally qualified) bank. When presenting anything to a bank, the homework must be done. Profit-and-loss statements on your business, your personal financial net worth statement, detailed projections, costs, methods of distribution and such related to the products you intend to import will be regarded. If you have limited knowledge of how to prepare such documents, have an accountant assist you. Professional arrangement and presentation will be a plus.

Banks provide several types of "bridge financing" for businesses needing funds to purchase products for resale. Probably the most common is the line of credit loan. Usually, the bank will ask for some form of collateral or security for the loan. You may pledge your business equipment, your house, or other financial assets, but the most common is based on your receivables. The bank sees that you have open account receivables of $100,000. That's money coming in. They may advance you a line of credit equal to 50% or more of that amount in lieu of security. Of course, they will make arrangements to have first dibs on that money should you default on your payments against the loan.

If you are in the distribution business, as opposed to a retail direct importer or end-user, a bank might offer what is called a back-to-back letter of credit. In this case, your customer/end-user provides a letter of credit to purchase the goods before they are imported, and the bank provides a companion letter of credit to purchase the goods from the supplier.

Another place to look is a foreign bank from the country that you intend to import from and that has offices in the U.S. Naturally, it will be interested in promoting sales of goods from their own country. Terms of loans may range from as little as 90 days to 5 years or more.

Besides banks, a few outside organizations will offer to purchase your receivables. This is known as factoring. You literally sell your collectibles to an agent, or factor, who will usually expedite the collection process. As an example, you have $50,000 in receivables, the factor offers to buy them for $40,000. The factor takes the risk of noncollection for a fee of $10,000, or 20%. You get to buy more products with the money.

Glossary of International Trade Terms

AAEI
American Association of Exporters and Importers.

abandonment
The act of refusing delivery of a shipment so badly damaged in transit that it is worthless, or damage to a vessel that is so severe that it is considered a constructive total loss.

abbrochment
The purchase at wholesale of all merchandise that is intended to be sold in a particular retail market for the purpose of controlling that market.

ABI
Automated Broker Interface, a module of ACS that provides a communications link for the transmission of entry and entry summary data on imported merchandise between all ABI users.

absolute advantage
An advantage of one nation or area over another in the costs of manufacturing an item in terms of used resources.

absorption
Investment and consumption purchases by households, businesses, and governments both domestic and international.

accelerated tariff elimination
The gradual reduction of import duties over time.

acceptance
An unconditional assent to an offer, an assent to an offer conditioned on only minor changes that do not affect any material terms of the offer, or receipt by the consignee of a shipment thus terminating the contract.

acceptance letter of credit
A letter of credit that, in addition to other required documents, requires presentation of a term draft drawn on the bank nominated as the accepting bank under the letter of credit.

accepted draft
A bill of exchange accepted by the drawee (acceptor) by putting his or her signature (acceptance) on its face. In doing so, the drawee commits to pay the bill upon presentation at maturity.

accepting bank
A bank that by signing a time draft accepts responsibility to pay when the draft becomes due.

acceptor
The party that signs a draft or obligation, thereby agreeing to pay the stated sum at maturity.

accession
The process by which a country becomes a member of an international agreement, such as the General Agreement on Tariffs and Trade (GATT).

accessions
Goods that are affixed to and become part of other goods.

accessorial charges
Charges made for additional, special, or supplemental services, normally over and above the line haul services.

accessorial services
Services performed by a shipping line or airline in addition to the normal transportation service.

accommodation
An action by one individual or legal entity that is taken as a favor, without any consideration, for another individual or legal entity.

accommodation note or paper
A commercial instrument of debt that is issued by or for an accommodated party (who is expected to pay the debt) and that contains the name of the accommodation party.

accord and satisfaction
A means of discharging a contract or cause of action by which the parties agree (the accord) to alter their obligations and then perform (the satisfaction) the new obligations.

account number
An identifying number issued by a carrier's accounting office to identify a shipper and/or consignee.

accounts payable
A current liability representing the amount owed by an individual or a business to a creditor(s) for merchandise or services purchased on an open account or short-term credit.

accounts receivable
Money owed a business enterprise for merchandise or services bought on open account.

accrual of obligation
The time at which an obligation matures or vests, requiring the obliger to perform.

ACE
Automated Commercial Environment, a U.S. Customs electronic data system that, when complete, will provide support for enforcing trade and contraband laws, ensuring trade compliance and providing service.

acquisition
The purchase of complete or majority ownership in a business enterprise, usually by another business.

ACS
Automated Commercial System, the comprehensive tracking, controlling, and processing system of the U.S. Customs Service. ACS is composed of many different modules or systems.

action ex contractu
A legal action for breach of a promise stated in an express or implied contract.

action ex delicto
A legal action for a breach of a duty that is not stated in a contract but arises from the contract, or a legal action that arises from a wrongful act, such as fraud.

act of God
An act of nature beyond human control, such as lightning, flood, earthquake or hurricane. Many shipping and other performance contracts include a "force majeure" clause which excuses a party who breaches the contract for these reasons.

ad valorem duty
A U.S. Customs duty assessed as a percentage rate or value of the imported merchandise.

ADD
Antidumping duties, assessed when merchandise is sold to purchasers in the U.S. at less than fair value, resulting in material injury to a U.S. industry.

address of record
The official or primary location for an individual, company, or other organization.

adhesion contract
Contract with standard, often printed, terms for sale of goods and services offered to consumers, who usually cannot negotiate any of the terms and cannot acquire the product unless they agree to the terms.

adjustment assistance
Financial, training, and reemployment technical assistance to workers, and technical assistance to firms and industries, to help them cope with adjustment difficulties arising from increased import competition.

admiralty
Any civil or criminal issue having to do with maritime law.

admiralty court
A court of law that has jurisdiction over maritime legal issues.

admission temporaire
The free entry of goods normally dutiable.

advance against collection
A short-term loan or credit extended to the seller (usually the exporter) by the seller's bank once a draft has been accepted by the buyer (generally the importer) of the seller's goods.

advance arrangements
The shipment of certain classes of commodities that require arrangements in advance with carriers.

advanced technology products (ATP)
Products whose technology is from a recognized high-technology field, represent leading-edge technology in that field, and constitute a significant part of all items covered in the selected classification code.

advice
A form of letter that relates or acknowledges a certain activity or result with regard to a customer's bill or charges due.

advised credit
A letter of credit whose terms and conditions have been confirmed by a bank.

advising bank
The bank that receives a letter of credit or amendment to a letter of credit from the issuing bank and forwards it to the beneficiary.

Advisory Committee on Export Policy
A U.S. government interagency dispute resolution body that operates at the assistant secretary level.

Advisory Committee on Trade Policy and Negotiation
A U.S. government group appointed by the president to provide advice on matters of trade policy and related issues, including trade agreements.

affiliate
A business enterprise located in one country but is directly or indirectly owned or controlled by a person of another country.

affiliated foreign group
Equivalent of the foreign parent or any foreign person associated with the foreign parent that is owned more than 50 percent by the person above it.

affreightment
The hiring or chartering of all or part of a vessel for the transport of goods.

affreightment contract
A contract with a shipowner to hire all or part of a ship for transporting goods.

afloat
Refers to a shipment of cargo that is currently on board a vessel between ports (as opposed to *on board*).

aft
Direction toward the stern of the vessel (ship or aircraft).

after date
A notation used on financial instruments (such as drafts or bills of exchange) to fix the maturity date as a fixed number of days past the date of drawing of the draft.

after sight
A notation on a draft that indicates that payment is due a fixed number of days after the draft has been presented to the drawee.

agent
A person or legal entity with the proper authorization to act on behalf of another person or legal entity.

agent bank
A bank acting on behalf of a foreign bank.

aggregated shipments
Several shipments from various shippers that are consolidated and treated as a single consignment.

agreed valuation
The set value of a shipping load that is agreed upon by both the shipper and the carrier to define the rate.

AIES
Automated Information Exchange System, provides an automated method of exchanging information between field import specialists and national import specialists.

air cargo
Property of any kind (excluding passenger baggage) that is transported by aircraft.

air express
Expediated (expedited) air freight service.

air parcel post
Term used to describe priority mail, consisting of first-class mail that weighs more than 13 ounces.

air waybill
Shipping document used for the transportation of air freight; it includes conditions, liability, shipping instructions, description of commodity, and applicable transportation charges.

alienable
Ability to be transferred or conveyed.

aliquot
A fractional share.

all-cargo aircraft.
Any aircraft that is used for the sole purpose of transporting cargo.

allowance
An amount paid by the seller as restitution or reimbursement if the receiving party was dissatisfied with the shipment for any number of reasons: faulty packaging, late arrival, and so on.

alternative tariff
A tariff with two or more rates for the same goods, to and from the same points, with the discretion to use the lowest of the charges.

amendment
An addition, deletion, or change made to a document.

amidships
In the middle of the vessel; often preferred by shippers because of minimal motion.

amortization
The gradual diminishment of any amount over a period of time.

AMS
Automated Manifest System, a module of ACS designed to control imported merchandise from the time a carrier's cargo manifest is electronically transmitted to U.S. Customs until control is relinquished to another party.

antidumping
The opposite of dumping as defined by the system of laws to remedy dumping.

any quantity
A cargo rating that applies to an article without consideration of weight.

appreciation
An increase in the value of one form of currency as compared with the currency of another nation.

appurtenance
An accessory connected to a primary property used in conjunction with the primary property, usually permanently affixed (i.e., a crane on a ship).

apron
Area of the airport where planes are parked for loading and unloading.

arrivals
Imported goods that have been placed in a bonded warehouse for which duty has not been paid.

as is
Indicates that goods for sale do not include a warranty or guarantee.

assembly service
A service under which an airline combines multiple shipments from multiple shippers into one shipment.

assessment
The placement of antidumping duties on imported goods.

athwartships
Across a vessel from side to side.

Auto Parts Advisory Committee
Established by an amendment to the Trade Act to set up an advisory committee to the U.S. Department of Commerce for dealing with U.S.–Japan trade issues involving the auto parts industry.

avoidance of contract
The legal cancellation of a contract because an event occurs that makes performance of the contract terms impossible or inequitable and that releases the parties from their obligations.

back haul
To haul a shipment back over part of a route it has already traveled.

back order
That portion of an order that cannot be delivered at the scheduled time, but will be delivered at a later time.

back-to-back borrowing
The process whereby a bank brings together a borrower and a lender so that they agree on a loan.

back-to-back loan
Operations whereby a loan is made in one currency in one country against a loan in another currency in another country.

bad faith
The intent to mislead or deceive. It does not include misleading by an honest, inadvertent, or unintentional action. A conscious act in bad faith.

bagged cargo
Goods shipped in sacks.

bailment
A delivery of goods or personal property by one person (the bailer) to another (the bailee) on an express or implied contract and for a particular purpose related to the goods. Bailee has express or implied obligation to perform or carry out a duty.

balanced economy
A condition of national finances in which imports and exports are equal.

balance of payments
A statement identifying all the economic and financial transactions between companies, banks, or private households and public authorities of one nation with those of other nations of the world over a specific time.

balance of trade
The difference in monetary terms between a country's imports and exports.

bale
A large bundle of compressed and bound goods, such as cotton.

bale Cargo
Bulky cargo shipped in bales, usually wrapped in burlap.

ballast
Heavy material placed on a ship to improve its stability.

bank draft
A check drawn by one bank against funds deposited to its account in another bank.

banker's bank
A bank that is established by mutual consent by independent and unaffiliated banks to provide a clearinghouse for financial transactions.

banker's draft
A draft payable on demand and drawn by, or on behalf of, a bank upon itself.

bank guarantee
Unilateral contract in which the bank commits itself to pay a certain sum if a third party fails to perform or if any other form of default occurs.

bank holding company
Any company that directly controls, with power to vote, more than 5% of voting shares of one or more other banks.

bank holiday
A day on which banks are closed.

bank note
Paper issued by a bank, redeemable as money and considered to be full legal tender.

bank release
A document issued by a bank, after it has been paid or given an acceptance, giving authority to a person to take delivery of goods.

bankruptcy
The condition of a legal entity that does not have the financial means to pay its incurred debts.

bareboat charter
The charter of a vessel whereby the party chartering becomes the owner for all practical purposes.

barge
A flat-bottomed cargo vessel primarily used on rivers and canals.

barratry
The intentional misconduct of the ship's master or crew; includes theft, intentional casting away of property, and inciting disobedience and results in injury.

barter
Trade of goods for other goods without the use of money or a third party.

basing point
A location used to determine rates between other points.

basing rate
A rate used for the sole purpose of determining other rates.

basket of currencies
A means of establishing value for a composite unit consisting of the currencies of designated nations.

battens
The protruding fixtures on the inside walls of a vessel's hold that keep cargo away from the walls of the ship.

bearer
The person in possession of someting.

beggar-thy-neighbor policy
A course of action through which a country tries to reduce unemployment and increase domestic output by raising tariffs and instituting nontariff barriers that impede imports.

belly pits or holds
Compartments beneath the cabin of an aircraft used for the transport of cargo or baggage.

beneficiary
An individual or company who gains upon the opening of a letter of credit.

berth
The place beside a docking area where the ship is secured and cargo can be loaded or unloaded.

bid bond
Guarantee established in connection with international tenders. Guarantees fulfillment of the offer to buy or perform a service. An indemnity bond.

bilateral investment treaty
A treaty between two countries with the goals of ensuring investments abroad of national or most-favored nations.

bilateral trade
The commerce between two countries.

bill
A written statement of contract terms.

billed weight
The designated weight shown on the freight bill.

billing third party
The transference of transportation charges to a party other than the shipper or consignee.

bill of credit
A written statement that authorizes the recipient to receive or collect money from a foreign bank.

bill of health
A certificate issued by customs declaring the proper health of crew or passengers of a vessel or airplane upon arrival or departure from a port.

bill of lading
A document issued by a carrier to a shipper; it provides written evidence regarding receipt of the goods, the conditions on which transportation is made, and the engagement to deliver goods at the prescribed location to the lawful holder of the bill of lading.

bill of parcels
A statement sent with a shipment and giving descriptions and prices for included items. Often referred to as a packing list.

bill of sale
A written document by which a party legally transfers ownership of goods to another party.

bill of sight
A customs document that allows a party to see the goods before they pay duties on them.

bill-to party
Refers to the party designated on a bill of lading as the one responsible for payment of the freight changes.

biological agents
A biologically active material.

black market
Buying or selling of products that violate government restrictions.

blanket rate
A special single rate applied to multiple articles in a single shipment.

blockade
Prevention of commercial exchange by physically preventing carriers from entering a specific port or country.

bona fide
In or with good faith, honesty, and sincerity.

bond
An interest-bearing certificate of debt by which the issuer is obligated to pay the principal amount at a specific time and interest periodically.

bonded
Goods stored by Customs until the import duties are paid or the goods are exported.

bonded terminal
An airline terminal approved by the U.S. Treasury Department for storage of goods until customs duties are paid.

bonded warehouse
An approved warehouse used for the storage of goods until duties are paid or the goods are properly dispersed.

bond of indemnity
An agreement made with a carrier that relieves it of any liability incurred under stated conditions.

bond system
A computerized bond control system (part of ACS).

booking
The act of recording arrangements for the movement of goods by vessel.

bounties
Government payments to producers to strengthen their competitive position.

box
Colloquial term referring to a trailer, semitrailer, or sea/land container.

box car
A closed freight car.

boycott
Refusing to deal commercially with a person, firm, or country.

breakage
A monetary allowance that a manufacturer allots to compensate a buyer for goods damaged in transit.

breakbulk
Unloading or distributing portions of a consolidated shipment for delivery.

breakbulk cargo
Cargo that is shipped as a unit but not containerized.

bribe
A payment that results in a benefit that would not have been received except for receipt of that money; a bribe is a criminal offense.

broker
One that acts as an agent for others, as in negotiating contracts, purchases, or sales, in return for a fee.

bulk cargo
Cargo that is made up of one commodity; examples include grain, oil, and ore.

bulk carrier
A vessel designed for the shipment of bulk cargo.

bulk freight
Freight not in packages or containers.

bulk sale
The transfer of a large amount of inventory in a single transaction not in the usual course of business.

bulk solids
Dry cargo shipped loose in containers.

bunker
A compartment on a ship for storage or fuel.

bunker adjustment factor
An adjustment in shipping charges to offset price fluctuations in the cost of bunker fuel.

bunker fuel
The fuel used to power a ship.

Bureau of Alcohol, Tobacco and Firearms
An agency of the U.S. Department of Treasury that regulates the alcohol, firearms and explosives industry, ensures the collection of federal taxes imposed on alcohol and tobacco, and investigates violations in connection with these goods.

Bureau of Export Administration
A U.S. government agency responsible for control of exports for reasons of national security, foreign policy, and short supply.

Buy American Acts
U.S. federal and state government statutes that give a preference to U.S.-produced goods in government procurement.

cabotage
Coastwide water transportation, navigation, or trade between ports of a nation.

call
A demand of payment on a loan, often because of failure on the part of the borrower to comply with an agreement.

call money
Currency lent by banks on a very short-term basis; it can be called the same day, at one day's notice, or at two days' notice.

capacity to contract
Legal competency to make a contract.

capital goods
Manufactured goods that are used in the production of other goods.

capital market
The market for buying and selling long-term loans, in the form of bonds, mortgages, and so on.

captain's protest
A document prepared by the captain of a vessel upon arrival in port that notes any unusual conditions encountered during the voyage; relieves the ship owner of liability.

cargo
Merchandise hauled by transportation lines.

cargo agent
An agent appointed by an airline shipping line to solicit and process international air and ocean freight.

cargo manifest
A list of a ship's cargo or passengers but without a listing of charges.

Cargo Selectivity System
An ACS module used to sort high-risk cargo from low-risk cargo.

cargo tonnage
The weight of a shipment or of ship's total cargo expressed in tons.

carnet
A customs document permitting the holder to carry or send merchandise temporarily into certain foreign countries (for display, demonstration, or similar purposes) without paying duties or posting bonds.

Carriage of Goods by Sea Act of 1936
A U.S. law that, among other provisions, establishes statutory responsibility for the carrier's liability for certain types of damage.

carrier
A legal entity that is in the business of transporting passengers or goods for hire.

carrier's certificate
A document issued by the shipping company that certifies the ownership of the goods to a named individual or company.

cartage agent
A ground service that provides transport and delivery of freight in areas not directly served by air or rail.

cartel
A collection of independent producers formed to regulate production, pricing, and marketing of members to maximize market power and limit competition.

casus major
A major casualty that is usually accidental, such as flood or shipwreck.

category groups.
Groupings of controlled products.

caveat emptor
The purchaser buys at his or her own risk.

CEBB
Customs Electronic Bulletin Board, an electronic bulletin board sponsored by U.S. Customs that provides the trade community with up-to-date information, requirements, and operation instructions.

cell
The on-board storage space for one shipping container on a ship.

census interface
An ACS module that captures U.S. Bureau of Census data.

central bank
An institution with the sole right to issue bank notes and power to dictate the monetary policy for a group of banks.

certificate of inspection
A document verifying the good condition of freight at the time of inspection, usually right before loading onto a carrier.

certificate of manufacture
A document certifying that the manufacture of goods is complete and the goods are now at the disposal of the carrier.

certificate of weight
A document stating the weight of a shipment.

certification
Official proof of authenticity.

cession of goods
A surrender of goods.

chargeable weight
The weight of a shipment used in determining freight charges.

chartered ship
A ship leased by its owner for a stated time, voyage, or voyages.

charter service
Temporary hiring of an aircraft for the transportation of cargo or passengers.

chassis
A special trailer or undercarriage on which containers are moved over the road.

city terminal service
A service provided by some airlines that involves transporting cargo to in-town terminals at lower rates than charged for door-to-door delivery.

claim
A demand of payment for loss due to negligence.

classification
The categorization of merchandise.

claused bill of lading
A notation on the bill of lading that denotes a deficient condition of the goods or packaging.

clean bill of lading
A bill of lading received by the carrier for goods delivered in "apparent good order and condition."

clearance
The completion of customs entry requirements that results in the release of goods to the importer.

closed-end transaction
A credit transaction with a fixed amount of time for repayment.

coastal trade
Trade between ports of one nation.

collar
An agreement that puts upper and lower limits on the interest rate of an agreement and is binding even if the market rate falls outside of this range.

collect charges
Transportation practice where the receiver of the goods pays the charges.

collection
The presentation for payment of an obligation and the payment thereof.

collection papers
All the documents given to the buyer to receive payments for a shipment; includes invoices, bills of lading, certificates of origin, insurance policies, and so on.

Collection System
An ACS module that controls and accounts for payments collected by the U.S. Customs Service.

collect on delivery
A service where the purchase price of a good is collected by the carrier upon delivery of the shipment and subsequently payed to the shipper.

combination aircraft
An aircraft capable of transporting both cargo and passengers on the same flight.

combined bill of lading
A bill of lading covering a shipment of goods by more than one mode of transportation.

combined transport
Consignment sent by means of various modes of transport.

comity
Courtesy, respect, and good will.

command economy
An economic system in which decisions about resources are made by a central government authority.

commercial bank
A bank that specializes in accepting demand deposits and granting loans.

commercial invoice
A document that identifies the seller and buyer of a shipment; also includes invoice number, date, shipping date, mode of transport, delivery and payment terms, and description of goods.

commercial letter of credit
An instrument by which a bank lends its credit to a customer to enable him or her to finance the purchase of goods or services.

commercial officers
Embassy officials who assist businesses by arranging appointments with local business and government officials and providing counsel on local trade regulations, laws, and customs.

commercial paper
Negotiable instruments used in commerce.

commercial set
The primary documents required to ship goods; usually includes an invoice, bill of lading, bill of exchange, and certificate of insurance.

commingling
The packing or mingling of various goods subject to different rates of duty so that the value of each class of goods cannot be readily determined.

commission
The amount payed to an agent for his or her role in the completion of a transaction involving the sale of goods.

commodity code
The system of identifying a commodity by a certain number to determine its commodity rate for transport.

commodity rate
The rate applicable to shipping a given commodity between points.

common point
A location serviced by two or more transportation lines.

compensatory trade
A form of countertrade in which any combination of goods and services is bartered.

competitive rate
Rate determined by one transportation line to compete with the rate of another transportation line.

complementary imports
Imports of raw materials or products that a country does not internally possess or produce.

compradore
An agent in a foreign country who is employed by a domestic businessman to facilitate transactions with local businesses within the foreign country.

concealed damage
Damage to the contents of a package that appears in good condition from an external view.

concealed loss
Loss from a package bearing concealed damage.

connecting carrier
A carrier that has a direct physical connection with another carrier or forms a connecting link between two points.

consignee
The person or firm named in a freight contract to whom goods have been shipped or turned over for care.

consignment
Delivery of merchandise from an exporter to an agent for sale by the agent, credited to the exporters account, with a commission earned by the agent.

consignor
The entity that ships goods to another for care; the exporter in a consignment relationship.

consolidated container
A shipping container that contains cargo from numerous shippers for delivery to numerous consignees.

consolidation
The combining of smaller shipments from a central location into a single shipment that is sent to a destination point at a lower shipping rate.

consolidator
A company that provides consolidation services.

consular invoice
An invoice covering the shipment of goods certified by the counsel of the country in which the goods originated.

consulate
The offices representing the commercial interests of one country located within the borders of another.

consumer goods
Any goods produced for the express use of individuals.

consumption entry
A customs entry in which the importer pays the applicable dues and the goods are released from customs.

container
A single rigid, sealed, reusable metal "box" in which merchandise is shipped by vessel, truck, or rail.

container freight charge
Charge made for the packing or unpacking of cargo from ocean freight containers.

container load
A shipment of cargo that according to weight or volume; will fit any number of standard containers.

container on flatcar
A container without wheels that is put on railcars for transport.

container part load
A shipment of cargo that according to weight or volume will not fit into any number of standard containers.

container vessel
An oceangoing vessel designed specifically to handle the loading, storage, and removal of freight.

contraband
Any product that a nation has labeled as unsuitable to possess, produce, or transport.

contract carrier
Excluding common carriers, any person who under special contract will transport passengers or goods for agreed-upon compensation.

convertibility
Ease of exchanging one currency for that of another nation or for gold.

core inflation
The basic level of inflation over a period of time as opposed to temporary fluctuations.

corporate dumping
The practice of exporting banned or out-of-date goods to a foreign market where restrictions on those items prevail.

cost plus
A pricing method in which the purchaser agrees to pay the production cost of the goods plus a fixed percentage to the seller for profit.

country of departure
The country from which a ship or shipment has or is scheduled to depart.

country of destination
The country that is the ultimate destination for a ship or shipment of goods.

country of dispatch
The country from which cargo was shipped.

country of exportation
Usually, the country in which the merchandise was manufactured and produced and from where it was shipped.

country of export destination
The country in which the goods are to be consumed, further processed, or manufactured, as known to the shipper at the time of exportation.

country of origin
The country in which merchandise was grown, mined, or manufactured.

country risk
The financial risks of a transaction that relate to the political, economic, or social instability of a country.

courier
Attendant who accompanies shipments.

custody bill of lading
A bill of lading issued by American warehouses as a receipt for goods stored.

customs
A government authority designated to regulate the flow of goods to and from a country and to collect duties levied upon imports and exports.

CVD
Countervailing duties, which are accessed when bounties or grants are paid or bestowed on merchandise exported to the U.S. from a foreign country with material injury to a U.S. industry.

damages
A loss or harm to a person or property.

dangerous goods
Goods capable of posing a health or safety risk when transported by air.

date draft
A draft that matures a specified number of days after the date it is issued, without regard to the date.

dating
Extended credit terms granted by the seller to induce buyers to receive goods in advance of required delivery date.

deadweight
The maximum carrying capacity of a ship.

dealer
An individual or firm acting as principal in the sale of merchandise.

debt-for-nature swap
Swap arranged by private conservation group to use the proceeds of debt conversions to finance conservation projects relating to park land or tropical forests.

debtor nation
A nation that is owed fewer foreign currency obligations than it owes other nations.

deck cargo
Cargo that is shipped on the deck of a vessel rather than in holds below.

declared value for carriage
The value of goods declared to the carrier by the shipper for the purposes of determining charges.

declared value for customs
The selling price of a shipment or the replacement cost if the goods are not for resale.

deductive value
A valuation of merchandise that is the resale price of imported merchandise in the U.S. with deductions for certain items.

deferred air freight
Air freight with less urgency, delivered over a period of days.

deferred payment letter of credit
A letter of credit that allows the buyer to take possession of goods by agreeing to pay the issuing bank.

del credere risk
Risk that a counterparty is either unable or unwilling to fulfill his or her payment obligations.

delivery
The act of transferring physical possession.

delivery carrier
The transport carrier whose responsibility it is to place a shipment at the disposal of the buyer.

delivery instructions
Specific delivery instructions for the freight forwarder or carrier stating exactly where the goods are to be delivered, the deadline, and naming a contact person should problems arise.

delivery order
A document from the consignee, shipper, or owner of freight ordering the delivery of freight to another party.

demise
A lease of property; a demise charter is a bareboat charter.

demurrage
The detention of a freight car or ship beyond time permitted for loading or unloading.

destination
The place to which a shipment is consigned.

detention
Delay in clearing goods through customs, usually resulting in storage fees and other charges.

devanning
The unloading of cargo from a container.

developed countries
A term used to describe more-industrialized nations.

developing countries
A term used to describe countries that lack strong amounts of industrialization, infrastructure, and economic means.

differential
An amount added to or deducted from a base shipping rate between two given locations to determine a new rate for another location.

discharge
The unloading of passengers or cargo from a vessel, vehicle, or aircraft.

discounting
The sale at less than original price value of a commodity or monetary instrument.

discrimination
The preferential rates or privileges granted to some shippers but not to others under similar circumstances.

dispatch
An amount paid by a vessel's operator to a charter if loading or unloading is completed in less time than stipulated in the charter agreement.

distribution license
A license that allows multiple exports of authorized commodities to foreign consignees approved in advance by the U.S. Bureau of Export Administration.

distribution service
A service that accepts one shipment from a single shipper and at a point of destination, separates the shipment and distributes it to many receivers.

distributor
An agent who sells directly for a supplier and maintains an inventory of the supplier's products.

diversion
Any change in the billing of a shipment once it has been received by the carrier at point of origin and prior to delivery at destination.

DOC
Department of Commerce.

dock
Loading or unloading platform at an industrial location or carrier terminal.

dock examination
A U.S. Customs examination that requires containers to be opened for a thorough inspection rather than just a visual one.

dock receipt
A receipt issued by a port officer that certifies that goods have been received by a shipper.

dolly
A piece of equipment with wheels used to move freight with or without a tractor.

domestic exports
Exports grown, produced, or manufactured in the U.S.

domicile
The place where a draft or acceptance is made payable.

door-to-door
Shipping service from shipper's door to consignee's door.

double-column tariff
A tariff schedule with two rates, one for preferred trading partners and one for imports.

downstream dumping
The sale of products by a manufacturer below cost to a secondary producer in its domestic market; the secondary producer then further processes the product and ships it to another country.

drawback
A refund of 99% of duties (and taxes) paid on imported merchandise that is immediately exported, subjected to manufacture or production and then exported, or destroyed in the same condition as it was.

drawback system
An ACS module that provides the means for processing and controlling all types of drawback entries.

dray
A vehicle used to haul cargo or goods.

drayage
The charge made for hauling freight or carts, drays or trucks.

dropoff
The delivery of a shipment by a shipper to a carrier for transportation.

dropoff charge
A charge made by a transportation company for delivery of a container.

drop shipment
A shipment of goods from a manufacturer directly to a dealer or consumer, avoiding shipment to a wholesaler or other interim destination.

dry-bulk container
A container designed to carry any of a number of free-flowing dry solids such as grain or sand.

dry cargo
Cargo that does not require temperature controls.

dry-cargo container
Any shipping container designed to transport goods other than liquids.

dual exchange rate
The existence of two or more exchange rates for a single currency.

dual pricing
The selling of identical products in different markets for different prices.

dumping
The sale of a commodity in a foreign market at less than fair value, usually considered to be a price lower than that at which it is sold within the exporting country or to third countries.

dunnage
Materials placed around cargo to prevent breakage or movement.

durable goods
Any product not consumed through use.

dutiable list
Items listed in a country's tariff schedule for which it charges import duty.

duty
A tax levied by a government on the import, export, or consumption of goods.

easement
A right to use another person's property.

edge act corporations
Banks that are subsidiaries either to bank holding companies or other banks established to engage in foreign-business transactions.

EDI
Electronic data interchange, The transmission of information and data through a computer system to another party.

electronic commerce
A system of integrated communications, data management, and security services that allow business applications within different organizations to automatically exchange information.

electronic funds transfer
System of transferring funds from one account to another using electronic pulses instead of paper.

electronic meat health certificate
A demonstration project that illustrates the electronic transmission of fresh meat health certificates.

ELVIS
Electronic Visa Information System, an electronic data prototype that provides information on non-U.S. issued textile visas.

embargo
A prohibition upon exports or imports with respect to specific products or specific countries.

en route
In transit (referring to goods, passengers, or vessels).

entrepot
An intermediary storage facility where goods are kept temporarily for distribution.

entrepot trade
The import and export of goods without the further processing of the goods. Usually refers to a party that buys and sells as a middleman.

entry
A statement of the kinds, quantities, and values of goods imported together with duties due and declared before a customs officer.

entry documents
The documents required to secure the release of imported merchandise.

entry summary
Documentation necessary to enable U.S. Customs to assess duties, collect statistics, and determine whether other requirements of law or regulations are met upon importation.

Entry Summary System
An ACS module that automates the entry-processing cycle.

Environmental Protection Agency
An independent agency in the executive branch whose mandate is to control and abate pollution in the areas of air, water, solid waste, pesticides, radiation, and toxic substances.

equalization
Money allotted to the customer if the goods are picked up at a destination other than the one named on the bill of lading.

escape clause
A provision in a bilateral or multilateral commercial agreement permitting a signatory nation to temporarily violate its obligations when imports threaten serious harm to the producers of competitive domestic goods.

ETA
The expected date and time of arrival.

ETD
The expected date and time of departure.

Eurobond
A bond issued in a foreign currency different from the one in which the bond is sold.

exception rates
Shipping rates set higher because the commodity requires special handling and care (e.g., live animals).

exchange rate
The price of one currency expressed in terms of another.

excise tax
A selective tax; sometimes referred to as a consumption tax.

exculpatory clause
A contractual clause that releases one party from liability in case of wrongdoing by the other party.

ex factory
A sale term by which the buyer gains ownership of goods when they leave the vendor's dock.

expiry date
A foreign exchange term for the last day that options can be executed; an expiration date.

export
To send or transport merchandise outside one's home country, especially for sale or trade.

export broker
A firm that specializes in bringing buyers and sellers together for a fee but does not participate in the actual business transaction.

export control
Retaining control over exports for statistical and strategic purposes.

export declaration
A required customs document for exportation from the U.S.

export draft
An order for the importing party to pay the seller for the exported goods.

export duty
A tax imposed on exports of some nations.

exporter
An individual or company that transports goods or merchandise from one country to another.

exporter identification number
An identification number required on the shipper's export declaration for all export shipments.

export license
A government document that gives permission to export a specified quantity of a specified commodity.

export management company
A private firm that serves as the export department for several manufacturers and handles the exporting aspect of the business for a commission or salary.

export merchant
A company that buys products directly from manufacturers, then packages and marks the merchandise for resale under its own name.

export processing zone
Industrial parks designated by a government to provide tax and other incentives to export firms.

export quotas
Specific restrictions on the value or volume of exports from a nation.

export restraints
Restrictions on the number of exports that are allotted for certain foreign markets.

export statistics
The statistics that contain the total volume or value of all exports leaving the U.S.

export subsidies
Government payments to induce exportation by domestic producers.

export trading company
A corporation organized for the principal purpose of exporting goods and services.

external value
The purchasing power of a currency abroad, converted using the exchange rate.

extradition
The return of an alleged criminal from one country to the country that has juris-diction.

facilitation
Any program designed to expedite the flow of international commerce.

factor
An agent who receives merchandise under a consignment or bailment contract, who sells it for the principal or in the factor's own name, and who is paid a com-mission for each sale.

factorage
The commission or other compensation paid to a factor.

factor's lien
The right of a factor to retain the principal's merchandise until the factor receives full compensation

fair value
The weighted average of a product's domestic market prices.

FDA
Federal Drug Administration.

Federal Reserve System
The central banking system of the United States; coordinator of monetary policy.

feeder vessel
A vessel used to connect to a line vessel that is unable to dock due to space or water depth requirements.

FEU
Forty-foot equivalent units (two 20-foot containers = 1 FEU).

financial instrument
A document that has monetary value or is evidence of a transaction.

financial market
Market for the exchange of capital and credit in an economy; it is divided into money markets and capital.

First World countries
Western, industrialized, noncommunist countries.

five dragons
Term used to describe the emerging economies of Hong Kong, Singapore, South Korea, Taiwan, and Thailand.

fixed charges
Charges that do not increase or decrease with a change in volume.

fixed exchange
An administratively fixed exchange rate that allows no rate fluctuations.

fixing
Establishing of the official exchange rate of a domestic currency against other negotiable currencies.

flag
A reference to the country or registry of a vessel.

flag of convenience
The national flag flown by a ship that is registered in a country other than that of its owners.

flight of capital
The movement of capital to avoid loss or to increase gain.

floating
Free determination of exchange rates based on supply and demand with no intervention on the part of government.

flotsam
Floating debris or wreckage of a ship and its cargo.

force majeure
Any condition or circumstance such as earthquakes, flood, or war that prevents the carrier from delivering the goods.

foreign bond
An international bond denominated in the currency of the country where it is issued.

foreign commerce
Trade between individuals or legal entities in different countries.

foreign currency
The currency of any foreign country that is the authorized medium of circulation.

foreign-exchange contract
A contract for the sale or purchase of foreign exchange specifying an exchange rate and delivery date.

foreign exchange rate
The price of one currency in terms of another.

foreign flag
A reference to a carrier not registered in a country but flying that country's flag.

foreign income
Income earned by Americans from work performed in another country.

foreign investment
The purchase of assets from abroad.

foreign market value
The price at which merchandise is sold in the principal markets of the country from which it is originally manufactured, mined, or grown.

foreign parent
The first foreign person or entity outside the U.S. in an affiliates's ownership chain and that has direct investment in the affiliate.

foreign person
A person who resides outside of the U.S. or is subject to the jurisdiction of a country other than one's own.

foreign remittances
The transfer of any monetary instrument across national boundaries.

forward foreign exchange
An agreement to purchase foreign currency at a future date at a predetermined rate.

foul bill of lading
A receipt for goods with the indication that they were received damaged or short in quantity.

fractional currency
Any currency that is smaller than a standard money unit.

franco
Free from duties, transportation charges, and other levies.

free-astray
A shipment dropped off at the wrong location is forwarded to the proper location free of charge.

free domicile
Term to describe when the shipper pays all the transportation charges and applicable duties.

free in
A pricing term indicating that the loading charges are for the account of the supplier.

free in and out
A pricing term indicating that the vessel operator is responsible for the cost of loading and unloading.

free list
A statement of items that are not liable to the payment of duties.

free market
Unrestricted movement of items in and out of a market, unhampered by the existence of tariffs or other fees.

free out
A pricing term indicating that unloading charges are for the account of the receiver.

free port
An area where imported goods may be brought without payment of duties.

free time
The time allowed shippers and receivers to load or unload cars before demurrage or detention.

free zone
An area within a country (a seaport, airport, warehouse, or any designated area) regarded as being outside its customs territory where importers may bring goods of foreign origin without paying customs duties or fees.

freight
All merchandise, goods, products, or commodities shipped by rail, air, road, or water, other than baggage, express mail, or regular mail.

freight charge
The charge assessed for transporting freight.

freight claim
A demand upon a carrier for the payment of overcharge or loss or damage sustained by shipper or carrier.

freighter
A ship or airplane used primarily to carry freight.

fungibles
Goods that are identical to other goods of the same nature.

futures contract
A contract for the future delivery of a specified commodity, currency, or security on a specific date at a rate determined in the present.

gang
A group of stevedores under a supervisor who are assigned to load or unload a portion of a vessel.

gangway
The opening or ramp through which a ship is boarded.

gantry crane
A specialized machine for the raising or lowering of cargo mounted on a structure spanning an open space.

gateway
A major airport or seaport, the port where customs clearance takes place, or a point at which freight moving from one territory to another is interchanged between transportation lines.

GATT
General Agreement on Tariffs and Trade.

geisha bond
Bond issued on the Japanese market in currencies other than yen.

General Agreement on Tariffs and Trade (GATT)
Both a multilateral trade agreement aimed at expanding international trade and the organization that oversees the agreement. The main goals of GATT are to liberalize world trade and place it on a secure basis.

general average
A loss that affects all cargo interests on board a vessel as well as the ship itself.

general cargo rate
The rate a carrier charges for the shipment of cargo that does not have a special class rate or commodity.

general cargo vessels
A vessel designed to handle breakbulk cargo such as bags, cartons, cases, crates and drums, either individually or in unitized loads or on pallets.

general commodity rate
A freight rate applicable to all commodities except those for which specific rates have been filed.

general imports
The total physical arrivals of merchandise from foreign countries, whether such merchandise enters consumption channels immediately or is entered into bonded warehouses or foreign trade zones under U.S. administration.

generalized system of preferences (GSP)
A program providing for free rates of duty for merchandise from beneficiary developing independent countries and territories to encourage their economic growth.

general liability
Unlimited responsibility for an obligation, such as payment of debts of a business.

general license
Authorized licenses by the U.S. Bureau of Export Administration that permit the export of nonstrategic goods to specified countries without the need for a validated license.

general order
Merchandise not entered within five working days after arrival of the carrier and stored at the expense of the importer.

general order warehouse
Warehouse where customs sends merchandise that has not been claimed within five days of arrival.

general partnership
A partnership where all partners have joint ownership and liability.

general tariff
A tariff that applies to countries that do not enjoy either preferential or most-favored-nation tariffs.

GITS
Government information technology services working groups.

global bond
A bond that can be traded immediately in any U.S. capital market and in the Euro-market.

global quota
A quota on the total imports of a product from all countries.

gold exchange standard
An international monetary agreement according to which money consists of fiat national currencies that can be converted into gold at established price ratios.

gold reserves
Gold, retained by a nation's monetary agency, forming the backing of currency that the nation has held in reserve.

gold standard
A monetary agreement whereby all national currencies are backed 100% by gold and the gold is utilized for payments of foreign activity.

gondola car
An open railway car with sides and ends, used principally for hauling coal, sand, and so on.

goods
Merchandise, supplies, raw materials, and completed products.

grantee
A corporation to which the privilege of establishing, operating, or maintaining a foreign trade zone has been extended.

green card
An identity card (visa) issued by the U.S. Immigration and Naturalization Service entitling a foreign national to enter and reside in the United States as a permanent resident.

grey list
A list of disreputable end-users in nations of concern for missile proliferation from the U.S.

grid
Fixed margin within which exchange rates are allowed to fluctuate.

gross
Twelve dozen, or 144, articles.

gross domestic product
A measure of the market value of all goods and services produced within the boundaries of a nation.

gross national product
A measure of the market value of all goods and services produced by the labor and property of a nation.

gross weight
The full weight of a shipment, including goods and packaging.

hallmark
Introduced in the beginning of the 14th century in England, an impression made on gold- and silverware to identify the quality of the metal used.

harbor fees
Charges assessed to users for use of a harbor, used generally for maintenance of the harbor.

harbor master
An officer who attends to the berthing, and so on, of ships in a harbor.

hard loan
A foreign loan that must be paid in hard money.

hard money
Currency of a nation having stability in the country and abroad.

harmonized system (HS)
A multipurpose international goods classification system designed to be used by manufacturers, transporters, exporters, importers, customs, statisticians, and others in classifying goods.

Harmonized Tariff Schedule of the U.S.
An organized listing of goods and their duty rates used by U.S. Customs as the basis for classifying imported products and therefore establishing the duty to be charged and providing the U.S. Census with foreign trade data.

Harter Act
Legislation protecting a ship's owner against claims for damage resulting from the behavior of the vessel's crew, provided the ship left port in proper condition.

hatch
The opening in the deck of a vessel giving access to the cargo hold.

haulage
The local transport of goods. Also the charge(s) made for hauling freight on carts, drays, or trucks. Also called cartage or drayage.

hazardous materials
A substance or material that has been determined by the U.S. Secretary of Transportation to be capable of posing an unreasonable risk to health, safety, and property when transported in commerce.

heavy lift
Articles too heavy to be lifted by a ship's tackle.

heavy lift charge
A charge made for lifting articles too heavy to be lifted by a ship's tackle.

heavy lift vessel
A vessel with heavy lift cranes and other equipment designed to be self-sustaining in the handling of cargo.

hedge
Generally referred to as accumulating a foreign currency in advance of a devaluation of that currency to save on the purchase of goods in that currency.

hedge ratio
The amount of an underlying instrument or the number of options needed to hedge a covered investment.

high density
The compression of flat or standard bales of cotton to high density of approximately 32 pounds.

hitchment
The combination of portions of a shipment with different geographical origins that move under one bill of lading from shipper to consignee.

hold
The space below deck in a vessel used to carry cargo.

hold-for pickup
Freight to be held at the carrier's destination location for pickup by the recipient.

hold-harmless contract
An agreement by which one party accepts responsibility for all damages and other liability that arise from a transaction, relieving the other party of any such liability.

honor
To pay or to accept a draft complying with the terms of credit.

horizontal export trading company
An export trading company that exports a range of similar or identical products supplied by a number of manufacturers or other producers.

house air waybill
A bill of lading issued by a freight forwarder for consolidated air freight shipments.

house-to-house
A term usually used to indicate a container-yard-to-container-yard shipment.

hub and spoke routing
Aircraft routing service pattern that feeds traffic from many cities into a central hub designed to connect with other flights to final destinations.

hull
The outer shell of a vessel.

hump
That part of a rail track that is elevated so that when a car is pushed up on it and uncoupled, the car runs down the other side by gravity.

hundredweight pricing
Special pricing for multiple-piece shipments traveling to one destination; rating is based on the total weight of the shipment as opposed to a per package basis.

identical merchandise
Used by U.S. Customs in establishing the customs value of merchandise exported to the U.S.

immediate delivery
An alternate U.S. Customs entry procedure that provides for immediate release of a shipment in certain circumstances.

immediate transportation entry
A form of U.S. Customs entry that allows imported merchandise to be forwarded from the port of original entry to another final destination for customs clearance.

immigration
The entry of foreign nationals into a country for the purpose of establishing permanent residence.

implied conditions
Certain conditions are not written into marine insurance policies, but they are so basic to understanding between underwriter and assured that the law gives them much the same effect as if written.

import
To bring in (goods or services) from a foreign country for trade or sale.

import credit
A commercial letter of credit issued for the purpose of financing the importation of goods.

import duty
Any tax on items imported.

importer
The individual, firm, or legal entity that brings articles of trade from a foreign source into a domestic market in the course of trade.

importer number
An identification number assigned by the U.S. Customs Service to each importer to track entries and other correspondence

Importers Manual USA
A reference book detailing specific requirements for importing 135 different product groups into the U.S. and other important information.

import license
A document required and issued by some national governments authorizing the importation of goods.

import quota
A protective ruling establishing limits on the quantity of a particular product that can be imported.

import quota auctioning
The process of auctioning the right to import specified quantities of quota-restricted goods.

import relief
Any of several measures imposed by a government to temporally restrict imports of a product or commodity to protect domestic producers from competition.

import restrictions
Any one of a series of tariff and nontariff barriers imposed by an importing nation to control the volume of goods coming into the country from other countries.

imports
Commodities of foreign origin as well as goods of domestic origin returned to the producing country with no change in condition or after having been processed and/or assembled in other countries.

imports for consumption
The total of merchandise that has physically cleared U.S. Customs and either enters domestic consumption channels immediately or enters after withdrawal for consumption from bonded warehouses under U.S. Customs custody.

import-sensitive producers
Domestic producers whose economic viability is threatened by competition (quality, price, or service) from imported products.

import substitution
A strategy which emphasizes the replacement of imports with domestically produced goods to encourage the development of domestic industry.

impost
A tax, usually an import duty.

impound
To seize or hold, or to place in protective custody by order of a court.

in bond
A procedure under which goods are transported or warehoused under customs supervision until they are either formally entered into the customs territory of the United States and duties paid, or until they are reshipped out of the U.S.

in-bond shipment
An import or export shipment that has not been cleared by U.S. Customs officials.

in-bond system
A part of U.S. Customs' Automated Commercial System, it controls merchandise from the point of unloading at the port of entry or exportation.

incentive
A motivational force that stimulates people to greater activity or increased efficiency.

income
Money or its equivalent, earned or accrued, arising from the sale of goods or services.

incoterms
A codification of international rules for the uniform interpretation of common contract clauses in international correspondence.

indemnify
To compensate for actual loss sustained.

indemnity
An agreement to reimburse another individual or legal entity who incurs a loss.

independent action
The right of a conference member to depart from the common freight rates, terms, or conditions of the conference without the need for prior approval of the conference.

indexed currency borrowings
Borrowings in a foreign currency in which the rate of interest is linked to an agreed scale.

indexed currency option note
A note denominated and paying interest in one currency but whose redemption value is linked to an exchange rate for another currency.

individual validated license
Written approval by the U.S. Department of Commerce to export a specified quantity or good to a single individual or company.

industrial list
A list issued by the Coordinating Committee for Multilateral Export Controls and containing dual-use items whose export is controlled for strategic reasons.

industrial policy
Encompasses traditional government policies intended to provide a favorable economic climate for the development of industry in general or specific industrial sectors.

infant industry argument
The view that "temporary protection" for a new industry or firm in a particular country through tariff and nontariff barriers to imports can help it to become established and eventually competitive in world trade.

inflation
Loss of purchasing power of money caused by growth of the amount of money in circulation.

informal entry
A simplified import entry procedure accepted at the option of customs for any baggage or commercial shipment that does not exceed $1,000.

informed compliance
A term that describes the improved ability of an entity (such as a company) to comply with federal rules and regulations through easy-access to up-to-date information.

infrastructure
The basic structure of a nation's economy.

inherent vice
Internal cause of damage to goods during shipping; damage caused by the qualities of the goods.

injury
A finding by the U.S. International Trade Commission that an import is causing harm or going to cause harm to a U.S. industry.

inland bill of lading
A bill of lading used in transporting goods overland to the exporter's international carrier.

inland carrier
A transportation line that hauls import/export traffic between ports and inland points.

inspection certificate
A document confirming that goods have been inspected for conformity.

instrument
Any written document that gives formal expression to a legal agreement or act.

integrated cargo service
A blend of all segments of the cargo system providing the combined services of carrier, forwarder, and customs broker.

integrated carriers
Carriers that have multiple varieties of fleets (e.g., air and ground, truck and rail, etc.).

intellectual property
An original piece of work that can be copyrighted or trademarked to confirm ownership.

interbank dealings
Dealings between the banks.

interchange agreement
An agreement that specifically lays out the terms of leasing equipment from a carrier.

interchange point
A location where one carrier delivers freight to another carrier.

interline shipping
The movement of a single shipment in two or more carriers.

intermodal compatibility
The capability of a shipment of goods to be shifted from one form of transportation to another.

intermodal transport
Coordinated transport of freight using multiple methods of transportation.

international trade
The business of buying and selling commodities outside of national boarders.

international trade data system
A proposed electronic system that would integrate the different government trade and transportation data processes into a system that provides a standard means of gathering, processing, storing and disseminating.

interstate carrier
A common carrier whose business extends beyond the boundaries of one state.

interstate commerce
Trade between or among several states of the United States; includes facsimile across state lines or transport by rail and roads.

invisible barriers to trade
Government regulations that do not directly restrict trade but hinder imports with excessive and obscure restrictions.

invisible trade balance
The balance of trade created by the import and export of services.

invoice
A document identifying the buyer and seller; includes all relevant information such as number, date, shipping date, mode of transport, and so on.

inward foreign manifest (IFM)
A U.S. Customs–mandated document requiring the complete listing by bill of lading numbers of an arriving ship's freight being imported into the U.S.

irrevocable letter of credit
A letter of credit that cannot be amended or canceled without prior mutual consent of all parties to the business contract.

issuance
The establishment of a letter of credit by the issuing bank based on the buyer's application and credit relationship with the bank.

issuance date of the documents
The date of shipment or loading on board of goods.

IT06
An initiative calling for the development of an international trade data system sponsored by the U.S. government that will meet the needs of federal agencies involved in international trade.

jetsam
Articles from a ship or ship's cargo that are thrown overboard, usually to lighten the load in times of emergency or distress, and that sink or are washed ashore.

jettison
To unload or throw overboard at sea a part of a ship's paraphernalia or cargo to lighten the ship.

JIG
Joint Industry Group.

joint agent
A person having authority to transact business for two or more transportation lines.

joint and several liability
Liability for damages imposed on two or more individuals or legal entities who are responsible together and individually, allowing the party harmed to seek full remedy against all or any number of the damages.

joint rate
A single through-rate on cargo moving via two or more carriers.

joint stock company
An unincorporated business association with ownership interests represented by shares of stock.

joint venture
A combination of two or more individuals or legal entities who undertake together a transaction for mutual gain or to engage in a commercial enterprise together with sharing of profits and losses.

jurat
A document signed by a person authorized to take oaths certifying the authenticity of a document or person.

juristic act
Action intended to have, and capable of having, a legal effect, such as the creation, termination, or alteration of a right.

just in time
The principle of production and inventory control that prescribes precise controls for the movement of raw materials, component parts, and work in progress.

Goods arrive when needed for production for use rather than being stockpiled for inventory.

keelage
The charges paid by a ship entering or remaining in certain ports.

key currency
A major currency in the global economy. Key currencies include the U.S. dollar, the British pound sterling, the German mark, the Swiss franc, the French franc, the Dutch guilder, and the Japanese yen.

kiosk
A small structure that incorporates a computer screen and input devices such as a keyboard or touch screen. Usually found in public places such as libraries or museums, it is used for the dissemination of information. Also any small, free-standing sales stand on a pedestrian right-of-way.

knocked down
An article taken apart and folded or telescoped in such a manner as to reduce its bulk at least two-thirds from its normal shipping cubage when set up or assembled.

known loss
A loss discovered before or at the time of delivery of a shipment.

laissez faire
A term used to describe minimal governmental involvement in an economy, allowing market forces and individuals to make their own decisions, with little or no regulation.

landbridge
The movement of containers from a foreign country by vessel, transiting a country by rail or truck, and then being loaded aboard another vessel for delivery to a second foreign country.

Lanham Act of 1947
Federal legislation governing trademarks and other symbols for identifying goods sold in interstate commerce.

lay order
The period during which imported merchandise may remain at the place of unloading without action being taken for its disposition.

legal entity
Any individual, proprietorship, partnership, corporation, association, or other organization that has, in the eyes of the law, the capacity to make a contract or an agreement, and the abilities to assume an obligation.

legal tender
Any money that is recognized as being lawful for use by a debtor to pay a creditor, who must accept same in the discharge of a debt unless the contract between the parties specifically states another type of consideration.

less than truckload
A shipment weighing less than the weight required for the application of the truckload rate.

letter of assignment
A document with which an assignor assigns rights to a third party.

letter of credit
A document issued by a bank stating its commitment to pay someone a stated amount of money on behalf of a buyer as long as the seller meets very specific terms and conditions.

letter of indemnity
A document that serves to protect the carrier/owner financially against possible repercussions in connection with the release of goods without presentation of an original bill of lading.

letter of intent
A document that describes the preliminary understanding between parties who intend to make a contract or join together in another action.

licensing agreement
A contract whereby the holder of a trademark, patent, or copyright transfers a limited right to use a process, sell or manufacture an article, or furnish specialized services covered by the trademark, patent, or copyright.

lift van
A wooden or metal container used for packing household goods and personal effects.

lighter
A barge towed by a tugboat and used mainly in harbors and inland waterways for the transport of cargo.

lighter aboard ship
A floatable large container (lighter) used in the combined ocean and inland waterway transport of goods.

lighterage
The loading or unloading of a ship by means of a lighter, especially when shallow waters prevent an oceangoing vessel from entering a waterway.

limitation period
A maximum period set by statute within which legal action can be brought or a right enforced. A statute may prohibit, for example, any individual or legal entity from bringing an action for breach of contract.

limited appointment
Persons appointed to the U.S. and Foreign Commercial Service (or to other foreign services) from the private sector or the federal government who are noncareer officers assigned overseas for a limited time.

limited liability
Restricted liability for the obligations of a business.

limited partnership
A partnership in which at least one partner has general liability and at least one of the other partners has limited liability.

line haul
The direct movement of freight between two major ports by a single ship.

line haul vessel
A vessel that is on a regularly defined schedule.

liner
A vessel carrying passengers and cargo that operates on a route with a fixed schedule.

line release system
A part of the U.S. Customs' Automated Commercial System that is designed for the release and tracking of shipments through the use of personal computers and bar code technology.

liner terms
Conditions under which a shipping company will transport goods, including the amount payable for freight and the cost both for loading and discharge of the vessel.

liquidated damages
A sum of money that a contracting party agrees to pay to the other party for breaching an agreement, particularly important in a contract in which damages for breach may be difficult to assess.

liquidation
The final review of a U.S. Customs entry and determination of the rate of duty and amount of duty.

liquidation system
A part of U.S. Customs' Automated Commercial System, it closes the file on each entry and establishes a batch filing number that is essential for recovering an entry for review or enforcement purposes.

liquidity
A company's ability to meet its obligations at all times, the availability of liquid funds in an economy, the possibility of being able to carry out financial transactions without influencing debt.

Lloyds of London
An association of English insurance underwriters, the oldest of its kind in the world.

Lloyds registry
An organization maintained for the surveying and classifying of ships so that insurance underwriters and other interested parties may know the quality and condition of the vessels offered by insurance or sale.

loading
The physical placing of cargo into a carrier's container or onto a vessel.

longshoreman
A laborer who loads and unloads ships at a seaport.

lose of intent
A document, such as a written memorandum, that describes the preliminary understanding between parties who intend to make a contract or join together in another action, such as a joint venture or a corporate merger.

lot labels
Labels attached to each piece of multiple-lot shipment for identification purposes.

lower-deck containers
Carrier-owned containers specially designed as an integral part of the aircraft to fit in the cargo compartments of a wide-body aircraft.

macroeconomics
The study of statistics of the economy as a whole rather than as single economic units.

mail entry
A means of shipping and entering goods into the customs territory of the U.S.

mala fide
In bad faith; a seller's representation that goods are usable for a particular purpose when in fact the seller knows that the goods are not.

manifest
A document giving the description of a ship's cargo or the contents of a car or truck.

maquiladora
A program that allows foreign manufacturers to ship components into Mexico duty free for assembly and subsequent reexport.

margin
The difference between the cost of sold items and the total net sales income.

marginal cost
The increase in the total cost of production that results from manufacturing one more unit of output.

maritime
Business pertaining to commerce or navigation by sea.

market access
The openness of a national market to foreign products.

market disruption
A situation in which a surge of imports of a certain product causes a sharp decline in the domestic sales of that product and creates a hardship for domestic producers.

market economy
An economic system in which resources are allocated and production of products determined by market forces rather than by government decree.

market price
The price established in the market where buyers and sellers meet to buy and sell similar products.

marking: country of origin
The physical markings on a product that indicate the country where the article was produced.

marks
Information placed on the outer surface of shipping containers or packages and include address labels, identifying numbers, box specifications, cautions, or directional warnings.

matador bond
Bond issued on the Spanish market, denominated in currencies other than the peseta.

mate's receipt
A declaration issued by an officer of a vessel in the name of the shipping company stating that certain goods have been received on board the vessel.

material contract terms
Terms in a contract that describe the goods, fix the price, and set the delivery date.

measurement cargo
Cargo on which the transportation charge is assessed on the basis of measurement.

medium of exchange
Any commodity that is widely accepted in payment for goods and services and in settlement of debts.

memorandum bill of lading
The duplicate copy of the bill of lading.

memorandum of understanding
An informal record, document, or instrument that serves as the basis of a future contact.

memorandum tariff
Publications that contain rule and rate information extracted from official tariffs.

merchant's credit
A letter of credit issued by the buyer him- or herself with no commitment on the part of a bank.

merchant's haulage
The inland move from or to a port with all arrangements made by the exporter.

merry-go-round
The circulation of money through various sources, ending up where it started.

microbridge
A landbridge movement in which cargo originating at or destined for an inland point is railed or trucked to or from the water port for a shipment to or from a foreign country.

MID
Originally, manufacturer identification number, a data element used by customs.

minibridge
Movement of cargo from a port over water then over land to a port on an opposite coast.

minimum charge
The lowest rate applicable on each type of cargo service no matter how small the shipment.

mixed credit
The combining of concessional and market rate export credit as an export promotion mechanism.

MOD Act
Customs Modernization and Informed Compliance Act, HR 3935, passed in 1992.

money
Any denomination of coin or paper currency of legal tender that passes freely as a medium of exchange; anything that is accepted in exchange for other things.

money creation
The increase in money supply by the central or commercial banks.

money market
The market for short-term financial instruments (e.g., commercial paper, treasury bills, discount notes).

money market operations
Comprises the acceptance and relending of deposits on the money market.

money supply
The amount of domestic cash and deposit money available in an economy.

moor
To secure a vessel to an anchor, buoy, or pier.

moorage
Charges assessed for mooring a vessel to a pier or wharf.

most-favored nation
A nondiscriminatory trade policy commitment on the part of one country to extend to another country the lowest tariff rate it applies to any other country.

motor carrier's terminal
The place where loaded or empty shipping containers are received or delivered by a motor carrier.

multilateral agreement
An international compact involving three or more parties.

multimodal transport
Shipping that includes at least two modes of transport, such as shipping by rail and by sea.

multinational corporation
A corporation having subsidiaries in more than one country.

NAFTA
North American Free Trade Agreement.

National Association of Export Companies
A nonprofit organization that acts as the information provider, support clearinghouse forum, and advocate for those involved in exporting and servicing exporters.

National Customs Brokers and Freight Forwarders Association
A nonprofit organization that serves as the trade organization of customs brokers and international freight forwarders in the U.S.

nationalization
Takeover by the government without compensation of a public or private activity.

national security controls
Restrictions placed on exports of U.S. goods and technology that would make a significant contribution to the military potential of another country and thus be detrimental to national security.

National Trade Data Bank (NTDB)
An electronic database that contains international economic and export promotion information supplied by 15 U.S. governmental agencies.

national treatment
Affords foreign individuals and firms the same competitive opportunities, including market access, as are available to domestic parties.

NCBFAA
National Customs Brokers and Forwarders Association of America.

Negotiable
Anything that can be sold or transferred to another for money or as payments of a debt.

negotiable bill of lading
Bill of lading transferred by endorsement.

negotiable warehouse receipt
A certificate issued by an approved warehouse that guarantees the existence and the grade of a commodity.

nested
Packed one within another.

net cash
Payment for goods sold usually within a short period of time with no deduction allowed from the invoice.

net national product
The market value of the net output of goods and services produced by the nation's economy.

net price
Price after all discounts, rebates, and so on, have been allowed.

net weight
The weight of goods without packaging.

neutral air waybill
A standard air waybill without identification of issuing carrier.

NII
National Information Infrastructure Task Force.

no show
Freight that has been booked to a ship, but has not physically arrived in time to be loaded that day.

notary public
A person commissioned by a state for a stipulated period to administer certain oaths and to attest and certify (with an official seal.)

notify address
Address mentioned in the transport document to which the carrier is to give notice when goods are due to arrive.

notify party
Name and address of a party in the transport document to be notified by the shipping company of the arrival of the goods.

NTDB
National Trade Data Bank, a database used as the central collection point for U.S. government–generated export promotion information.

Nuclear Energy Agency
Promotes the safe and effective use of nuclear energy through the exchange of information among technical experts, the sharing of analytical studies, and undertaking joint research and development projects.

Nuclear Regulatory Commission (NCR)
A U.S. agency that regulates the transfer of nuclear facilities, materials, and parts.

ocean bill of lading
A receipt for the cargo and a contract for transportation between a shipper and the ocean carrier.

offer
A proposal that is made to a certain individual or legal entity to enter into a contract, definite in its terms, and that indicates the offeror's intent to be bound by an acceptance.

Office of Export Licensing (OEL)
An agency under the Bureau of Export Administration that administers export licenses.

Office of Management and Budget
An executive office of the president that evaluates, formulates, and coordinates management procedures and program objectives within and among federal departments and agencies.

official development assistance
Financial flows to developing countries and multilateral institutions provided by official government.

offshore
A reference to financial operations transacted outside the country in question.

offshore bank
Bank located outside the country in question.

offshore banking center
Financial center where many of the financial institutions have little connection with that country's financial system; usually done for tax purposes.

old-to-market
A committed-to-export, experienced, larger-scale firm with export sales volume in excess of 15%.

on board
Notation on a bill of lading indicating that the goods have been loaded on board a named ship.

on deck
Notation on a bill of lading that indicates that the goods have been loaded on the deck of the ship.

on-deck bill of lading
Bill of lading containing the notation that goods have been placed on deck.

open account
Credit extended that is not supported by a note, mortgage, or other formal written evidence of obligation.

open conference
A shipping conference in which there are no restrictions upon membership other than ability and willingness to serve the trade.

open economy
An economy free of trade restrictions.

open-end contract
An agreement by which the buyer may purchase goods from a seller for a certain time without changes in the price or the contract terms.

operator
A corporation that operates a foreign trade zone under the terms of an agreement with a foreign trade zone.

order
A request to deliver, sell, receive, or purchase goods or services.

order bill
A bill of lading that states that goods are consigned to the order of the person named in the bill.

order notify
A bill of lading term to provide for surrender of the original bill of lading before freight is delivered.

outright
A forward purchase or sale of foreign exchange not offset by a corresponding spot transaction.

outward swap
Spot purchase of foreign exchange and forward resale of the same currency against domestic currency.

overnight
Swap from settlement date until the following business day.

over the counter
Securities trading that takes place outside the normal exchanges.

packing list
A document prepared by the shipper listing the kinds and qualities of merchandise in a particular shipment.

pallet
A platform with or without sides, on which a number of packages or pieces may be loaded to facilitate shipment.

palletizing
The loading and securing of a number of sacks, bags, boxes, or drums on a pallet base.

pallet loader
A device employing one or more vertical lift platforms for the mechanical loading or unloading of palletized freight at planeside.

pallet transporter
A vehicle for the movement of loaded pallets between an aircraft and the freight terminal.

parcel post air freight
An airline service through which a shipper can consolidate a number of parcel post packages with destination postage affixed by the shipper, for shipment as air freight to the postmaster at another city.

parent Bank
A bank in a major industrial country that sets up a subsidiary in a developing country.

par exchange rate
The free market price of one country's money in terms of the currency of another.

parity
Equality in amount or value.

par of exchange
The market price of money in one national currency that is exchanged at the official rate for a specific amount in another national currency, or another commodity of value (gold, silver, etc.).

parol
Oral expression. A parol contract is one that is verbal only and that has not been put into writing by the parties thereto.

partnership
An unincorporated business owned and operated by two or more persons, who may have general or limited liability according to the agreement of the partnership.

patent
A grant by law to an inventor of a device of the right to exclude other persons from making, using, or selling it.

payable in exchange
The requirement that a negotiable instrument be paid in the funds of the place from which it was originated.

payee
The person or organization to whom a check or draft or note is made payable.

payer
The party primarily responsible for the payment of the amount owed as evidenced by a given negotiable instrument or contract.

payments surplus
The excess of the value of a nation's exports over its imports.

performance
The proper fulfillment of a contract or obligation.

peril point
A hypothetical limit beyond which a reduction in tariff protection would cause serious injury to an industry.

perishable freight
Freight subject to decay or deterioration.

petrodollars
Huge sums of money from oil-producing nations other than the U.S. or Great Britain.

phytosanitary inspections certificate
A certificate issued by the U.S. Department of Agriculture indicating that a U.S. export shipment has been inspected and is free from harmful pests and plant diseases.

pickup and delivery service
An optional service for the surface transport of shipments from shipper's door to originating carrier's terminal and from the terminal of destination to receiver's door.

pickup order
An order from a broker to a carrier to pick up freight at a location.

pier-to-pier
Shipment of cargo by carrier from origin pier to discharge pier.

piggyback
The transportation of truck trailers and containers on specially equipped railroad flatcars.

pilferage
The loss of goods due to steady theft in small amounts.

pilot
A person whose occupation is to steer ships, particularly along a coast or into and out of a harbor.

Plimsoll mark
The horizontal line on the outside of a ship representing the depth to which the vessel may be safely loaded; this mark must stay above the water surface.

point of origin
The location at which a shipment is received by a transportation line from the shipper.

point-to-point
Represents service and rates for shipments in door-to-door service.

port
A harbor or haven where ships may anchor and discharge or receive cargo.

port charge
A charge made for services performed at ports.

portfolio investment
In general, any foreign investment that is not direct investment.

port of discharge
The port at which a shipment is offloaded by a transportation line.

port of entry
A port at which foreign goods are admitted into the receiving country.

port of export
The port, airport, or customs point from which an export shipment leaves a country for a voyage to another country.

port-of-origin air cargo clearance
U.S. Customs clearance at inland airports to facilitate the procedures before the goods reach a gateway.

postdated check
A check bearing a date still in the future.

postshipment verification
An inspection to determine that an exported strategic commodity is being used for the purposes for which its export was licensed.

preference
A creditor's right to be paid before other creditors of the same debtor.

prelicense checks
Checks that are conducted to determine that a request for a license to export a controlled commodity represents a legitimate order.

premium
The amount above a regular price, paid as incentive to do something.

prepaid
A notation on a shipping document indicating that shipping charges have already been paid by the shipper.

prepaid charges
The transportation trade practice under which the shipper pays transportation charges.

price support
Subsidy or financial aid offered to specific growers, producers, or distributors, in accordance with governmental regulations, to keep market prices from dropping below a certain minimum level.

priority air freight
Reserved air freight or air express service wherein shipments have a priority after mail and small packages have been loaded.

private corporation
A business corporation whose shares of stock are not traded among the general public.

procurement and lead time
The time required by the buyer to select a supplier and to place and obtain a commitment for specific quantities of materials at specified times.

product groups
Commodity groupings used for export control purposes.

productivity
A measurement of the efficiency of production.

project license
A U.S. license that authorizes large-scale exports of a wide variety of commodities and technical data for specified activities.

proof of delivery
Information provided to payor containing name of person who signed for the package with the date and time.

proprietor
A person who has an exclusive right or interest in property or in a business.

proprietorship
A business owned by one person.

protectionism
The deliberate use or encouragement of restrictions on imports to enable relatively inefficient domestic producers to compete successfully with foreign producers.

protective service
Offered by many airlines, it allows shippers to arrange to have their shipments under carrier surveillance at each stage of transit.

protective tariff
A duty or tax on imported products to make them more expensive in comparison with domestic products.

protest
The means by which an importer, consignee, or other designated party may challenge a customs decision.

public corporation
A business corporation with shares traded among the general public, such as through a stock exchange.

published rate
The charges for a particular class of cargo as published in a carrier's tariff.

purchase order
A purchaser's written offer to a supplier formally stating all terms and conditions of a proposed purchase.

quadrilateral meetings
Meetings involving trade ministers from the U.S., European Community, Canada, and Japan to discuss trade.

quantitative restrictions
Explicit limits, or quotas, on the physical amounts of particular commodities that can be imported or exported during a specified time period, usually measured by volume but sometimes by value.

quarantine
The term during which an arriving ship or airplane, including its passengers, crew, and cargo, suspected of carrying a contagious disease, is held in isolation to prevent the possible spread of the disease.

quay
A structure built for the purpose of mooring a vessel; also called a pier.

queue
A line or group of people waiting for service, such as a line of people waiting in a teller line at a bank, paperwork in a stack waiting for processing; or items on a waiting list waiting for processing.

quid pro quo
A mutual consideration; securing an advantage or receiving a concession in return for a similar advantage or concession.

quota
A limitation on the quantity of goods that may be imported into a country from all countries or from specific countries during a set period of time.

quota system
A part of the U.S. Customs Service Automated Commercial System, it controls quota levels (quantities authorized) and quantities entered against those levels.

rail waybill
Freight document that indicates that goods have been received for shipment by rail.

rate of exchange
The amount of funds of one nation that can be bought, at a specific date, for a sum of currency of another.

realignment
Simultaneous and mutually coordinated re- and devaluation of the currencies of several countries.

real rights
Rights in real estate or in items attached to real estate.

receipt
Any written acknowledgment of value received.

received for shipment bill of lading
A bill of lading that confirms the receipt of goods by the carrier, but not their actual loading on a ship, truck, or plane.

receiving papers
Paperwork that accompanies a shipment when it is brought to the dock.

reciprocal trade agreement
An international agreement between two or more countries to establish mutual trade concessions that are expected to be of equal value.

reciprocity
The process by which governments extend similar concessions to each other.

reconsignment
A change in the name of the consignor, a change in the place of delivery, or relinquishment of shipment at a point before delivery.

redeliver
A demand by U.S. Customs to return previously released goods to customs custody for reexamination, reexport, or destruction.

reefer container
A controlled temperature shipping container (usually refrigerated).

reevaluation
The restoration of the value of a nation's currency that had once been devalued in terms of the currency.

reexport
The export of imported goods without added value.

refund
An amount returned to the consignor as a result of the carrier having collected charges in excess of the originally agreed-upon charges.

remittance
Funds forwarded from one person to another as payment for bought items or services.

remittance following collection
In instances when the shipper has performed services incident to the transportation of goods, a carrier will collect payment for these services from the receiver and remit such payment to the shipper.

replevin
A legal action for recovering property; brought by the owner or party entitled to repossess the property against a party who has wrongfully kept it.

request for quotation
A negotiating approach whereby the buyer asks for a price quotation from a potential seller for specific goods or services.

rescind
To cancel a contract.

reserved freight space
A service offered by some airlines enabling shippers to reserve freight space on designated flights.

restricted letter of credit
A letter of credit that is restricted to a bank specifically mentioned.

restrictive business practices
Actions in the private sector designed to restrict competition so as to keep prices relatively high.

retaliation
Action taken by a country to restrain its imports from a country that has increased a tariff or imposed other measures that adversely affect its exports.

reverse preferences
Tariff advantages once offered by developing countries to imports from certain developed countries that granted them preferences.

revolving letter of credit
A letter of credit that is automatically restored to its full amount after the completion of each transaction.

risk position
An asset or liability that is exposed to fluctuations in value through changes in exchange rates.

road waybill
Transport document that indicates goods have been received for shipment by road haulage carrier.

roll-on, roll-off
A category of ships designed to load and discharge cargo that rolls on wheels.

rollover credit
Any line of credit that can be borrowed against up to a stated credit limit and into which repayments go.

route
The course or direction that a shipment moves.

royalty
Compensation for the use of a person's property based on an agreed percentage of the income arising from the sale of that property.

sales agreement
A written document by which a seller agrees to convey property to a buyer for a stipulated price under specific terms and conditions.

sales tax
A tax placed by a state or municipality on items at the time of their purchase.

salvage
Compensation paid for the rescue of a ship, its cargo, or passengers from a loss at sea; the act of saving a ship or its cargo from possible loss; or property saved from a wreck or fire.

samurai bond
Bond issued on the Japanese market in yen from a point outside Japan.

sanction
An embargo imposed against an individual country by the UN or a group of nations in an effort to influence its conduct or its policies.

seal
A mark or sign that is used to witness and authenticate the signing of an instrument, contract, or other document.

seaworthiness
The fitness or safety of a vessel for its intended use.

secured
Guaranteeing a payment by the pledge of something valuable.

security
Property pledged as collateral.

seizure
The act of taking possession of property.

seller's market
Exists when goods cannot easily be secured and when the economic forces of business tend to cause goods to be priced at the vendor's estimate of value.

selling rate
Rate at which a bank is willing to sell foreign exchange or to lend money.

service a loan
To pay interest due on a loan.

service commitments
Pickup or delivery commitments agreed to by carrier and shipper.

settlement date
The date on which payment for a transaction must be made.

shared foreign sales corporation
A foreign sales corporation consisting of more than 1 and less than 25 unrelated exporters.

shipment
Cargo tendered by one shipper, on one bill of lading, from one point of departure, for one consignee, to one destination, at one time, via a single port of discharge.

shipment record
A repository of information for each shipment that reflects all activity throughout each step of the process.

shipped on deck
Annotation in a bill of lading that the goods have been shipped on the deck of a vessel.

shipper
The company or person who ships cargo to the consignee.

shipping order
Instructions of shipper to carrier for forwarding of goods.

ship's manifest
A list of the individual shipments constituting the ship's cargo.

ship's papers
The documents a ship must carry to meet the safety, health, immigration, commercial, and customs requirements of a port of call or of international law.

ship's stores
The food, medical supplies, spare parts, and other provisions carried for the day-to-day running of a ship.

short form bill of lading
A bill of lading on which the detailed conditions of transportation are not listed in full.

short of exchange
The position of a foreign exchange trader who has sold more foreign bills than the quantity of bills he or she has in possession to cover sales.

shortage
A deficiency in quantity shipped.

short weight
Notation of a shipment's weight as less than noted on the original bill of lading, indicating loss during transit.

signature service
A service designed to provide continuous responsibility for the custody of shipments in transit, so named because a signature is required from each person handling the shipment.

sling
A contrivance into which freight is placed to be hoisted into or out of a ship.

slip
A vessel's berth between two piers.

small package service
A specialized service to guarantee the delivery of small parcels within specified express time limits.

smuggling
Conveying goods or persons across borders without permission.

soft currency
The funds of a country that are controlled by exchange procedures, thereby having limited convertibility into gold and other currencies.

soft loan
A loan made with easy or generous terms such as low or no interest and long payback.

sovereign credit
A borrowing guaranteed by the government of a sovereign state.

sovereign risk
The risk to a lender the government of a sovereign state may default on its financial obligations.

special rates
Rates that apply to cargo traffic under special conditions and usually a limited number of cities.

specific commodity rate
Rate applicable to certain classes of commodities, usually commodities moving in volume shipments.

specific rate of duty
A specified amount of duty per unit of weight or other quantity.

spot cash
Immediate cash payment in a transaction.

spot exchange
The purchase and sale of foreign exchange for delivery and payment at the time of the transaction.

spot exchange rate
The price of one currency expressed in terms of another currency at a given moment in time.

spot market
The market for a commodity or foreign exchange available for immediate delivery.

spot operations
Foreign exchange dealing in which settlement of the mutual delivery commitments is made at the latest two days after the transaction was carried out.

spot price
A price quotation for immediate sale and delivery of a commodity or currency.

spot rate
The rate for purchase or sale of a commodity for immediate delivery.

spotting
The placing of a container where required to be loaded or unloaded.

standard of living
The level of material affluence of a nation as measured by per capita output.

standby commitment
A bank commitment to loan money up to a specified amount for a specific period, to be used only in a specific situation.

steamship indemnity
An indemnity received by an ocean carrier issued by a bank indemnifying the carrier for any loss incurred for release of goods to the original bill of lading.

stevedore
A person charged with loading and unloading ships in port.

storage
The keeping of goods in a warehouse.

storage demurrage
A charge made on property remaining on the dock past the prescribed free-time period.

storage in transit
The stopping of freight traffic at a point located between the point of origin and destination to be stored and reforwarded at a later date.

store-door delivery
The movement of goods to the consignee's place of business, customarily applied to movement by truck.

stowage
The arranging and packing of cargo in a vessel for shipment.

stowage instructions
Specific instructions given by the shipper or shipper's agent concerning the way in which cargo is to be handled and stowed.

stowplan
A diagram showing how cargo containers have been placed on a vessel; also called a stowage plan.

straight bill of lading
A nonnegotiable bill of lading that designates a consignee who is to receive the goods and obligates the carrier to deliver the goods to that consignee only.

strategic level of controls
Commodity groupings used for export control purposes.

strike clause
An insurance clause included in policies to cover against losses as a result of strikes.

stripping
The unloading of cargo from a container; also called devanning.

stuffing
The loading of cargo into a container.

subsidiary
Any organization more than 50% of whose voting stock is owned by another firm.

subsidy
A grant paid by a government to producers of goods to strengthen their competitive position.

supply access
Assurances that importing countries will, in the future, have fair and equitable access at reasonable prices to supplies of raw materials and other essential imports.

surcharge
A charge above the usual or customary charge.

surety
A bond, guaranty, or other security that protects a person, corporation, or other legal entity in cases of another's default in the payment of a given obligation, improper performance of a given contract, or malfeasance.

survey
To examine the condition of a vessel for purposes of establishing seaworthiness or value.

sushi bond
Eurodollar bonds issued by Japanese corporations on the Japanese market for Japanese investors.

switch arrangements
A form of countertrade in which the seller sells on credit and then transfers the credit to a third party.

Table of Denial Orders
A list of individuals and firms that have been disbarred from shipping or receiving U.S. goods or technology.

tare weight
The weight of a container or packing materials, but without the goods being shipped. The gross weight of a shipment less the net weight of the goods being shipped.

tariff
A comprehensive list or "schedule" of merchandise with applicable rates to be paid or charged for each listed article; or a schedule of shipping rates charged, together with governing rules and regulations.

tariff anomaly
Exists when the tariff on raw materials or semimanufactured goods is higher than the tariff on the finished product.

tariff escalation
A situation in which tariffs on manufactured goods are relatively high, tariffs on semiprocessed goods are moderate, and tariffs on raw materials are nonexistent or very low.

tariff quotas
Application of a higher tariff rate to imported goods after a specified quantity of the item has entered the country at a lower prevailing rate.

tariff schedule
A comprehensive list of the goods a country may import and the import duties applicable to each.

tariff war
When one nation increases the tariffs on goods imported from, or exported to, another country, and that country then follows by raising tariffs itself in a retaliatory manner.

tax haven
A nation offering low tax rates and other incentives for individuals and businesses of other countries.

tender
A small vessel that serves a larger vessel in a port for the purpose of supplying provisions and carrying passengers from ship to shore.

tenor
The period between the formation of a debt and the date of expected payment.

terminal
The area at the end of a rail, ship, air, or truck line that serves as a loading, unloading, transfer point, and storage/repair facility.

terminal charge
A charge made for services performed at terminals.

terms of trade
The volume of exports that can be traded for a given volume of imports.

Third World countries
Developing countries, especially in Asia, Africa, and Latin America, but excluding communist countries.

through bill of lading
A single bill of lading covering receipt of cargo at the point of origin for delivery to the ultimate destination.

through rate
A shipping rate applicable from point of origin to destination.

tied loan
A loan made by a government agency that requires a foreign borrower to spend the proceeds in the lender's country.

to order
A term on a financial instrument or title document indicating that it is negotiable and transferrable.

tracer
A request upon a transportation line to trace a shipment for the purpose of expediting its movement or delivery.

tracking
A carrier's system of recording movement intervals of shipments from origin to destination.

trade deficit
A nation's excess of imports over exports over a period of time.

trade name
The name under which an organization conducts business, or by which the business or its goods and services are known.

trade promotion
Encouragement of the progress, growth, or acceptance of trade.

trade surplus
A nation's excess of exports over imports over a period of time.

trade terms
The setting of responsibilities of the buyer and seller in a sale including sale price, shipping, and so on.

trailer
A vehicle without motor power designed to be drawn by another vehicle.

tramp line
A transportation line operating tramp steamers.

tramp steamer
A steamship that does not operate under any regular schedule from one port to another, but calls at any port where cargo may be obtained.

transaction value
The price actually paid or payable for merchandise.

transfer of technology
The movement of modern or scientific methods of production or distribution from one enterprise to another.

transfers (mail, wire, cable)
The remittance of money by a bank to be paid to a party in another town or city.

transit zone
A port of entry in a coastal country that is established as a storage and distribution center for the convenience of a neighboring country lacking adequate port facilities or access to the sea.

transmittal letter
A list of the particulars of a shipment and a record of the documents being transmitted together with instructions for disposition of documents.

transparency
The extent to which laws, regulations, agreements, and practices affecting international trade are open, clear, measurable, and verifiable.

transportation and exportation entry
Customs entry used when merchandise arrives in the U.S. and is destined for a foreign country.

transport documents
All types of documents evidencing acceptance, receipt, and shipment of goods.

transship
To transfer goods from one transportation line to another, or from one ship to another.

traveler
A person who stays for a period of less than one year in a country of which he or she is not a resident.

traveler's checks
A form of check especially designed for travelers, including persons on vacation and business trips.

triangular trade
Trade between three countries, in which an attempt is made to create a favorable balance for each.

tri-temp
A container that can maintain three exact temperature zones in difference compartments simultaneously.

tropical products
Agricultural goods of export interest to developing countries in the tropical zones of Africa, Latin America, and East Asia (coffee, tea, spices, bananas, and tropical hardwoods).

trust receipt
A declaration by a client to a bank that ownership of goods released by the bank are retained by the bank, and that the client has received the goods in trust only.

turnkey
A method of construction whereby the contractor assumes total responsibility from design through completion.

turnkey contract
An agreement under which a contractor agrees to complete a product so that it is ready for use when delivered to the other contracting party.

two-tier market
An exchange rate regime that normally insulates a country from the balance of payments effects of capital flows while it maintains a stable exchange rate for current account transactions.

tying arrangement
A condition that a seller imposes on a buyer, requiring that if the buyer desires to purchase one product (tying product), the buyer must also agree to purchase another product (tied product), which the buyer may or want to purchase. Also called bundling.

ultimate consignee
The person who is the true party in interest, receiving goods for the designated end-user.

ultimo day
The last business day or last stock-trading day of a month.

unconfirmed
A documentary letter of credit for which the advising bank makes no commitment to pay, accept, or negotiate.

unconscionable
Unfair or oppressive.

underdeveloped country
A nation in which per capita real income is proportionately low when contrasted with the per capita real income of nations where industry flourishes.

UN/EDIFACT
United Nations Electronic Data Interchange for Administration, Commerce and Transport; a nationally accepted electronic data interchange standard.

unfair trade practice
Unusual government support to firms such as export subsidies or certain anti-competitive practices by firms themselves such as dumping, boycotts, or discriminatory shipping arrangements that result in restraint of competition.

Uniform Commercial Code
A set of statutes purporting to provide some consistency among states' commercial laws.

UN Conference on Trade and Development
A part of the UN General Assembly that promotes international trade and seeks to increase trade between developing countries and countries with different social and economic systems.

UN Industrial Development Organization (UNIDO)
Established in 1967 under the UN Secretariat, UNIDO serves as a specialized agency to foster industrial development in lesser developed countries through offering technical assistance in both the governmental and industrial sectors.

U.S. and Foreign Commercial Service
An agency of the U.S. Department of Commerce that helps U.S. firms be more competitive in the global marketplace.

U.S.–Canada Free Trade Agreement
Provisions adopted by the US with the enactment of the ETA Implementation Act of 1988. The ETA reduced tariffs on imported merchandise between Canada and the U.S. It was superceded by NAFTA.

U.S. Code (USC)
A set of volumes containing the official compilation of U.S. law available from local offices of the U.S. Government Printing Office in major U.S. cities.

U.S. Customs Service (USCS)
U.S. governmental agency whose primary duties include the assessment and collection of all duties, taxes, and fees on imported merchandise, and the enforcement of customs and related laws and treaties.

U.S. International Trade Commission
An independent fact-finding agency of the U.S. government that studies the effects of tariffs and other trade restraints on the U.S. economy. It conducts public hearings to assist in determining whether or not potential or real damage has been done.

U.S. price
In the context of dumping investigations, this term refers to the price at which goods are sold in the U.S. compared with their foreign market value. The comparisons are used in the process of determining whether foreign firms importing into the U.S. are being competitive.

U.S. Trade and Development Agency
An independent agency within the executive branch. Its mandate is to promote economic development in, and simultaneously export U.S. goods and services to, developing and middle-income countries.

U.S. trade representative
A cabinet-level official with the rank of ambassador who is the principal adviser to the president on international trade policy and has responsibility for setting and administering overall trade policy.

U.S. Travel and Tourism Administration
An organization within the Department of Commerce that stimulates demand internationally for travel to the United States and coordinates marketing projects and programs with U.S. and international travel interests.

unit load
The strapping or banding together of a number of individual cargo containers to create a single unit.

unit load device
Term commonly used when referring to containers and pallets.

unitization
The practice or technique of consolidating many small pieces of freight into a single unit for easier handling.

Universal Copyright Convention
An international agreement that was concluded to afford copyright protection to literary and artistic works in all countries that voluntarily agree to be bound by the convention terms.

unloading
The physical removal of cargo from a carrier's container.

unrestricted letter of credit
A letter of credit that may be negotiated through any bank of the beneficiary's choice.

Uruguay Round
The eighth round of multilateral trade negotiations concerning the General Agreement on Tariffs and Trade (GATT). The Uruguay Round (so named because meetings began in Punta del Este, Uruguay, in 1987) concluded in December 1993 after seven years of existence and was replaced by the World Trade Organization (WTO).

USCS
U.S. Customs Service.

USDA
U.S. Department of Agriculture.

user's fees
Assessments collected by the U.S. Customs Service as part of the entry process to help defray various costs involved in the importation of goods to the U.S.

usuance
The time allowed for payment of an international obligation.

validated export license
A document issued by the U.S. government authorizing the export of commodities for which written export authorization is required.

validity
The time period for which a letter of credit is valid.

valuation
The appraisal of the worth of imported goods by customs officials for the purpose of determining the amount of duty payable in the importing country.

valuation charges
Transportation charges assessed shippers who declare a value of goods higher than the value of the carriers' limits of liability.

value added
That part of the value of produced goods developed in a company. It is determined by subtracting from sales the costs of materials and supplies, energy costs, contract work, and so on, and it includes labor.

value-added tax
An indirect tax on consumption that is assessed on the increased value of goods at each discrete point in the chain of production and distribution, from the raw material stage to final consumption.

vendor
A company or individual that supplies goods or services.

vertical export trading company
An export trading company that integrates a range of functions taking products from suppliers to buyers.

vessel ton
A unit of measurement in the shipping industry assuming that 100 cubic feet of cargo equals 1 ton.

visa
A license issued by the government of an exporting country for the export to a specific importing country of a certain quantity of a quota-controlled commodity subject to a voluntary export restriction or a voluntary quota.

visa waiver
A program of selected countries that eliminates their visa requirement on a test basis.

volatility
The measure of the relative deviation of a price from the mean.

volume rate
A rate applicable in connection with a specified volume of freight.

voluntary export restriction
An understanding between trading partners in which the exporting nation, to reduce trade friction, agrees to limit exports of a particular good.

voluntary restraint agreements
Informal bilateral or multilateral arrangements through which exporters voluntarily restrain certain exports, usually through export quotas to avoid economic dislocation in an importing country.

war clause
An insurance clause included in policies to cover against losses as a result of war.

warehouse, U.S. Customs bonded
A federal warehouse where goods remain until duty has been collected from the importer.

warehouse receipt
A document listing the goods or commodities deposited in a warehouse. It is a receipt for the commodities listed and for which the warehouse is the bailee.

warranty
A promise by a contracting party that the other party can rely on certain facts or representations.

war risk
The risk to a vessel, its cargo, and passengers by aggressive actions of a hostile nation or group.

Warsaw Convention
An international multilateral treaty that regulates, in a uniform manner, the conditions of international transportation by air.

waybill
A document prepared by a transportation line at the point of a shipment, showing the point or origin, destination, route, consignor, consignee, description of shipment, and amount charged for the transportation.

Webb-Pomerene Act of 1918
Federal legislation exempting exporters' associations from antitrust regulations.

Webb-Pomerene association
Associations engaged in exporting that combine the products of similar producers for overseas sales. These associations have partial exemption from U.S. antitrust laws.

weight break
Levels at which the freight rate per 100 pounds decreases because of substantial increases in the weight.

wharfage
A charge assessed by a pier or dock owner for handling incoming or outgoing cargo.

without reserve
A term indicating that a shipper's agent or representative is empowered to make definitive decisions and adjustments abroad without approval of the group or individual represented.

World Bank
The International Bank for Reconstruction and Development (IBRD), commonly referred to as the World Bank, an intergovernmental financial institution located in Washington, DC.

World Bank Group
An integrated group of international institutions that provides financial and technical assistance to importers and exporters.

world trade clubs
Local or regional-based organizations in the U.S. and around the world of importers, exporters, customs brokers, freight forwarders, attorneys, bankers, manufacturers, and shippers.

WTO
World Trade Organization. Assumed duties of GATT as of January 1995. See Chapter 9.

zip code
A numerical code, established by the U.S. Postal Service, used for the purpose of routing and to identify delivery zones. Some U.S. carriers apply this code for freight in the same manner.

zone
Any one of a number of sections or districts in the U.S. or of the world used for the purpose of establishing proper rates for parcels, mail, pickup, and delivery.

zone status
The legal status of merchandise that has been admitted to a U.S. foreign trade zone, thereby becoming subject to the provisions of the Foreign Trade Zone Act (FTZA).

zone user
A corporation, partnership, or party that uses a U.S. foreign trade zone for storage, handling, processing, or manufacturing merchandise in zone status, whether foreign or domestic.

International Trade Contacts

Australia
Australian Consulate-General
611 N. Larchmont Boulevard
Los Angeles, CA 90004-1321
Phone: 213-469-9176

Austria
Trade Commissioner
Austrian Trade Commission
150 E. 52nd Street, 32nd Floor
New York, NY 10022
Phone: 212-421-5250
Fax: 212-751-4675

Bahamas
The Bahamas Chamber of Commerce
Shirley Street and Collins Avenue
P.O. Box N-155
Nassau, Bahamas
Phone: 809-322-2145
Fax: 809-322-4649

Chile
PROCHILE
866 United Nations Plaza, Suite 302
New York, NY 10017
Phone: 212-207-3266
Fax: 212-207-3649

PROCHILE
1900 Avenue of the Stars, Suite 2470
Los Angeles, CA 90067
Phone: 310-553-4541, 310-553-4542
Fax: 310-553-6817

PROCHILE
1110 Brickell Avenue, Suite 300
Miami, FL 33131
Phone: 305-374-0697
Fax: 305-374-4270

Costa Rica
Export-Investment Promotion Center
  (Cenpro)
Attn: Marco Rivera
P.O. Box 1278-1007
San Jose, Costa Rica
Phone: 506-221-7166

Cyprus
Permanent Secretary
Ministry of Commerce, Industry and
 Tourism
2 A. Araouzos Street
Nicosia, Cyprus
Phone: 011-357-2-303264
Fax: 011-357-2-366120

Secretary General
Cyprus Chamber of Commerce and
 Industry
38 Deligeorgis Street
Nicosia, Cyprus
Phone: 011-357-2-449500
Fax: 357-2-449048

Czech Republic
Economic Chamber of the Czech
 Republic
Argentinska 38
170 05 Praha 7, Czech Republic
Phone: 011-42-2-6679-4111
Fax: 011-42-2-6671-0805

Czech Ministry of Trade and Industry
Na Frantisku 32
110 15 Praha 1, Czech Republic
Phone: 011-42-2-285-1111
Fax: 011-42-2-481-1089

Centre for Foreign Economic Relations
Politickych veznu 20
111 21 Praha 1, Czech Republic
Phone: 011-42-2-2422-1586
Fax: 011-42-2-2422-1575

Denmark
Royal Danish Consulate General
10877 Wilshire Boulevard, Suite 1105
Los Angeles, CA 90024
Phone: 310-443-2090
Fax: 310-443-2099

Royal Danish Embassy
3200 Whitehaven Street NW
Washington, DC 20008
Phone: 202-234-4300
Fax: 202-382-1470

Royal Danish Consulate General
John Hancock Center, Suite 3430
875 N. Michigan Avenue
Chicago, IL 60611-1901
Phone: 312-787-8780
Fax: 312-787-8744

Royal Danish Consulate General
One Dag Hammerskjold Plaza
885 Second Avenue, 18th Floor
New York, NY 10017
Phone: 212-223-4545
Fax: 212-754-1904

The Dominican Republic
Centro Dominicano de Promocion de
 Exportaciones
Avenue 27 de Febrero
Plaza de la Independencia
Santo Domingo, The Dominican
 Republic
Telephone: 809-530-5505
Fax: 809-566-9131

Asociacion Dominicana de
 Exportadores, Inc.
Avenue Winston Churchill 5
Santo Domingo, The Dominican
 Republic
Phone: 809-532-6779, 809-533-9734
Fax: 809-532-1926

Ethiopia
Embassy of Ethiopia
1800 K Street NW, Suite 624
Washington, DC 20006
Phone: 202-452-1272
Fax: 202-223-0137

Fiji
Fiji Trade and Investment Board
Town Hall Road, 3rd Floor Civic
 House
Suva, Fiji
Phone: 679-315-988
Fax: 679-301-783

Germany

German American Chamber of
  Commerce
401 N. Michigan Avenue, Suite 2525
Chicago, IL 60611-4212
Phone: 312-644-2662
Fax: 312-644-0738

German American Chamber of
  Commerce
5520 Pacific Concourse Drive, Suite
  280
Los Angeles, CA 90045
Phone: 310-297-7979
Fax: 310-297-7966

German American Chamber of
  Commerce
5555 S. Felipe, Suite 1030
Houston, TX 77056
Phone: 713-877-1114
Fax: 713-877-1602

German American Chamber of
  Commerce
1515 Market Street, Suite 505
Philadelphia, PA 19102
Phone: 215-665-1585
Fax: 215-665-0375

German American Chamber of
  Commerce
465 California Street, Suite 910
San Francisco, CA 94104
Phone: 415-392-2262
Fax: 415-392-1314

German American Chamber of
  Commerce
40 W. 57th Street, 31st Floor
New York, NY 10019
Phone: 212-974-8857
Fax: 212-974-8863

German American Chamber of
  Commerce
3475 Lenox Road NE, Suite 620
Atlanta, GA 30326
Phone: 404-239-9494
Fax: 404-264-1761

Greece

Greek Consulate General
Office of the Commercial Counselor
150 East 58th Street, Suite 1701
New York, NY 10022
Phone: 212-751-2404
Fax: 212 593 2278

Greek Consulate General
Office of the Commercial Attache
168 N. Michigan Avenue
Chicago, IL 60601
Phone: 312-332-1716
Fax: 312-236-5127

Embassy of Greece
Office of the Commercial Counselor
2211 Massachusetts Avenue NW
Washington, DC 20008
Phone: 202-332-2844
Fax: 202-328-3105

Consulate General of Greece
Trade Section
12424 Wilshire Boulevard, Suite 800
Los Angeles, CA 90025
Phone: 310-442-9902
Fax: 310-442-9972

Hungary

Hungarian Economic and Trade
  Representation
130 East Randolph Drive
Prudential Plaza, Suite 1130
Chicago, IL 60601
Phone: 312-856-0274
Fax: 312-856-1080

Hungarian Economic and Trade
  Representation
150 E. 58th Street, 33rd Floor
New York, NY 10022
Phone: 212-752-3060
Fax: 212-486-2958

Hungarian Economic and Trade
  Representation
2401 Calvert Street NW, Suite 1021
Washington, DC 20008
Phone: 202-387-3191
Fax: 202-387-3140

Ireland
Irish Trade Board
345 Park Avenue, 17th Floor
New York, NY 10154-0037
Phone: 212-371-6398
Fax: 212-371-3600

Italy
Italy-America Chamber of Commerce
    West
11520 San Vicente Boulevard, Suite
    203
Los Angeles, CA 90049
Phone: 310-826-9898
Fax: 310-826-2876

Italy-America Chamber of Commerce
126 West Grand Avenue
Chicago, IL 60610
Phone: 312-661-1336
Fax: 312-767-3299

Italy-America Chamber of Commerce
Mid-Atlantic Chapter
2400 Eleven Penn Center
Philadelphia, PA 19103-2962
Phone: 215-963-8700

Italy-America Chamber of Commerce
Empire State Building
730 Fifth Avenue, Suite 600
New York, NY 10019
Phone: 212-459-0044
Fax: 212-459-0090

Italy-America Chamber of Commerce,
    Inc.
Southeast Chapter
1 S.E. 15th Road, Suite 150
Miami, FL 33312
Phone: 305-577-9868
Fax: 305-577-3956

Korea
KOTRA
Marquis One Tower, Suite 2802
245 Peachtree Center Ave.
Atlanta, GA 30303
Phone: 404-524-2234

KOTRA
12720 Hillcrest Road, Suite 390
Dallas, TX 75230-2040
Phone: 1-214-934-8644
Fax: 214-239-4191

KOTRA
One Biscayne Tower, Suite 1620
Miami, FL 33131
Phone: 1-305-374-4648
Fax: 1-305-375-9332

KOTRA
460 Park Avenue, Suite 402
New York, NY 10022
Phone: 1-212-826-0900
Fax: 1-212-888-4930

KOTRA
1 California Street, 19th Floor, Suite
    1905
San Francisco, CA 94111
Phone: 1-415-434-8400
Fax: 415-434-8450

KOTRA
111 E. Wacker Drive, Suite 319
Chicago, IL 60601
Phone: 1-312-644-4324
Fax: 312-644-4879

KOTRA
1129 20th Street NW, Suite 410
Washington, DC 20036
Phone: 1-202-857-7919 / 7921
Fax: 202-857-7923

Kuwait
Kuwait Information Office
2600 Virginia Avenue NW, Suite 404
Washington, DC 20037
Phone: 202-338-0211
Fax: 202-338-0957

Kuwait Chamber of Commerce and
    Industry
P.O. Box 775
Safat, Kuwait
Phone: 965-243-3864
Fax: 965-240-4110

Latvia
Latvian Chamber of Commerce and
  Industry
21 Brivibas Bulvaris
Riga, LV-1849, Latvia
Phone: 371-2-225595
Fax: 371-2-332276

World Trade Center in Riga
Elizabetes iela 2
Riga, LV-1340, Latvia
Phone: 371-2-322242
Fax: 371-7-830035

Latvian Customs Department
Kr. Valdemara iela 1A
Riga, LV-1841, Latvia
Phone: 371-2-323858
Fax: 371-2-322440

Madagascar
Chambre de Commerce, d'Industrie et
  d'Agriculture
B.P. 166
Antananarivo (101), Madagascar
Phone: 261-2-282-11
Fax: 261-2-202-13

Ministere du Commerce
B.P. 354
Ambohidahy
Antananarivo (101), Madagascar
Phone: 261-2-271-92
Fax: 261-2-312-80

Malawi
Malawi Investment Promotion Agency
Private Bag 302
Lilongwe 3, Malawi
Phone: 202-797-1007
Fax: 202-265-0976

Malaysia
Malaysian Trade Commission
South Hope Street, Suite 400
Los Angeles, CA 90071
Phone: 213-892-9034
Fax: 213-955-9142

Malaysian Trade Commission
313 E. 43rd Street, 3rd Floor
New York, NY 10017
Phone: 212-682-0232
Fax: 212-983-19987

Mali
Ambassade de la Republique du Mali
2130 R Street
Washington, DC 20008
Phone: 202-332-2249

Malta
Malta Export Trade Corporation
  (METCO)
Attn: General Manager
Trade Centre
San Gwann SGN 09, Malta
Phone: 356-446186 to 88
Fax: 356-496687

Morocco
Moroccan Center for Export Promotion
23 Rue Bnou Majed El Bahar
Casablanca, Morocco
Phone: 2-30-22-10
Fax: 2-30-17-93 / 31-86-87

Casablanca World Trade Center
100 Avenue De l'Armee Royale
20 000 Casablanca, Morocco
Phone: 2-31-78-78
Fax: 2-31-51-36

Association of Importers and Exporters
  of Moroccan Products
7 Rue Ahmed Touki
Casablanca, Morocco
Phone: 2-26-87-51
Fax: 2-27-19-79

The Netherlands
Netherlands Foreign Trade Agency—
  EVD
P.O. Box 20101
2500 EC The Hague, The Netherlands
Phone: 31-70-379-8933
Fax: 31-70-379-7878

Netherlands Wholesale and
International Trade Federation
P.O. Box 29822
2502 LV The Hague, The Netherlands
Phone: 31-70-354-6811
Fax: 31-70-351-2777

Royal Netherlands Embassy
Economic Division
4200 Linnean Avenue NW
Washington, DC 20008
Phone: 202-244-5300
Fax: 202-966-0737

International Procurement Agency B.V.
P.O. Box 190
1400 AD Bussum, The Netherlands
Phone: 31-35-691-5077
Fax: 31-35-693-6016

Paraguay
Proparaguay General Promotion Office
for Export and Investment
Padre Cardozo 469
Asuncion, Paraguay
Phone: 595-21-208276-7
Fax: 595-21-200425

The Philippines
Office of the Commercial Counselor
1600 Massachusetts Avenue NW
Washington, DC 20036
Phone: 202-467-9419 / 9361
Fax: 202-467-99428

Poland
Consulate General of the Republic of
Poland
Commercial Section
12400 Wilshire Boulevard, Suite 555
Los Angeles, CA 90025
Phone: 310-442-8500
Fax: 310-442-8526

Embassy of the Republic of Poland
Office of the Economic Counselor
1503 21st Street NW
Washington, DC 20036
Phone: 202-467-6690
Fax: 202-833-8343

Consulate General of the Republic of
Poland
Commercial Section
333 E. Ontario Street, Suite 3906B
Chicago, IL 60611
Phone: 312-642-4102
Fax: 312-642-8829

Polish Chamber of Commerce
Promotion Center
ul. Trebacka 4
00-916 Warsaw, Poland
Phone: 48-22-26-0221 / 7376
Fax: 8-22-27-4673, 48-2-635-5137

Embassy of the Republic of Poland
Office of the Economic Counselor
820 Second Avenue, 17th Floor
New York, NY 10017
Phone: 212-370-5300
Fax: 212-818-9623

Portugal
Portuguese Trade and Tourism Office
590 Fifth Avenue
New York, NY 10036
Phone: 212-354-4610
Fax: 212-575-4737

Ministry of Commerce and Tourism
A/C Gabinete de Relacoes Publicas
Av. da Republica, 79-4
1000 Lisbon, Portugal
Phone: 01-386-40-60

Spain
Commercial Offices of Spain
500 N. Michigan Avenue, Suite 1500
Chicago, IL 60611
Phone: 312-644-1154/55
Fax: 312-527-5531

Commercial Offices of Spain
Home Savings Tower, Suite 1050
660 South Figueroa Street
Los Angeles, CA 90017
Phone: 213-627-5284
Fax: 213-627-0883

Commercial Offices of Spain
2558 Massachusetts Avenue, NW
Washington, DC 20008
Phone: 202-265-8600
Fax: 202-265-9478

Commercial Offices of Spain
Chrysler Building
405 Lexington Avenue
New York, NY 10174-0331
Phone: 212-661-4959
Fax: 212-972-2494

Sudan
Ministry of Ecomomic Planning and
    Investment
Khartoum, Sudan
Phone: 011-249-11-770156 / 770454
Fax: 011-249-11-770730

Suriname
The Chamber of Commerce and
    Industry
10 Mr. Dr. J.C. De Mirandastraat
Paramaribo, Suriname
Phone: 011-597-474536 / 473526
Fax: 011-597-4747799

Sweden
Swedish Trade Council
150 N. Michigan Avenue, Suite 1200
Chicago, IL 60601-7594
Phone: 1-800-SWEDEN-4
Fax: 312-346-0683

Switzerland
Directorate General of Swiss Customs
Monbijourstr. 40
CH-3003 Bern, Switzerland
Phone: 011-41-31-322-6511
Fax: 011-41-31-322-78-72

Switzerland
Federal Department of Foreign Trade
Bundeshaus Ost
CH-3003 Bern, Switzerland
Phone: 031-322-22-11

Taiwan
Headquarters for Taipei Economic and
    Cultural Representative Office in the
    U.S. (TECRO)
133 Po-ai Road, Taipei
Taiwan, R.O.C.
Tel.: (02) 311 9212
Fax: (02) 382-2651

Taipei Economic and Cultural
    Representative Office in the U.S.A.
4201 Wisconsin Ave., NW
Washington, DC 20016-2137
Tel.: 1 (202) 895-1800

Tunisia
Union Tinisienne de l'Industrie du
    Commerce et de l'Artisanat
103 Avenue de la Liberte
1002 Tunis, Tunisia
Phone: 216-1-780-366
Fax: 216-1-783-143

Export Promotion Centre (CEPEX)
28, rue Gandhi
1001 Tunis, Tunisia
Phone: 216-1-350-801
Fax: 216-1-353-683

Ministere de la Cooperation
    Internationale et de l'Investissement
    Exerieur
149, Avenue de la Liberte
1002 Tunis Belvedere, Tunisia
Phone: 216-1-798-522
Fax: 216-1-799-169

Turkey
Export Promotion Center (IGEME)
Mithatpasa Cad. No: 60 06420
Kizilay-Ankara, Turkey
Phone: 90-312-417-22-23
Fax: 90-312-714-22-33

Union of Chambers of Commerce
Ataturk Bulvari No: 149
Bakanliklar, Turkey
Phone: 0-312-417-7700
Fax: 90-312-418-3268 / 418-1002

West Africa
The Chief Executive
National Investment Promotion
  Authority
Independence Drive
Banjul, The Gambia, West Africa
Phone: 220-228332
Fax: 220-229220

The Chief Executive
Gambia Chamber of Commerce and
  Industry
59 Buckle Street
Banjul, The Gambia, West Africa
Phone: 220-2299671/227042
Fax: 220-2299671

APPENDIX B

Importers' Resources
(Includes Internet Web Sites)

Argentina
Association of Importers and Exporters of the Republic of Argentina (Asociacion de Importadores y Exportadores de la Republica Argentina)
Sarmiento 767 P1
1041 Capital Federal
Buenos Aires, Argentina

Camara de Consorcios de Exportacion
Gral. Peron 2630-6d
1041 Capital Federal
Buenos Aires, Argentina

Chamber of Exporters of the Republic of Argentina (Camera de Exportadores de la Republica Argentina)
Av. Roque S. Pena 741 P.1
1005 Capital Federal
Buenos Aires, Argentina

Confederation of Producers and Exporters of the Republic of Argentina (Confederacion de Productores y Exportadores de la Republica Argentina)
Bartolome Mitre 2241/43
P.O. Box 1013
Buenos Aires, Argentina

Australia
Australian Institute of Export
National Office
281 Sussex Street, Suite 9
Sydney, NSW 2000 Australia

Bahrain
Bahrain Chamber of Commerce and Industry
http://www.arabbiz.com/bahrain/bah cha.html
P.O. Box 248, M 3,000
Manama, Bahrain

Bolivia
National Chamber of Exporters of
Bolivia (Camera Nacional De
Exportadores De Bolivia)
Avenida Arce 2017
P.O. Box 12145
La Paz, Bolivia

Brazil
National Confederation of Commerce—
Brazil (Confederacao Nacional do
Commercio)
Scs Q-02b1 "C" No. 227 Edificio
Presidente Dutra Cep 70300
Brasilia, Brazil

Brunei
Brunei Bumiputra Chamber of
Commerce and Industry
Dewan Ushawan Den Perdagangan
Bumiputra Brunei
P.O. Box 203
Gadong Post Office
Bandar Seri Begawan 3102
Brunei Darussalam

Burundi
Agence Promotion du Exchanges
Exterieurers
B.p. 3535
Bujumbura, Burundi

Canada
Association Canadienne D'exportation
99, Rue Bank, Bureau 250
Ottawa, Ontario K1P 6B9 Canada

Canadian Exporters' Association
http://www.achilles.net@cea1.aec/
99 Bank Street, Suite 250
Ottawa, Ontario K1P 6B9 Canada
Email: cea1aec@achilles.net

Export Development Corporation
http://www.edc.ca/english/index.html
151 O'Connor Street
Ottawa, Ontario K1A 1K3 Canada
Email: export@.edc4.edc.ca

Chile
Asociacion de Exportadores de Chile
A.g. Moneda 920
Santiago, Chile

China
China Chamber of International
Commerce
(China Council for the Promotion of
International Trade)
http://wwwl.usa1.com@ibnet/
cpithp.html
1, Fuxingme Nwai Street
P.O. Box 100860
Beijing, China

China International Trade Association
2 E. Chang'an Avenue
Beijing 100731
People's Republic of China

Colombia
Pro Expo (Fondo de Promocion de
Exportacione S)
Calle 28 No. 13a-15
Pisos 35 Al 42
Bogota, Colombia

Costa Rica
Centre for Promotion of Exports and
Investments
Edificio Murray, Calle 7, Ave. 1 Y 3
P.O. Box 5418-1000
San Jose, Costa Rica

Chamber of Exporters of Costa Rica
(Camera de Exportadores de Costa
Rica)
Apartado 218-2101
Zapote, Costa Rica

Denmark
Foreign Trade Register of the Danish
Chamber of Commerce
Borsen
Dk- 1217 Copenhagen K, Denmark

Ecuador
Fondo de Promocion de Exportaciones
Juan Leon Mera 130 Y Avda Patria
P.O. Box 163
Quito, Ecuador

Estonia
Foreign Trade Association ("Estimpex")
Ws 32-34
Tallinn, Estonia

Trading Center ("INREKO")—Estonia
Adala 4a
Tallinn, Estonia

Fiji
Fiji Trade and Investment Board
Civic House, 3rd Floor
Government Building
P.O. Box 2303
Suva, Fiji

Finland
Federation of Finnish Commerce and
  Trade
Kaupan Keskusliitto
Mannerheimintie 76 a
Sf-00250 Helsinki, Finland

Finnish Foreign Trade Association
Suomen Ulkomaankauppaliitto
Arkadiankatu 2
Postilokero 908 Sf-00100
Helsinki, Finland

France
French Foreign Trade Center
Centre Francaise du Commerce
  Exterieur
10, Avenue D'iena
F-75016 Paris, France

French National Center for Foreign
  Commerce
10, Avenue D'iena
Paris 75016 France

Germany
Foreign Trade Association
Mauritiusstei NW
W-5000 Cologne 1, Germany

Ghana
Ghana Export Promotion Council
Republic House
Tudu Road
P.O. Box M 146
Accra, Ghana

Ghana National Trading Company
P.O. Box 67, Ghana House
Accra, Ghana

Greece
Hellenic Export Promotion
  Organization
86-88 Marinou Antypa
Heliopoulis 163 46 Greece

Guatemala
Guatemalan Chamber of Exports
11 Calle 5-66, Zona 9
5 Nivel
Ediecio Tivoli
Guatemala City, Guatemala

Honduras
Foundation for Investment and
  Development of Exports (Fundacion
  Pare la Inversion y Desarrollo de
  Exportaciones)
Apartado Postal 2029
Tegucigalpa, Honduras

Hong Kong
Hong Kong Exporters' Association
Star House, Room 825
3 Salisbury Road
Tsimshatsui
Kowloon, Hong Kong

Hong Kong General Chamber of
  Commerce
22/Floor, United Centre
95 Queensway, Hong Kong

Hong Kong Trade Development
  Council
http://www.tdc.org.hk/38/f
Office Tower
Connection Plaza
1 Harbour Road
Wanchai, Hong Kong

Hungary
Hungarian Investcenter Tradeinform
Dorottya U. 4, H- 1051
Budapest, Hungary

Hungarian Investment and Trade
  Promotion Agency
Honvedu. 13-15,h-1880
Budapest, Hungary

India
Federation of Indian Export
  Organizations
PHD House, 3rd Floor
4/2 Siri Institutional Area
Hauz Khas
New Delhi, Delhi, India

Indian Institute of Foreign Trade
B-21 Institutional Area, South of Iit
New Delhi 110 029 India

Trade Development Authority
Bank of Baroda Building
16 Parliament Street
New Delhi 110 001 India

Indonesia
Association of Indonesian Export
  Companies
J1. Kramat Raya 4-6
Jakarta-Pusat, Indonesia

Importers Association of Indonesia
Jalan Kesejahteraan, No. 98, Aprj
Box 2744
10110 Jakarta, Indonesia

Indonesian Exporters Association
Jl. Biom 21
Jakarta, Indonesia

Indonesian Exporters Federation
J1. Kramat Raya 406
Jakarta, Indonesia

Ireland
Irish Exporters Association
Marshalsea House
17 Merchants' Quay
Dublin, Ireland

Jamaica
Jamaica Exporters Association
http://www.sbed.com/
13 Dominica Drive
P.O. Box 9
Kingston 5 Jamaica

Japan
Council of All Japan Exporters'
  Associations
Kikai Shinko Kaikan, 5-8
Shibakoen 3-chome
Minato-ku
Tokyo 105, Japan

Japan Foreign Trade Council, Inc.
World Trade Center Building
4-1, Hamamatsu-cho 2-chome
Minato-ku
Tokyo 105, Japan

Korea
Korea Foreign Trade Association
http://www.ktfa.co.kr/
159-1, Samsong-dong
Kang-nam-gu, Seoul, Republic of
  Korea

Korean Overseas Information Services
http://www.kois.go.kr/intro.html

Korea Trade Promotion Corporation (KOTRA)
http://ikjoon.isisnet.co.kr/kotra/
159, Samsung-dong, Kangnam-ku
Korea Trade Center
P.O. Box 123
Seoul, Korea

Macao
Macao Exporters Association (Associacao Dos Exportadores De Macau)
Avenida do Infante
D. Henrique 60-64, Andar 3 Macao

Malaysia
Malaysian International Chamber of Commerce and Industry
http://www1.usa1.com@eibnet/
miccihp.html
Tingkat 10 Wisma Damansara
Jalan Semantan
P.O. Box 10192
50706 Kuala Lumpur, Malaysia
Email: micc@ibnet.com

National Chamber of Commerce and Industry of Malaysia
http://www.undp.org/tcdc/
mal4571.htm
17th Floor, Plaza Pekeliling Jalan Tun Razak 50400 Kuala Lumpur, Malaysia

Mexico
Bancomext: Mexican Bank for Foreign Trade
http://www.quicklink.com/mexico/
bancomext/banc1.html
Camino a Sta Teresa no. 1679
Delegacion Alvaso
Obregon 01900 Mexico, D.F.

Confederation of National Chambers of Commerce (Confederac Ion de C Amaras Nac ional es de Comercio)
Balderas No. 144,
Piso 3 06079 Mexico, D.F.

Importers and Exporters Association— Mexico (Associacion Nacional de Importadores y Exportadores de la Republica Mexicana)
Monterrey 130,
Col. Roma 06700
Mexico, D.F.

U.S.-Mexico Chamber of Commerce
http://www.cais.com/usmcofc/
1726 M Street NW, Suite 704
Washington, DC 20036 USA
Email: news-hq@usmcoc.org

Morocco
Association of African Trade Promotion Organizations
Boite Postale 23
Tangier, Morocco

Islamic Centre for Development of Trade (Centre Islamique pour le Developement du Commerce)
Tours des Habous
Avenue des Far
Boite Postale 13545
Casablanca, Morocco

The Netherlands
Netherlands Wholesale and International Trade Federation
Adriaan Goekooplaan 5 Postbus 29822 Nl-2502 LV
The Hague, Netherlands

Peru
Asociacion de Exportadores del Peru
Avenida Salaverry 1910,
Apartado 1806 Jesus Maria
Lima 11 Peru

Philippines
Confederation of Small and Medium Exporters
Ground Floor, ABC Building
2251 Pasong Tamo Street
Makati, Metro Manila, Philippines

Export Assistance Center (Exponet)
6th Floor, New Solid Building
357 Gil Puyat Avenue
Makati City, Metro Manila, Philippines

Foreign Buyers Association of the
  Philippines
512 4th Floor, Cityland Condominium
Herrera Corner Ormaza and Esteban
  Street
Legaspi Village
Makati, Metro Manila, Philippines

International Trade Group
6th Floor, New Solid Building
357 Gil Puyat Avenue
Makati City, Metro Manila, Philippines

Philippine Exporters Confederation, Inc.
(PHILEXPORT, Inc.)
http://is.eunet.ch/astarte/export.htm
Ground Floor, Money Museum
Philippino International Convention
  Center Ccp Complex, Roxas
  Boulevard
Pasay City, Philippines

Poland
Polish Chamber of Foreign Trade
4 Trebacka Str.
00-074 Warszawa, Poland

Polish Chamber of Private and Trade
  Industry
Ul.hoza 35
00-681 Warszawa, Poland

Russia
Russian American Chamber of
  Commerce
http://www.nar.com/racc/
The Marketplace Tower II
3025 South Parker Road, Suite 735
Aurora, CO 80014 USA
Email: Russianbus@.AOL.com

Russian Federation Chamber of
  Commerce and Industry
Ulitsa Kuibysheva 6
Moscow 103684 Russia

Singapore
Economic Development Board
http://asia-online.com/edb/index.html
250 North Bridge Road, 24-00
Raffles City Tower
Singapore 0617 Singapore

South Africa
National African Federated Chamber of
  Commerce
Private Bag X81
Sushanguwe 0152 South Africa

South African Foreign Trade
  Organization
P.O. Box 782706
Export House, 5th Floor
Sandton 2146 Republic of South Africa

Switzerland
International Federation of Freight
  Forwarders Association (Federation
  Internationale des Associations de
  Transitaires et Assimilies)
Baumackerstrasse 24 Postfach 8493
  Ch-8050
Zurich, Switzerland

International Trade Center
Palais Des Nations
1211 Geneva 10, Switzerland

Taiwan
Chamber of Commerce and Trade
Associations of Taiwan
Listings -http://tptaiwan.org.tw/astn/
  eunion.htm

China External Trade Association
  (CETRA)
http://tptaiwan.org.tw/
4-8 F. 333 Keelung Road, Sec. 1
Taipei 10548, Taiwan
Republic of China
Email: Mi@.cetra.tptaiwan.org.tw

Chinese National Association of
Industry and Commerce
F1.13, No. 390, Section 1
Fu-hsin S. Road, Taipei, Taiwan, ROC

Taiwan Importers and Exporters
  Association
http://www.obn.com.sg/gb/chamber/
  data/chm052.html
14f, 2 Fu Shing N. Road
Taipei 10559 Taiwan

Thailand
Thai Chamber of Commerce
150 Rajabopit Road
Bangkok 10200 Thailand

Turkey
Export Promotion Center (Igeme)
Mithatpasa Cad. No: 60
Kizilay, Ankara, Turkey

General Secretariat of Mediterranean
  Exporters Unions
Uray Cad. Turan Ishani Kat:3-4
Mersin, Turkey

Promotion Foundation of Turkey
Ugur Mumcu Caddesi 24
Gaziosmanpasa, Ankara, Turkey

Union of Chambers of Commerce,
  Industry, Maritime Commerce and
  Commodity Exchanges of Turkey
Ataturk Bulvari No:149
Bakanliklar, Ankara, Turkey

United States
American Association of Exporters and
  Importers
11 W. 42nd Street, 30th Floor
New York, NY 10036 USA
Phone: 212-944-2230
Fax: 212-382-2606

American Chambers of Commerce
http://www1.usa1.com@ibnet/usachams.
  html

Atlantic Council of the United States
910 17th Street NW, #1000
Washington, DC 20006 USA
Email: Info@.Acgate.acus.org

American League for Exports and
  Security Assistance
122 C Street NW, #310
Washington, DC 20001 USA

American National Metric Council
4330 East West Highway, Suite 1117
Bethesda, MD 20814 USA

Asia Pacific Chamber of Commerce
http://oneworld.wa.com/apcc/apcc.html
  Email: APCC@Halcyon.com

Association of Foreign Trade
  Representatives
P.O. Box 300
New York, NY 10024-0300

The Brookings Institution
http://www.brook.edu/
Foreign Policy Studies
1775 Massachusetts Avenue NW
Washington, DC 20036-2188 USA
Email: brookinfo@brook.edu

Consumers for World Trade
2000 L Street NW, #200
Washington, DC 20036 USA
Email: Mcameron@cap.gwu.edu

European-American Chamber of
   Commerce
101 Pennsylvania Avenue NW
Washington, DC 20004 USA

Federation of International Trade
   Associations
http://www.webhead.com/fita/home.html
1851 Alexander Bell Drive
Reston, VA 22091 USA

International Center for Foreign Trade
   and Industry
3800 Moore Place
Alexandria, VA 22305 USA

International Trade Action Council
1225 19th Street NW, Suite 210
Washington, DC 20036 USA

International Trade Council
3114 Circle Hill Road
Alexandria, VA 22305

International Trade Facilitation Council
   (NCTID)
1800 Diagonal Road, Suite 220
Alexandria, VA 22314 USA

International Traders Association
c/o the Mellinger Company
6100 Variel Avenue
Woodland Hills, CA 91367 USA

Minority International Network for
   Trade
P.O. Box 1483
Murray Hill Station
New York, NY 10156 USA

National Association of Foreign Trade
   Zones
http://www.emtron.com/members/
   index.htm
1825 I Street NW, Suite 400
Washington, DC 20006 USA

National Association of
   Manufacturers—Trade and
   Technology Policy
1331 Pennsylvania Avenue NW,
   #1500n
Washington, DC 20004-1790 USA

National Customs Brokers and
   Forwarders Association of America,
   Inc.
http://www.tradecompass.com/ncbfaa/
   index.html
1 World Trade Center, Suite 1153
New York, NY 10048 USA
Email: Webmaster@ncbfaa.org

National Foreign Trade Council
http://www.ahrm.org/nftc/nttc.htm
1625 K Street NW, #1090
Washington, DC 20006 USA
1270 Avenue of the Americas
New York, NY 10020 USA

North American Free Trade
   Agreement—Information
http://the-tech.mit.edu/bulletins/
   nafta.html

North American Institute (NAMI)
http://www.santafe.edu/~naminet/
   index.html
708 Paseo De Peralta
Santa Fe, NM 87501 USA
Email: Naminet@Santafe.edu

Organization of Women in
   International Trade
750 17th Street NW, Suite 901
Washington, DC 20006 USA

Overseas Development Council
1875 Connecticut Avenue NW #1012
   Washington, DC 20009-5728 USA

Overseas Private Investment
Corporation (OPIC)
1100 New York Avenue NW
Washington, DC 20527 USA

Pacific Basin Development Council
567 King Street, Suite 325
Honolulu, Hawaii 96813-3070 USA

Partners of the Americas
1424 K Street NW, Seventh Floor
Washington, DC 20005 USA

Trade Relations Council of the United
States
7311 Grove Road, Suite X
Frederick, MD 21701 USA

World Export Processing Zones
Association
P.O. Box 986
Flagstaff, AZ 86002 USA

World Trade Centers Association
http://www.wtca.org/
1 World Trade Center, Suite 7701
New York, NY 10048 USA

Vietnam
Vietnam Chamber of Commerce and
Industry
http://coombs.anu.edu.au/~vern/
vninfo/vcci.htm
33 Ba Trieu Str
Hanoi, Vietnam

APPENDIX C
U.S. Foreign Trade Zones

This list gives the address and phone number of the contact person for each FTZ project. If the contact person is not an employee of the grantee, the name of the grantee organization is also given. If assistance is needed from FTZ staff, U.S. Department of Commerce, call (202) 482-2862.

Zone No. 1, New York, New York
Grantee: City of New York
Operator: S & F Warehouse, Inc.
Brooklyn Navy Yard, Building 77,
   Brooklyn, NY 11205
Sol Braun 718-834-0400

Zone No. 2, New Orleans, Louisiana
Grantee/Operator: Board of
   Commissioners of the Port of New
   Orleans
P.O. Box 60046, New Orleans, LA
   70160
Baldwin Van Benthuysen 504-897-0189

Zone No. 3, San Francisco, California
Grantee: San Francisco Port
   Commission
Operator: Foreign Trade Services, Inc.
Pier 23, San Francisco, CA 94111
Tom Faenzi 415-391-0176

Zone No. 4 Grant Expired

Zone No. 5, Seattle, Washington
Grantee/Operator: Port of Seattle
   Commission
P.O. Box 1209, Seattle, WA 98111
Scott Pattison 206-728-3628

Zone No. 6, Grant Expired

Zone No. 7, Mayaguez, Puerto Rico
Grantee/Operator: Puerto Rico
   Industrial Dev. Co.
P.O. Box 362350, San Juan, PR 00936-
   2350
Gerardo Toro 809-834-0620

Zone No. 8, Toledo, Ohio
Grantee: Toledo-Lucas County Port
   Authority
1 Maritime Plaza, Toledo, OH 43604-
   1866
Kelly Rivera 419-243-8251

343

Zone No. 9, Honolulu, Hawaii
Grantee/Operator: State of Hawaii
Pier 2, 521 Ala Moana, Honolulu, HI 96813
Gordon Trimble 808-586-2509

Zone No. 10, Grant Expired

Zone No. 11, Grant Expired

Zone No. 12, McAllen, Texas
Grantee/Operator: McAllen Economic Development Corp.
6401 South 33rd Street, McAllen, TX 78501
Joyce Dean 210-682-4306

Zone No. 13, Grant Expired

Zone No. 14, Little Rock, Arkansas
Grantee: Arkansas Dept. of Industrial Development
Operator: Little Rock Port Authority
7500 Lindsey Road, Little Rock, AR 72206
Thomas S. Moore 501-490-1468

Zone No. 15, Kansas City, Missouri
Grantee/Operator: Greater Kansas City FTZ, Inc.
River Market Office Building, 20 E. 5th Street, Suite 200
Kansas City, MO 64106
Chris N. Vedros 816-421-7666

Zone No. 16, Sault Ste. Marie, Michigan
Grantee/Operator: Economic Development Corp. of Sault Ste. Marie
1301 W. Easterday Avenue
Sault Ste. Marie, MI 49783
James F. Hendricks 906-635-9131

Zone No. 17, Kansas City, Missouri
Grantee/Operator: Greater Kansas City FTZ, Inc.
River Market Office Building

20 E. 5th Street, Suite 200
Kansas City, MO 64106
Chris N. Vedros 816-421-7666

Zone No. 18, San Jose, California
Grantee: City of San Jose
50 W. San Fernando Street, Suite 900
San Jose, CA 95113
Joseph Hedges 408-277-5880

Zone No. 19, Omaha, Nebraska
Grantee/Operator: Dock Board of the City of Omaha
Omaha/Douglas Civic Center, 1819 Farnam Street, Suite 1100
Omaha, NE 68183
Scott Knudsen 402-444-5381

Zone No. 20, Suffolk, Virginia
Grantee: Virginia Port Authority
600 World Trade Center, Norfolk, VA 23510
Bob Merhige 757-683-8000

Zone No. 21, Dorchester County, South Carolina
Grantee: South Carolina State Ports Authority
P.O. Box 22287, Charleston, SC 29413-2287
Jacqueline B. Sassard 803-577-8164

Zone No. 22, Chicago, Illinois
Grantee: Illinois International Port District
3600 E. 95th Street, Chicago, IL 60617-5193
Matt Dosen 312-646-4400

Zone No. 23, Buffalo, New York
Grantee: County of Erie
424 Main Street, Suite 300
Buffalo, NY 14202
Paul R. Leone 716-856-6525

Zone No. 24, Pittston, Pennsylvania
Grantee/Operator: Eastern Distribution
  Center, Inc.
1151 Oak Street, Pittston, PA 18640-3795
Michael J. Horvath 717-655-5581

Zone No. 25, Port Everglades, Florida
Grantee/Operator: Port Everglades Port
  Authority
1850 Eller Drive, Ft. Lauderdale, FL
  33316
Karen M. Varner 305-523-3404, ext. 320

Zone No. 26, Atlanta, Georgia
Grantee: Georgia Foreign Trade Zone,
  Inc.
P.O. Box 95546, Atlanta, GA 30347
Penn Worden 404-636-7811

Zone No. 27, Boston, Massachusetts
Grantee: Massachusetts Port Authority
World Trade Center, Suite 321
Boston, MA 02210
Andrew Bendheim 617-478-4100

Zone No. 28, New Bedford,
  Massachusetts
Grantee/Operator: City of New
  Bedford
Office of City Planning, 133 William
  Street, Room 211
New Bedford, MA 02740-6172
Marc R. Rousseau 508-979-1488

Zone No. 29, Louisville, Kentucky
Grantee/Operator: Louisville and
  Jefferson County Riverport Authority
6900 Riverport Drive
P.O. Box 58010
Louisville, KY 40268
C. Bruce Traughber 502-935-6024

Zone No. 30, Salt Lake City, Utah
Grantee: Redevelopment Agency of
  Salt Lake City
451 South State Street, Room 404
Salt Lake City, UT 84111
Allison Gregorson 801-535-7230

Zone No. 31, Granite City, Illinois
Grantee/Operator: Tri-City Regional
  Port District
2801 Rock Road, Granite City, IL 64040
Robert Wydra 618-452-3337

Zone No. 32, Miami, Florida
Grantee: Greater Miami Foreign Trade
  Zone, Inc.
Omni International Complex, 1601
  Biscayne Boulevard
Miami, FL 33132
Rodell Holzberg 305-350-7700

Zone No. 33, Pittsburgh, Pennsylvania
Grantee: Regional Industrial
  Development Corporation of
  Southwestern Pennsylvania
Seventh Floor, 907 Penn Avenue
Pittsburgh, PA 15222-3805
Frank Brooks Robinson 412-471-3939

Zone No. 34, Niagara County, New
  York
Grantee: County of Niagara
Operator: North American Trading and
  Drayage
2221 Niagara Falls Boulevard
Niagara Falls, NY 14304
Jodyne Morphy 716-731-4900

Zone No. 35, Philadelphia,
  Pennsylvania
Grantee: Philadelphia Regional Port
  Authority
210 W. Washington Square
Philadelphia, PA 19106
Elizabeth Murphy 215-426-6791

Zone No. 36, Galveston, Texas
Grantee: City of Galveston
Operator: Port of Galveston
123 Rosenberg, P.O. Box 328
Galveston, TX 77553
Diane Falcioni 409-766-6121

Zone No. 37, Orange County, New York
Grantee: County of Orange
265 Main Street
Goshen, NY 10924
Geoffrey Chanin 914-294-5151, ext. 1130

Zone No. 38, Spartanburg County,
   South Carolina
Grantee: South Carolina State Ports
   Authority
P.O. Box 22287, Charleston, SC 29413-
2287
Jacquelin B. Sassard 803-577-8164

Zone No. 39, Dallas/Fort Worth, Texas
Grantee/Operator: Dallas/Fort Worth
   International Airport Board
P.O. Drawer 619428
DFW Airport, TX 75261-9428
Tracy Kaplan 214-574-3121

Zone No. 40, Cleveland, Ohio
Grantee: Cleveland Port Authority
101 Erieside Avenue, Cleveland, OH
   44114
Steven L. Pfeiffer 216-241-8004

Zone No. 41, Milwaukee, Wisconsin
Grantee: Foreign Trade Zone of
   Wisconsin, Ltd.
P.O. Box 340046, Milwaukee, WI
   53224
Vincent J. Boever 414-769-2956

Zone No. 42, Orlando, Florida
Grantee/Operator: Greater Orlando
   Aviation Authority
9675 Tradeport Drive, Orlando, FL
   32827
Linda Smith 407-825-2213

Zone No. 43, Battle Creek, Michigan
Grantee: City of Battle Creek
Operator: BC/CAL/KAL Inland Port
   Authority of South Central Michigan
   Development Corporation
P.O. Box 1438, Battle Creek, MI 49016
Jan Burland 616-962-7526

Zone No. 44, Morris County, New
   Jersey
Grantee: N.J. Department of Commerce
   and Economic Development,
   Division of International Trade
P.O. Box 47024, Newark, NJ 07102
H. Edward Burton 609-633-3606

Zone No. 45, Portland, Oregon
Grantee/Operator: Port of Portland
P.O. Box 3529, Portland, OR 97208
Peggy J. Krause 503-731-7537

Zone No. 46, Cincinnati, Ohio
Grantee/Operator: Greater Cincinnati
   FTZ, Inc.
300 Carew Tower, 441 Vine Street
Cincinnati, OH 45202-2812
Neil Hensley 513-579-3122

Zone No. 47, Campbell County,
   Kentucky
Grantee/Operator: Greater Cincinnati
   FTZ, Inc.
300 Carew Tower, 441 Vine Street
Cincinnati, OH 45202-2812
Neil Hensley 513-579-3122

Zone No. 48, Tucson, Arizona
Grantee: Papago-Tucson FTZ
   Corporation
P.O. Box 11246, Mission Station
Tucson, AZ 85734
William Tatom 520-746-3692

Zone No. 49, Newark/Elizabeth, New
   Jersey
Grantee/Operator: Port Authority of
   NY and NJ
1 World Trade Center, Suite 34S
New York, NY 10048-0642
Lucy Ambrosino-Marchak 212-435-6727

Zone No. 50, Long Beach, California
Grantee: Board of Harbor
   Commissioners of the Port of Long
   Beach

P.O. Box 570, Long Beach, CA 90801-0570
Fritz Bergman 310-590-4162

Zone No. 51, Duluth, Minnesota
Grantee/Operator: Seaway Port
Authority of Duluth
1200 Port Terminal Drive, P.O. Box 16877
Duluth, MN 55816-0877
Ray Skelton 218-727-8525

Zone No. 52, Suffolk County, New York
Grantee/Operator: County of Suffolk
1 Trade Zone Drive, Ronkonkoma, NY 11779
John E. Dobbs 516-588-5757

Zone No. 53, Rogers County, Oklahoma
Grantee/Operator: City of Tulsa—
Rogers County Port Authority
5350 Cimarron Road, Catoosa, OK 74015-3027
Robert W. Portiss 918-266-2291

Zone No. 54, Clinton County, New York
Grantee/Operator: Clinton County Area
Development Corp.
61 Area Development Drive,
Plattsburgh, NY 12901
Gerard E. Kelly 518-563-3100

Zone No. 55, Burlington, Vermont
Grantee/Operator: Greater Burlington
Industrial Corporation
P.O. Box 786, 7 Burlington Square
Burlington, VT 05402
C. Harry Behney 802-862-5726

Zone No. 56, Oakland, California
Grantee: City of Oakland
Operator: Pacific American
Warehousing and Trucking Co.
9401 San Leandro, Oakland, CA 94603
Linda Childs 510-568-8500

Zone No. 57, Mecklenburg County, North Carolina
Grantee: North Carolina Department of Commerce
Operator: Piedmont Distribution Center
P.O. Box 7123, Charlotte, NC 28241-7123
Betty Robinson 704-587-5573

Zone No. 58, Bangor, Maine
Grantee/Operator: City of Bangor
Economic Development Office, City Hall
73 Harlow Street, Bangor, ME 04401
Stephen A. Bolduc 207-945-4400

Zone No. 59, Lincoln, Nebraska
Grantee/Operator: Lincoln Chamber of Commerce
Lincoln Foreign-Trade Zone, Inc.
1221 N Street, Suite 320
Lincoln, NE 68508
Duane S. Vicary 402-476-7511

Zone No. 60, Nogales, Arizona
Grantee: Nogales-Santa Cruz County
Economic Development Foundation, Inc.
P.O. Box 1688, Nogales, AZ 85628
Steve Colontuoni 520-761-7800, ext. 3050

Zone No. 61, San Juan, Puerto Rico
Grantee/Operator: Commercial and
Farm Credit and Development
Corporation of Puerto Rico
Box 195009, San Juan, PR 00919-5009
Lionel A. Lopez 787-793-3090

Zone No. 62, Brownsville, Texas
Grantee/Operator: Brownsville
Navigation District
Foreign-Trade Zone #62
1000 Foust Road, Brownsville, TX 78521
Jo Lynne Saban 210-831-4592

Zone No. 63, Prince George's County,
Maryland
Grantee: Prince George's County
Government Office of the County
Executive
14741 Governor Oden Bowie Drive
Upper Marlboro, MD 20772
Don Spicer 301-985-5002

Zone No. 64, Jacksonville, Florida
Grantee: Jacksonville Port Authority
P.O. Box 3005, 2831 Talleyrand
Avenue
Jacksonville, FL 32206-0005
Deborah G. Claytor 904-630-3053

Zone No. 65, Panama City, Florida
Grantee/Operator: Panama City Port
Authority
P.O. Box 15095, Panama City, FL
32406
Rudy Etheredge 904-763-8471

Zone No. 66, Wilmington, North
Carolina
Grantee: North Carolina Department of
Commerce
Operator: N.C. State Port Authority
P.O. Box 9002, Wilmington, NC 28402
Robin Ormsby 910-763-1621

Zone No. 67, Morehead City, North
Carolina
Grantee: North Carolina Department of
Commerce
Operator: N.C. State Port Authority
P.O. Box 9002, Wilmington, NC 28402
Robin Ormsby 910-763-1621

Zone No. 68, El Paso, Texas
Grantee: City of El Paso
5B Butterfield Trail Boulevard
El Paso, TX 79906-4945
Robert C. Jacob, Jr. 915-771-6016

Zone No. 69, Grant Expired

Zone No. 70, Detroit, Michigan
Grantee: Greater Detroit Foreign-Trade
Zone, Inc.
8109 E. Jefferson, Detroit, MI 48214
W. Steven Olinek 313-331-3842

Zone No. 71, Windsor Locks,
Connecticut
Grantee: Industrial Development
Commission of Windsor Locks
Town Office Building, 50 Church Street
P.O. Box L
Windsor Locks, CT 06096
James E. Maitland 203-627-1444

Zone No. 72, Indianapolis, Indiana
Grantee: Indianapolis Airport Authority
Operator: Greater Indianapolis FTZ,
Inc.
FTZ No. 72, P.O. Box 51681
Indianapolis, IN 46251
William Herber 317-487-7200

Zone No. 73, Baltimore/Washington
International Airport, Maryland
Grantee: Maryland Department of
Transportation
Maryland Aviation Administration
P.O. Box 8766, BWI Airport, MD
21240-0766
Gary E. Davies 410-859-7002

Zone No. 74, Baltimore, Maryland
Grantee: City of Baltimore
Baltimore City Development
Corporation
36 S. Charles Street, Suite 1600
Baltimore, MD 21201
Tom Buser 410-837-9305

Zone No. 75, Phoenix, Arizona
Grantee: City of Phoenix Community
and Economic Development
Department
200 W. Washington Street, 20th Floor
Phoenix, AZ 85003-1611
Robert Wojtan 602-262-5040

Zone No. 76, Bridgeport, Connecticut
Grantee/Operator: City of Bridgeport
City Hall, 45 Lyon Terrace
Bridgeport, CT 06604
Edward Lavernoich 203-576-7221

Zone No. 77, Memphis, Tennessee
Grantee: The City of Memphis
Memphis and Shelby County, Division
  of Planning and Development
City Hall, 125 North Main Street
Memphis, TN 38103-2084
Connie Binkowitz 901-576-7107

Zone No. 78, Nashville, Tennessee
Grantee: Metropolitan Nashville Port
  Authority
214 Second Avenue North, Suite 1
Nashville, TN 37201
Robert Gowan 615-862-6029

Zone No. 79, Tampa, Florida
Grantee: City of Tampa
Tampa Foreign-Trade Zones Board
2112 N. 15th Street, Second Floor
Tampa, FL 33601
John Darsey 813-242-5442

Zone No. 80, San Antonio, Texas
Grantee: City of San Antonio
Economic Development Department
P.O. Box 839966, San Antonio, TX
  78283-3966
Margaret Anaglia 210-207-8093

Zone No. 81, Portsmouth, New
  Hampshire
Grantee/Operator: New Hampshire
  State Port Authority
555 Market Street, Box 506
Portsmouth, NH 03801
Thomas Orfe 603-436-8500

Zone No. 82, Mobile, Alabama
Grantee: City of Mobile
Operator: Mobile Airport Authority
1840 South Broad, Brookley Complex
Mobile, AL 36615
Greg Jones 334-433-1222

Zone No. 83, Huntsville, Alabama
Grantee/Operator: Huntsville-Madison
  County Airport Authority
1000 Glenn Hearn Boulevard, Box
  20008
Huntsville, AL 35824
Craig Pool 205-772-3105

Zone No. 84, Harris County, Texas
Grantee: Port of Houston Authority
111 East Loop North
Houston, TX 77029
Jack Beasley 713-670-2400

Zone No. 85, Everett, Washington
Grantee: Port of Everett
P.O. Box 538, Everett, WA 98206
Edward Paskovskis 206-259-3164

Zone No. 86, Tacoma, Washington
Grantee: Port of Tacoma
1 Sitcom Plaza, Tacoma, WA 98421
Jerry Ahmann 206-383-5841

Zone No. 87, Lake Charles, Louisiana
Grantee/Operator: Lake Charles Harbor
  and Terminal District
P.O. Box 3753, Lake Charles, LA 70602
Linda Manuel 318-439-3661

Zone No. 88, Great Falls, Montana
Grantee/Operator: Great Falls
  International Airport Authority
2800 Terminal Drive, Great Falls, MT
  59404-5599
M. J. Attwood 406-727-3404, ext. 392

Zone No. 89, Clark County, Nevada
Operator: Nevada International Trade
  Corporation
1111 B Grier Drive, Las Vegas, NV
  89119
Jerry Sandstrom 702-791-0000
Grantee: Nevada Development
  Authority

Zone No. 90, Onondaga, New York
Grantee: County of Onondaga, c/o
  Greater Syracuse FTZ, Ltd.
572 S. Salina Street, Syracuse, NY
  13202-3320
LouAnn Hood 315-470-1884

Zone No. 91, Newport, Vermont
Grantee/Operator: Northeastern
  Vermont Development Association
44 Main Street, P.O. Box 630
St. Johnsbury, VT 05819
Charles E. Carter 802-748-5181

Zone No. 92, Harrison County,
  Mississippi
Grantee: Greater Gulfport/Biloxi
  Foreign-Trade Zone, Inc.
P.O. Box 40
Gulfport, MS 39502
Bruce Frallic 601-863-5951

Zone No. 93, Raleigh/Durham, North
  Carolina
Grantee: Triangle J Council of
  Governments
100 Park Drive, P.O. Box 12276
Research Triangle Park, NC 27709
Pamela Davison 919-558-9394

Zone No. 94, Laredo, Texas
Grantee: City of Laredo
Operator: Laredo International Airport
4719 Maher Avenue, Building #132
Laredo, TX 78041
Humberto Garza 210-795-2000

Zone No. 95, Starr County, Texas
Grantee/Operator: Starr County
  Industrial Foundation
P.O. Box 502, Rio Grande City, TX
  78582
Chris Salinas 210-487-2709

Zone No. 96, Eagle Pass, Texas
Grantee: City of Eagle Pass

Operator: Maverick Co. Development
  Corp.
P.O. Box 3693, Eagle Pass, TX 78853
Diane Galaviz 210-773-6166

Zone No. 97, Del Rio, Texas
Grantee/Operator: City of Del Rio
114 W. Martin Street
Del Rio, TX 78841
Juan Aguirre 210-774-8553

Zone No. 98, Birmingham, Alabama
Grantee: City of Birmingham
Operator: Shaw Warehouse
3000 Second Avenue South
Birmingham, AL 35222
Warren Crow 205-251-7188

Zone No. 99, Wilmington, Delaware
Grantee/Operator: State of Delaware
Delaware Development Office
99 Kings Highway
Dover, DE 19903
Dorothy Sbriglia 302-739-4271

Zone No. 100, Dayton, Ohio
Grantee/Operator: Greater Dayton
  Foreign-Trade Zone, Inc.
c/o Dayton Area Chamber of
  Commerce
1 Chamber Plaza, Dayton, OH 45402-
  2400
Verity Snyder 513-226-1444

Zone No. 101, Clinton County, Ohio
Grantee/Operator: Airborne FTZ, Inc.
145 Hunter Drive, Wilmington, OH
  45177
Mike Kuli 513-382-5591

Zone No. 102, St. Louis, Missouri
Grantee/Operator: St. Louis County
  Port Authority
121 S. Meramec, Suite 900
St. Louis, MO 63105
Butch Miller 314-889-7663

Zone No. 103, Grand Forks, North Dakota
Grantee: Grand Forks Regional Airport Authority
2787 Airport Drive, Grand Forks, ND 58203
Robert Selig 701 746 2580

Zone No. 104, Savannah, Georgia
Grantee/Operator: Savannah Airport Commission
Savannah International Airport
400 Airways Avenue, Savannah, GA 31408
A. W. Barbee, Jr. 912-964-0904

Zone No. 105, Providence and North Kingstown, Rhode Island
Grantee: Rhode Island Economic Development Corp.
1330 Davisville Road, North Kingstown, RI 02852
John Riendeau 401-277-3134

Zone No. 106, Oklahoma City, Oklahoma
Grantee: The City of Oklahoma City
Operator: South Oklahoma City Chamber of Commerce
Foreign-Trade Zone 106, 701 S.W. 74th Street
Oklahoma City, OK 73139-4599
Alba Castillo 405-634-1436

Zone No. 107, Des Moines, Iowa
Grantee: The Iowa Foreign Trade Zone Corporation
604 Locust Street, Suite 309
Des Moines, IA 50309
James D. Polson 515-284-1270

Zone No. 108, Valdez, Alaska
Grantee: The City of Valdez, Alaska
P.O. Box 307, Valdez, AK 99686
Tim Lopez 907-835-4981

Zone No. 109, Watertown, New York
Grantee: The County of Jefferson
c/o Jefferson County Industrial Agency
800 Starbuck Avenue, Suite 800
Watertown, NY 13601
Stephen Mitchell 315-782-5865

Zone No. 110, Albuquerque, New Mexico
Grantee: The City of Albuquerque
P.O. Box 1293, Albuquerque, NM 87103
Simon Shima 505-768-3269

Zone No. 111, JFK International Airport, New York
Grantee: The City of New York
110 William Street, New York, NY 10038
Hugh Frasier 212-312-3867

Zone No. 112, Colorado Springs, Colorado
Grantee: Colorado Springs Foreign-Trade Zone, Inc.
90 S. Cascade Avenue, Suite 1050
Colorado Springs, CO 80903
Robert K. Scott 719-661-0955

Zone No. 113, Ellis County, Texas
Grantee: Midlothian Trade Zone Corporation
Operator: Trade Zone Operations, Inc.
1500 N. Service Road Highway 67
P.O. Box 788, Midlothian, TX 76065
Lawrence A. White 214-723-5522

Zone No. 114, Peoria, Illinois
Grantee: Economic Development Council, Inc.
124 S.W. Adams, Suite 300
Peoria, IL 61602-1388
William Rigley 309-676-7500

Zone No. 115, Beaumont, Texas
Grantee: Foreign-Trade Zone of
 Southeast Texas, Inc.
2748 Viterbo Road, Box 9
Beaumont, TX 77705
Bill Kimbrough 409-835-5367

Zone No. 116, Port Arthur, Texas
Grantee: Foreign-Trade Zone of
 Southeast Texas, Inc.
2748 Viterbo Road, Box 9
Beaumont, TX 77705
Bill Kimbrough 409-835-5367

Zone No. 117, Orange, Texas
Grantee: Foreign-Trade Zone of
 Southeast Texas, Inc.
2748 Viterbo Road, Box 9
Beaumont, TX 77705
Bill Kimbrough 409-835-5367

Zone No. 118, Ogdensburg, New York
Grantee: Ogdensburg Bridge and Port
 Authority
1 Bridge Plaza
Ogdensburg, NY 13669
Doug McDonald 315-393-4080

Zone No. 119, Minneapolis-St. Paul,
 Minnesota
Grantee: Greater Metropolitan Area
 FTZ Commission
1000 Minnesota World Trade Center
30 E. Seventh Street, St. Paul, MN
 55101
Steven J. Anderson 612-725-8361

Zone No. 120, Cowlitz County,
 Washington
Grantee: Cowlitz Economic
 Development Council
1452 Hudson Street, P.O. Box 1278
U.S. Bank Building, Suite 208
Longview, WA 98632
Clint Page 360-423-9921

Zone No. 121, Albany, New York
Grantee: Capital District Regional
 Planning Commission
214 Canal Square, Second Floor
Schenectady, NY 12305
Chungchin Chen 518-393-1715

Zone No. 122, Corpus Christi, Texas
Grantee/Operator: Port of Corpus
 Christi Authority
222 Power Street, P.O. Box 1541
Corpus Christi, TX 78403
Larry Cunningham 512-882-5633

Zone No. 123, Denver, Colorado
Grantee: City and County of Denver
216 16th Street, Suite 1000
Denver, CO 80202
Steve TeSelle 303-640-7049

Zone No. 124, Gramercy, Louisiana
Grantee: South Louisiana Port
 Commission
P.O. Box 909, La Place, LA 70069-0909
Glenda Jeansonne 504-536-8300

Zone No. 125, South Bend, Indiana
Grantee: St. Joseph County Airport
 Authority
Operator: K.A.K. LLC
1507 S. Olive, P.O. Box 3559
South Bend, IN 46619
Kenneth Kanczuzewski 219-232-9357

Zone No. 126, Sparks, Nevada
Grantee: Economic Development
 Authority of Western Nevada
5190 Neil Road, Suite 111
Reno, NV 89502
Ken Lynn 702-829-3700

Zone No. 127, West Columbia, South
 Carolina
Grantee/Operator: Richland-Lexington
 Airport District
Columbia Metropolitan Airport

P.O. Box 280037, Columbia, SC 29228-0037
Robert Waddle 803-822-5010

Zone No. 128, Whatcom County, Washington
Grantee: Lummi Indian Business Council
2616 Kwina, Bellingham, WA 98226
Clayton Finkbonner 360-384-2374

Zone No. 129, Bellingham, Washington
Grantee: Port of Bellingham
625 Cornwall Avenue, Bellingham, WA 98225-5017
Bob Hilpert 206-676-2500

Zone No. 130, Blaine, Washington
Grantee: Port of Bellingham
625 Cornwall Avenue, Bellingham, WA 98225-5017
Bob Hilpert 206-676-2500

Zone No. 131, Sumas, Washington
Grantee: Port of Bellingham
625 Cornwall Avenue, Bellingham, WA 98225-5017
Bob Hilpert 206-676-2500

Zone No. 132, Coos County, Oregon
Grantee: International Port of Coos Bay Commission
P.O. Box 1215, Coos Bay, OR 97420
Martin Callery 503-267-7678

Zone No. 133, Quad-City, Iowa/Illinois
Grantee: Quad-City Foreign-Trade Zone, Inc.
1830 Second Avenue, Suite 200
Rock Island, IL 61201-8038
John Gardner 309-788-7436

Zone No. 134, Chattanooga, Tennessee
Grantee: RiverValley Partners, Inc.
835 Georgia Avenue, Suite 500
Chattanooga, TN 37402
J. Steven Hiatt 615-265-3700

Zone No. 135, Palm Beach County, Florida
Grantee: Port of Palm Beach District
P.O. Box 9935, Riviera Beach, FL 33419
Henry McKay 407-842-4201

Zone No. 136, Brevard County, Florida
Grantee: Canaveral Port Authority
P.O. Box 267, Port Canaveral Station
Cape Canaveral, FL 32920
Susan Cossey 407-783-7831

Zone No. 137, Washington Dulles International Airport, Virginia
Grantee: Washington Dulles Foreign-Trade Zone
P.O. Box 17349, Dulles International Airport
Washington, D.C. 20041
Joseph R. Trocino 703-471-2120

Zone No. 138, Franklin County, Ohio
Grantee: Rickenbacker Port Authority
Rickenbacker International Airport
7400 Alum Creek Drive, Columbus, OH 43217-1232
Bruce Miller 614-491-1401

Zone No. 139, Sierra Vista, Arizona
Grantee: Sierra Vista Economic Development Foundation, Inc.
P.O. Box 2380, Sierra Vista, AZ 85636
Barry Albrecht 520-458-6948

Zone No. 140, Flint, Michigan
Grantee: City of Flint
City Hall, 1101 S. Saginaw Street
Flint, MI 48502
Constance Scott 810-766-7346

Zone No. 141, Monroe County, New York
Grantee: County of Monroe
Rochester International Development Corp.
55 St. Paul Street, Rochester, NY 14604
Charles Goodwin 716-454-2220

Zone No. 142, Salem, New Jersey
Grantee: South Jersey Port Corporation
P.O. Box 129, Second and Beckett
Streets, Camden, NJ 08101
John R. Maier 609-757-4905

Zone No. 143, West Sacramento,
California
Grantee: Port of Sacramento
Operator: California Free Trade Zone
2650 Industrial Boulevard
West Sacramento, CA 95691
Tim O'Connor 916-372-8322

Zone No. 144, Brunswick, Georgia
Grantee: Brunswick Foreign-Trade
Zone, Inc.
100 Shipyard Drive, Brunswick, GA
31520
Deborah G. Stubbs 912-267-7181

Zone No. 145, Shreveport, Louisiana
Grantee: Caddo-Bossier Parishes Port
Commission
P.O. Box 52071, Shreveport, LA 71135-
2071
John W. Holt, Jr. 318-861-4981

Zone No. 146, Lawrence County,
Illinois
Grantee: Bi-State Authority
Mid-America FTZ, Inc., P.O. Box 514
Lawrenceville, IL 62439
Terry L. Denison 618-943-5219

Zone No. 147, Reading, Pennsylvania
Grantee: FTZ Corporation of
Southeastern Pennsylvania
645 Penn Street, Reading, PA 19601
Anthony Grimm 610-376-6766

Zone No. 148, Knoxville, Tennessee
Grantee: Industrial Development Board
of Blount County
Operator: Greater Knoxville Foreign-
Trade Zone
c/o Integral Services Group

P.O. Box 6506
Maryville, TN 37802
Jeff Deardorff 423-977-8704

Zone No. 149, Freeport, Texas
Grantee: Port of Freeport
Brazos River Harbor Navigation District
P.O. Box 615, Freeport, TX 77541
Phyllis Saathoff 409-233-2667, ext. 258

Zone No. 150, El Paso, Texas
Grantee: Westport Economic
Development Corporation
P.O. Box 9368
El Paso, TX 79984
Patricia A. Minor 915-533-1122, ext. 230

Zone No. 151, Findlay, Ohio
Grantee: Community Development
Foundation
Municipal Building, Room 310
Findlay, OH 45840
John Kovach 419-424-7095

Zone No. 152, Burns Harbor, Indiana
Grantee: The Indiana Port Commission
150 W. Market Street, Suite 603
Indianapolis, IN 46204
Don Miller 317-232-9201

Zone No. 153, San Diego, California
Grantee: City of San Diego
Civic Center Plaza, 1200 Third Avenue
Suite 1620
San Diego, CA 92101-4178
Lydia Moreno 619-236-6005

Zone No. 154, Baton Rouge, Louisiana
Grantee: Greater Baton Rouge Port
Commission
P.O. Box 380, Port Allen, LA 70767-0380
Karen St. Cyr 504-342-1660

Zone No. 155, Calhoun/Victoria
Counties, Texas
Grantee: Calhoun-Victoria Foreign-
Trade Zone, Inc.

P.O. Drawer 397, Point Comfort, TX 77978
Robert Van Borssum 512-987-2813

Zone No. 156, Weslaco, Texas
Grantee: City of Weslaco
500 S. Kansas, Weslaco, TX 78596
Allan Romer 210-968-3181

Zone No. 157, Casper, Wyoming
Grantee: Natrona County International Airport
Airport Terminal Unit, Box 1
Casper, WY 82604
Eddie F. Storer 307-472-3521

Zone No. 158, Vicksburg/Jackson, Mississippi
Grantee: Vicksburg/Jackson Foreign-Trade Zone, Inc.
P.O. Box 709, Vicksburg, MS 39180-0709
Francis M. Biedenharn 601-636-6914

Zone No. 159, St. Paul, Alaska
Grantee: City of St. Paul
P.O. Box 901, St. Paul Island, AK 99660
John R. Merculief 907-546-2331

Zone No. 160, Anchorage, Alaska
Grantee: Port of Anchorage
P.O. Box 196650, Anchorage, AK 99519-6650
Tom Jensen 907-343-6209

Zone No. 161, Sedgwick County, Kansas
Grantee: Board of Commissioners of Sedgwick County
County Courthouse, 525 N. Main Suite 320
Wichita, KS 67203-3759
Louanna Honeycutt 316-268-7575

Zone No. 162, North Haven, Connecticut
Grantee: Greater New Haven Chamber of Commerce
195 Church Street, New Haven, CT 06510
Martin Tristine 203-469-1391, ext. 240

Zone No. 163, Ponce, Puerto Rico
Grantee: CODEZOL C.D.
Corporacion para el Desarrollo de la Zona Libre de Ponce
Apartado 384, Marginal 301-C La Rambla
Ponce, PR 00731
Enrique Amy, Jr. 809-259-4445

Zone No. 164, Muskogee, Oklahoma
Grantee: Muskogee City-County Port Authority
4901 Harold Scoggins Drive, Muskogee, OK 74401
Scott Robinson 918-682-7886

Zone No. 165, Midland, Texas
Grantee: City of Midland
c/o Midland International Airport
9506 Laforce Boulevard, P.O. Box 60305
Midland, TX 79711
Carroll Thomas 915-560-2200

Zone No. 166, Homestead, Florida
Grantee: Vision Council, Inc.
43 N. Krome Avenue, Homestead, FL 33030
Richard H. Bauer 305-247-7082

Zone No. 167, Brown County, Wisconsin
Grantee: Brown County, Wisconsin
305 E. Walnut, P.O. Box 23600
Green Bay, WI 54305-3600
Jeff Finley 414-448-4001

Zone No. 168, Dallas/Fort Worth, Texas
Grantee: Dallas/Fort Worth Maquila
Trade Development Corp.
Operator: Foreign Trade Zone
Operating Company of Texas
P.O. Box 742916
Dallas, TX 75374-2916
Dennis Konopatzke 214-991-9955

Zone No. 169, Manatee County,
Florida
Grantee: Manatee County Port
Authority
13231 Eastern Avenue
Palmetto, FL 34221-6608
Joseph Gontarski 941-722-6621

Zone No. 170, Clark County, Indiana
Grantee: Indiana Port Commission
150 W. Market Street, Suite 603
Indianapolis, IN 46204
Don Miller 317-232-9201

Zone No. 171, Liberty County, Texas
Grantee: Liberty County Economic
Development Corporation
Foreign-Trade Zone 171, P.O. Box 857
Liberty, TX 77575
John Hebert 409-336-7311

Zone No. 172, Oneida County, New
York
Grantee: County of Oneida
Operator: Oneida County Industrial
Development Corporation
153 Brooks Road, Rome, NY 13441-
4105
Joseph G. Karam 315-338-0393

Zone No. 173, Grays Harbor,
Washington
Grantee: Port of Grays Harbor
P.O. Box 660, Aberdeen, WA 98520-
0141
Ron Popham 360-533-9541

Zone No. 174, Pima County, Arizona
Grantee: City of Tucson

Office of Economic Development
P.O. Box 27210, Tucson, AZ 85726-
7210
Kendall Bert 520-791-5093

Zone No. 175, Cedar Rapids, Iowa
Grantee: Cedar Rapids Airport
Commission
2515 Wright Brothers Boulevard SW
Cedar Rapids, IA 52404
Kurt Eilers 319-362-3131

Zone No. 176, Rockford, Illinois
Grantee: Greater Rockford Airport
Authority
60 Airport Drive, Rockford, IL 61109-
2902
Victoria Benson 815-965-8639, ext. 331

Zone No. 177, Evansville, Indiana
Grantee: Indiana Port Commission
Operator: Morton Avenue Warehouse,
Inc.
1700 Lynch Road, Evansville, IN 47711
Owen Snodgrass 812-464-3180

Zone No. 178, Presidio, Texas
Grantee/Operator: Presidio Economic
Development Corporation
P.O. Box 1414, Presidio, TX 79845
Jose Leyva 915-229-3724

Zone No. 179, Madawaska, Maine
Grantee: Madawaska Foreign Trade
Zone Corporation
Operator: Northern Trading Co. Inc.
P.O. Box 250, 190-202 E. Main St.
Madawaska, ME 04756
Jacqueline Clark 207-728-4273

Zone No. 180, Miami (Wynwood),
Florida
Grantee/Operator: Wynwood
Community Economic Development
Corp.
3000 Biscayne Boulevard, Suite 210
Miami, FL 33137
William Rios 305-576-0440

Zone No. 181, Akron-Canton, Ohio
Grantee: Akron-Canton Regional
 Airport Authority
5400 Lauby Road NW, North Canton,
 OH 44720
Frederick J. Krum 216-499-4059

Zone No. 182, Fort Wayne, Indiana
Grantee: City of Fort Wayne
City-County Building, Room 840
Fort Wayne, IN 46802
Trisha Gensic 219-427-1127

Zone No. 183, Austin, Texas
Grantee: Foreign Trade Zone of
 Central Texas, Inc.
P.O. Box 142114, Austin, TX 78714-
 2114
Lawrence Hart 512-452-8848

Zone No. 184, Klamath Falls, Oregon
Grantee: City of Klamath Falls Dock
 Commission
City of Klamath Falls
P.O. Box 237, Klamath Falls, OR
 97601-0361
Joseph Riker 541-883-5361

Zone No. 185, Culpeper County,
 Virginia
Grantee: Culpeper-County Chamber of
 Commerce, Inc.
133 W. Davis Street, Culpeper, VA 22701
Norma Dunwody 540-825-8628

Zone No. 186, Waterville, Maine
Grantee: Maine International Foreign-
 Trade Zone, Inc.
P.O. Box 2611, Waterville, ME 04903-
 2611
John Nale 207-873-4304

Zone No. 187, Toole County, Montana
Grantee/Operator: Northern Express
 Transportation, Inc.
301 First Street South, Suite 3
Shelby, MT 59474
John Kavanagh 406-434-5203

Zone No. 188, Yakima, Washington
Grantee: Yakima Air Terminal Board
2400 W. Washington Avenue, Yakima,
 WA 98903
Bob Clem 509-575-6149

Zone No. 189, Kent/Ottawa/Muskegon
 Counties, Michigan
Grantee: KOM Foreign Trade Zone
 Authority
KOM FTZ #189, Grand Valley State
 University
Seidman School of Business
301 W. Fulton Avenue
Eberhard Center Room 718
Grand Rapids, MI 49504-6495
Michael Michalski 616-771-6653

Zone No. 190, Butte-Silver Bow,
 Montana
Grantee: City and County of Butte-
 Silver Bow
P.O. Box 3641, Butte, MT 59702
Bill Fogarty 406-723-4321

Zone No. 191, Palmdale, California
Grantee: City of Palmdale
38300 N. Sierra Highway, Palmdale,
 CA 93550-4798
Al McCord 805-267-5100

Zone No. 192, Meridian, Idaho
Grantee/Operator: City of Meridian
33 E. Idaho, Meridian, ID 83642
Shari Stiles 208-888-4433

Zone No. 193, Pinellas County, Florida
Grantee: Pinellas County Industry
 Council
c/o St. Petersburg/Clearwater
 Economic Development Council
Building 1200, Suite 1
7990 114th Avenue N, Largo, FL 34643
Patsy Beyer 813-541-8080

Zone No. 194, Rio Rancho, New
  Mexico
Grantee: City of Rio Rancho
3900 Southern Boulevard, P.O. Box
  15550
Rio Rancho, NM 87174
James Lewis 505-891-7201

Zone No. 195, Fairbanks, Alaska
Grantee: Fairbanks Industrial
  Development Corp.
515 7th Avenue, Suite 320
Fairbanks, AK 99701
Ronald Ricketts 907-452-2185

Zone No. 196, Fort Worth, Texas
Grantee: Alliance Corridor, Inc.
2421 Westport Parkway, Suite 200
Fort Worth, TX 76177
Timothy Ward 817-890-1000

Zone No. 197, Dona Ana County, New
  Mexico
Grantee: Board of County
  Commissioners of the County of
  Dona Ana
Economic Development Department
180 W. Amador Avenue, Las Cruces,
  NM 88001
Judy Price 505-647-7248

Zone No. 198, Volusia and Flagler
  Counties, Florida
Grantee: County of Volusia, Florida
c/o Daytona Beach International
  Airport
700 Catalina Drive, Suite 300
Daytona Beach, FL 32114
Mike Ulrich 904-248-8030

Zone No. 199, Texas City, Texas
Grantee: Texas City Foreign-Trade
  Zone Corporation
P.O. Box 2608, Texas City, TX 77592
Randy Dietel 409-948-3111

Zone No. 200, Mercer County, New
  Jersey
Grantee: County of Mercer
Joyce McDade Administration Building
640 S. Broad Street, Trenton, NJ 08611
Robert D. Prunetti 609-989-6518

Zone No. 201, Holyoke, Massachusetts
Grantee: Holyoke Economic
  Development and Industrial Corp.
City Hall, Room 10
Holyoke, MA 01040
Robert H. Bateman 413-534-2200

Zone No. 202, Los Angeles, California
Grantee: Board of Harbor
  Commissioners of the City of Los
  Angeles
425 S. Palos Verdes Street, San Pedro,
  CA 90731
Karen Tozer 310-732-3846

Zone No. 203, Moses Lake,
  Washington
Grantee: Moses Lake Public
  Corporation
Port of Moses Lake, Grant County
  Airport
Building 1202, 7810 Andrews Street NE
Moses Lake, WA 98837-3218
David M. Bailey 509-762-5363

Zone No. 204, Tri-City,
  Tennessee/Virginia
Grantee: Tri-City Airport Commission
P.O. Box 1055, Blountville, TN 37617-
  1055
Terry W. Barnes 615-323-6288

Zone No. 205, Port Hueneme,
  California
Grantee: Board of Harbor
  Commissioners, Oxnard Harbor
  District
Port of Hueneme, P.O. Box 608
105 E. Port Hueneme Road
Port Hueneme, CA 93044-0608
Kam Quarles 805-488-3677

Zone No. 206, Medford-Jackson
County, Oregon
Grantee: Jackson County, Oregon
10 S. Oakdale, Medford, OR 97501
Burke M. Raymond 503-776-7269

Zonc No. 207, Richmond, Virginia
Grantee: Capital Region Airport
Commission
Richmond International Airport,
Box A-3
Richmond, VA 23231-5999
Timothy Doll 804-236-2102

Zone No. 208, New London,
Connecticut
Grantee: New London Foreign Trade
Zone Commission
111 Union Street, New London, CT
06320
Phil Biondo 860-447-5203

Zone No. 209, Palm Beach County,
Florida
Grantee: Palm Beach County
Department of Airports
Palm Beach International Airport
Building 846, West Palm Beach, FL
33406-1491
Bruce V. Pelly 407-471-7412

Zone No. 210, St. Clair County,
Michigan
Grantee: Port Huron-St. Clair County
Industrial
Development Corporation
800 Military Street, Suite 320
Port Huron, MI 48060
H. Thomas Rowland 810-982-3510

Zone No. 211, Anniston, Alabama
Grantee: Anniston Metropolitan Airport
Board of Commissioners
Operator: Foreign Trade Zone
Corporation
P.O. Box 6241, Huntsville, AL 35824-
0241
Greg Jones 205-772-3105

Zone No. 212, Tacoma, Washington
Grantee: Puyallup Tribal Foreign-Trade
Zone Corporation
3702 Marine View Drive NE, Suite 200
Tacoma, WA 98422
James May 206-383-2820

Zone No. 213, Fort Myers, Florida
Grantee: Lee County Port Authority
Southwest Florida International Airport
16000 Chamberlin Parkway, Suite 8671
Fort Myers, FL 33913
Donald L. Davenport 941-768-4307

Zone No. 214, Lenoir County, North
Carolina
Grantee: North Carolina Global
TransPark Authority
P.O. Box 27406
Raleigh, NC 27611-7406
Stacey Burks 919-733-1365

Zone No. 215, Sebring, Florida
Grantee: Sebring Airport Authoirty
Sebring Regional Airport
128 Authority Lane, Sebring, FL 33870
Mike Willingham 941-655-6444

Zone No. 216, Olympia, Washington
Grantee: Port of Olympia
915 Washington Street NE, P.O. Box 827
Olympia, WA 98507-0827
John M. Mohr 360-586-6150

Zone No. 217, Ocala, Florida
Grantee: Economic Development
Council, Inc.
Operator: Ocala Regional Airport
P.O. Box 1270
Ocala, FL 34478-1270
Maritza R. Baker 352-629-8401

Zone No. 218, St. Lucie County, Florida
Grantee: Central Florida Foreign-Trade
Zone, Inc.
2300 Virginia Avenue, Fort Pierce,
FL 34982
T. Morris Adger 407-462-1732

APPENDIX D

Glossary of Antidumping Terms and Phrases

This glossary is intended to provide parties with a basic understanding of many technical terms. These explanations are not regulations or rules with the force of law. As difficult or detailed questions arise, parties should seek clarification from the statute, regulations, and the Department of Commerce, rather than attempts to derive precise guidance from these general explanations.

1. Administrative protective order
2. Affiliated persons
3. Antidumping law
4. Arm's-length transactions (between affiliates)
5. Certification of accuracy
6. Circumstances of sale
7. Comparison market
8. Constructed export price
9. Constructed export price offset
10. Constructed value
11. Contemporaneous sales

12. Cost of manufacture
13. Cost of production
14. Credit expense
15. Date of sale
16. Difference in merchandise adjustments
17. Direct versus indirect expenses
18. Discounts
19. Dumping
20. Export price and constructed export price
21. Facts available
22. Foreign like product
23. Further manufacturing adjustment
24. Home market
25. Identical merchandise
26. Imputed expenses
27. Indirect expenses
28. Inventory carrying costs
29. Level of trade adjustment
30. Normal value
31. Ordinary course of trade
32. Proprietary information
33. Proprietary treatment
34. Rebates
35. Similar merchandise
36. Subject merchandise
37. Technical service expenses
38. Third-country market
39. Verification
40. Viability

1. Administrative protective order

An administrative protective order is the legal mechanism by which the Department of Commerce controls the limited disclosure of business proprietary information to representatives of interested parties. The department authorizes the release of proprietary information under administrative protective order only when the representatives file a request in which they agree to the following four conditions: (1) to use the information only in the antidumping proceeding, (2) to secure the information and protect it from disclosure to any person not subject to an administrative protective order, (3) to report any violation of the terms of the protective order, and (4) to acknowledge that they may be subject to sanctions if they violate the terms of the order. (Section 777[c] of the act. See also *proprietary information* and *proprietary treatment*.)

2. Affiliated persons

Under the antidumping law, transactions between affiliated persons are subject to particular scrutiny. Affiliated persons (affiliates) include (1) members of a family, (2) an officer or director of an organization and that organization, (3) partners, (4) employers and their employees, and (5) any person or organization directly or indirectly owning, controlling, or holding, with power to vote, 5% or more of the outstanding voting stock or shares of any organization. In addition, affiliates include (6) any person who controls any other person and that other person, and (7) any two or more persons who directly control, are controlled by, or are under common control of, any person. "Control" exists where one person or organization is legally or operationally in a position to exercise restraint over or direct the other person or organization (Section 771[33] of the Act.)

3. Antidumping law

The U.S. antidumping laws are set forth in Title VII of the Tariff Act of 1930, as amended. (19 U.S.C. 1673 et seq.)

4. Arms-length transactions (between affiliates)

Generally, the department may use transactions between affiliates as a basis for normal value, cost of production, and constructed value only if the transactions are at arm's length. Arm's-length transactions are those in which the selling price between the affiliated parties is comparable to the selling prices in transactions involving persons who are not affiliated. The department accounts for terms of sale, conditions of delivery, and other circumstances related to the sales in deciding if the selling prices are comparable.

5. Certification of accuracy

Any person who submits factual information to the department must include with the submission a certification of the completeness and accuracy of the factual information. Certification must be made by a knowledgeable official responsible for presentation of the factual information and by the party's legal counsel or other representative, if any. A sample certification form is included as Appendix V to the questionnaire. (Section 782 [b] of the act.)

6. Circumstances of sale

In comparing the normal value to the export price or constructed export price, the department makes adjustments for differences in circumstances of sale. This adjustment normally is limited to differences in direct selling expenses (and assumptions of expenses on behalf of the buyer) that the department does not adjust for under other more specific provisions. (Section 773[a][6][C][iii] of the act. See also *direct versus indirect expenses.*)

7. Comparison market

The comparison market is the home or third-country market from which the department selects the prices used to establish normal values. (see also *viability.*)

8. Constructed export price

(See *export price and constructed export price.*)

9. Constructed export price offset

To the extent practicable, the department attempts to base normal value on sales made at the same level of trade as the export price or constructed export price. Where this is impossible, the law provides, subject to certain conditions, for an adjustment to normal value to account for differences in level of trade. However, where the department establishes different functions at the different levels of trade, but the data available do not form an appropriate basis for determining a level of trade adjustment, the law provides for a limited adjustment in the form of the "constructed export price offset." This adjustment does not apply in export price comparisons, and the department will make the adjustment only when normal value is established at a level of trade more remote from the factory than the level of trade of the constructed export price. The offset is a deduction from normal value in the amount of indirect selling expenses incurred in the comparison market. The amount of this deduction may not exceed (i.e., it is "capped" by) the amount of indirect selling expenses deducted in calculating constructed export price. (Section 773[a][7][B] of the act. See also *level of trade adjustment*.)

10. Constructed value

When there are no sales of the foreign like-product in the comparison market suitable for matching with the subject merchandise (including, for example, when the department disregards sales because they are below the cost of production), the department uses constructed value as the basis for normal value. The constructed value is the sum of (1) the cost of materials and fabrication of the subject merchandise; (2) the selling, general, and administrative expenses and profit in the comparison market; and (3) the cost of packing for exportation to the U.S. (Section 773[e] of the act.)

11. Contemporaneous sales

In investigations, the department normally compares average export prices (or constructed export prices) with average normal values. The averages normally are based on sales made over the course of the period of investigation. In administrative reviews of existing antidumping orders, on the other hand, the department normally compares the export price (or constructed export price) of an individual U.S. sale to an average normal value for a "contemporaneous month." The preferred month is the month in which the particular U.S. sale was made. If, during the preferred month, there are no sales in the comparison market of a foreign like product that is identical to the subject merchandise, the department will then employ a six-month window for the selection of contemporaneous sales. For each U.S. sale, the department will calculate an average normal value for sales of identical merchandise in the most recent of the three months prior to the month of the U.S. sale. If there are no such sales, the department will use sales of identical merchandise in the earlier of the two months following the month of the U.S. sale. If there are no sales of identical merchandise in any of these months, the department will apply the same progression to sales of similar merchandise.

12. Cost of manufacture

The cost of manufacture is the sum of material, fabrication, and other processing costs incurred to produce the products under investigation. (See also *cost of production.*)

13. Cost of production

Cost of production means the cost of producing the foreign like product. The cost of production is the sum of (1) material, fabrication, and other processing costs; (2) the selling, general, and administrative expenses; and (3) the cost of containers and other packing expenses. The department may disregard comparison market sales in calculating normal value if they are made at prices that are less than the cost of production. The department will disregard all sales below cost if made: (1) within an extended period of time (normally one year) in substantial quantities (at least 20% of the volume of the product examined is sold below cost or the weighted-average unit price is below the weighted-average cost for the period examined), and (2) at prices that do not permit recovery of costs within a reasonable period of time (i.e., the price is not greater than the weighted-average cost of production during the period examined). Although the department initiates any cost of production inquiries for all sales of the foreign like product, this determination is made on a product-specific basis. (Section 773[b] of the act.)

14. Credit expense

Credit expense is a type of expense for which the department frequently makes circumstances-of-sale adjustments. It is the interest expense incurred (or interest revenue foregone) between shipment of merchandise to a customer and receipt of payment from the customer. The department normally imputes the expense by applying a firm's annual short-term borrowing rate, prorated by the number of days between shipment and payment, to the unit price. If actual payment dates are not kept in a way that makes them accessible, the calculation may be based on the average of the number of days that accounts receivable remain outstanding. (See also *imputed expenses.*)

15. Date of sale

Because the department attempts to compare sales made at the same time, establishing the date of sale is an important part of the dumping analysis. Generally, the date of sale is the date on which the basic terms of the sale, particularly price and quantity, are agreed upon by the buyer and the seller. Typically, the date of sale is the sale contract date, purchase order date, or the order confirmation date. For long-term or requirements contracts, the date of the sale is the date of contract. If basic terms of sale have changed up to, or even subsequent to, the date of shipment, then the date of shipment is the date of sale. However, the date of sale cannot occur after the date of shipment. Thus, the department treats postshipment price modifications as price adjustments.

16. Difference in merchandise adjustments

When normal value is based on sales in the comparison market of a product that is similar, but not identical, to the product sold in the U.S., the department will adjust normal value to account for differences in the variable costs of producing the two products. Generally, the adjustment is limited to differences in the cost of materials, labor, and variable production costs that are attributable to physical differences in the merchandise. The department will not adjust for differences in fixed overhead or administrative expenses or profit.

17. Direct versus indirect expenses

In calculating export price, constructed export price, and normal value, the department treats selling expenses differently depending on whether they are direct expenses or indirect expenses. For instance, circumstances-of-sale adjustments normally involve only direct expenses (and assumptions of expenses on behalf of the buyer, see below), while the constructed export price offset involves indirect expenses. The department uses a two-step test to distinguish between direct and indirect expenses. Direct expenses generally must be (1) variable and (2) traceable in a company's financial records to sales of the merchandise under investigation. 1. Variable versus fixed expenses: direct expenses are typically variable expenses that are incurred as a direct and unavoidable consequence of the sale (i.e., in the absence of the sale these expenses would not be incurred). Indirect expenses are fixed expenses that are incurred whether or not the sale is made. The same expense may be classified as fixed or variable depending on how the expense is incurred. For example, if an exporter pays an unaffiliated contractor to perform a service, this fee would normally be considered variable and treated as a direct expense (provided that condition 2, below, is also satisfied). However, if the exporter provides the service through a salaried employee, the fixed-salary expense will be treated as an indirect expense. 2. Tying of the expense to sales of the merchandise under investigation: Selling expenses must be reasonably dependent upon sales of the merchandise under investigation to qualify as direct selling expenses. However, even if a fixed expense is allocable to the merchandise under investigation, the department normally will not treat the expense as a direct expense. Common examples of direct selling expenses include credit expenses, commissions, and the variable portions of guarantees, warranty, technical assistance, and servicing expenses. Common examples of indirect selling expenses include inventory carrying costs, salesmen's salaries, and product liability insurance. The department also allocates the fixed portion of expenses, such as salaries for employees who perform technical services or warranty repairs, as indirect expenses. The Department also treats assumptions of expenses as if they were direct expenses, provided they are attributable to a later sale of the merchandise. For example, the department treats expenses incurred for advertising aimed at retailers as if they were direct selling expenses when the exporter is selling to wholesalers.

18. Discounts

A discount is a reduction to the gross price that a buyer is charged for goods. Although the discount need not be stated on the invoice, the buyer remits to the seller only the face amount of the invoice, less discounts. Common types of discounts include early-payment discounts, quantity discounts, and loyalty discounts.

19. Dumping

Dumping occurs when imported merchandise is sold in or for export to the U.S. at less than the normal value of the merchandise, that is, a price that is less than the price at which identical or similar merchandise is sold in the comparison market, or less than the constructed value of the merchandise. The dumping margin is the amount by which the normal value exceeds the export price or constructed export price of the subject merchandise. The weighted-average dumping margin is the sum of the dumping margins divided by the sum of the export prices and constructed export prices.

20. Export price and constructed export price

Export price and constructed export price refer to the two types of calculated prices for merchandise imported into the U.S. The department compares these prices with normal values to determine whether goods are dumped. Both export price and constructed export price are calculated from the price at which the subject merchandise is first sold to a person not affiliated with the foreign producer or exporter. Generally, a U.S. sale is classified as an export price sale when the first sale to an unaffiliated person occurs before the goods are imported into the U.S. Generally, a U.S. sale is classified as a constructed export price sale when the first sale to an unaffiliated person occurs after importation. However, if the first sale to the unaffiliated person is made by a person in the U.S. affiliated with the foreign exporter, constructed export price applies even if the sale occurs prior to importation, unless the U.S. affiliate performs only clerical functions in connection with the sale. To ensure that a fair comparison with the normal value is made, the department makes adjustments to the price charged to the first unaffiliated customer in calculating the export price or constructed export price. For both export price and constructed export price the department adds packing charges, if not already included in the price, rebated import duties, and, if applicable, certain countervailing duties. Also for both, the department deducts transportation costs and export taxes or duties. No other adjustments are made in calculating export price. However, in calculating the constructed export price, the department also deducts selling commissions and other expenses incurred in selling the subject merchandise in the U.S., the cost of any further manufacture or assembly performed in the U.S., and a portion of profit. (Section 772 of the act.)

21. Facts available

The department seeks to make its antidumping determinations on the basis of responses to its antidumping questionnaires. However, for a variety of reasons, the data needed to make such determinations may be unavailable or unusable. In such instances, the law requires the department to make its determinations on the basis of "the facts otherwise available" (more commonly referred to as "the facts available"). More specifically, the department must use the facts available if necessary information is unavailable on the record of an antidumping proceeding. In addition, the department must use the facts available where an interested party or any other person: (1) withholds information requested by the department, (2) fails to provide requested information by the requested date or in the form and manner requested, (3) significantly impedes an antidumping proceeding, or (4) provides information that cannot be verified. In selecting the information to use as the facts available, the law authorizes the department to make an inference that is adverse to an interested party if the department finds that party failed to cooperate by not acting to the best of its ability to comply with a request for information. However, the law also provides that when the department relies on secondary information rather than on information obtained in the course of an antidumping proceeding, the department must, to the extent practicable, corroborate that information from independent sources that are reasonably at the department's disposal. The department will consider using submitted information that does not meet all of the department's requirements if: (1) the information is submitted within applicable deadlines, (2) the information can be verified, (3) the information is not so incomplete that it cannot serve as a reliable basis for a determination, (4) the party establishes that it acted to the best of its ability, and (5) the department can use the information without undue difficulties. Finally, if an interested party promptly informs the department of difficulties it is having in responding to a request for information, the department will consider modifying its request to the extent necessary to avoid imposing an unreasonable burden on the party. (Sections 776 and 782[c]–[e] of the act.)

22. Foreignlike-product

The term *foreignlike product* refers to merchandise that is sold in the comparison market and that is identical or similar to the subject merchandise. When used, foreignlike-product means all merchandise that is sold in the comparison market and that fits within the description of merchandise provided in Appendix III to the questionnaire. (Section 771 [16] of the act. See also *Identical Merchandise* and *Similar Merchandise*.)

23. Further manufacturing adjustment

In calculating constructed export price, the department normally deducts from the price of the merchandise sold in the U.S. the cost of any further manufacture or assembly performed in the U.S. by, or for, the exporter or an affiliate. However, if the value of the further processing is likely to exceed substantially the value of the subject merchandise as imported, the department may instead use an alternative basis for the constructed export price. If possible, the department would use the price of subject merchandise sold to an unaffiliated customer by the producer, exporter, or affiliated seller. If there is an insufficient quantity of such sales, the department may rely on any other reasonable basis. (Sections 772[d][2] and 772[e] of the act.)

24. Home Market

The home market refers to the market for sales of the foreign like product in the country in which the merchandise under investigation is produced. Home market sales are the preferred basis for normal value. (See also *third-country market* and *viability*.)

25. Identical merchandise

Identical merchandise is the preferred category of foreignlike product for purposes of the comparison with subject merchandise. The identical merchandise is merchandise that is produced by the same manufacturer in the same country as the subject merchandise and that the department determines is identical or virtually identical in all physical characteristics to the subject merchandise, as imported into the U.S. (See also *foreignlike product* and *similar merchandise*.)

26. Imputed expenses

Imputed expenses generally are opportunity costs (rather than actual costs) that are not reflected in the financial records of the company being investigated but that must be estimated and reported for purposes of an antidumping inquiry. Common examples of imputed expenses include credit expenses and inventory carrying costs.

27. Indirect expenses

(See *direct versus indirect expenses*.)

28. Inventory carrying costs

Inventory carrying costs are the interest expenses incurred (or interest revenue foregone) between the time the merchandise leaves the production line at the factory and the time the goods are shipped to the first unaffiliated customer. The department normally calculates these costs by applying the firm's annual short-term borrowing rate, prorated by the number of days between leaving the production line and shipment to the customer, to the unit cost or price. (See also *imputed expenses*.)

29. Level of trade adjustment

To the extent practicable, the department calculates normal values based on sales at the same level of trade. When the U.S. sale is an export price sale, the level of trade of the U.S. sale is determined by the level of trade of the starting price. When the U.S. sale is a constructed export price sale, the level of trade of the U.S. sale is determined by the level of trade, not of the starting price but of the constructed export price. When the department is unable to find sales in the comparison market at that same level of trade as the U.S. sale, the department may adjust the normal value to account for differences in levels of trade between the two markets. The department will make these adjustments only when there is a difference in the levels of trade (i.e., there is a difference between the actual functions performed by the sellers at the different levels of trade in the two markets) and that difference affects price comparability. The department will measure the effect on price comparability by determining whether there is a consistent pattern of price differences between sales at the different levels of trade in the comparison market. The department normally will calculate any adjustment for level of trade based on the percentage difference between an average of the prices at the different levels of trade in the comparison market, less any expenses adjusted for elsewhere in the normal value calculation. (Sections 773[a][1] and [7] of the act.)

30. Normal value

Normal value is the general term applied to the adjusted price of the foreign like product in the home or third-country (comparison) market, or to the constructed value of the subject merchandise. The department compares the normal value with the export price or constructed export price to determine the margin of dumping, if any. The department initially seeks to calculate normal values based on price. If there are adequate sales in the home market (see *viability*), the department calculates normal value based on the price at which the foreignlike product is first sold (generally, to unaffiliated parties) in that market; otherwise, if there are adequate sales in a third-country market, the department calculates normal value based on the price at which the foreignlike product is first sold (generally, to unaffiliated parties) in the third-country market. If there are no appropriate home or third-country market sales, the department determines normal value by calculating the constructed value. To ensure that a fair comparison with the export price or constructed export price is made, the department makes adjustments to the price used to calculate the normal value. The department adds U.S. packing charges and deducts any of the following expenses included in the comparison market price: packing charges, transportation costs, and any internal tax that was rebated or not collected on the subject merchandise. The department may make additional adjustments to account for differences in the conditions under which sales are made in the U.S. and the comparison market. Thus, the department may increase or decrease the normal value to account for differences in quantities, physical characteristics of the merchandise, levels of trade, and other circumstances of sale. (Section 773[a] of the act.)

31. Ordinary course of trade

In calculating normal value, the department will consider only those sales in the comparison market that are in the ordinary course of trade. Generally, sales are in the ordinary course of trade if made under conditions and practices that, for a reasonable period of time prior to the date of sale of the subject merchandise, have been normal for sales of the foreignlike product. (Section 771 [IS] of the act. See also *arm's-length transactions.*)

32. Proprietary information

Proprietary information is sensitive business data that would cause substantial harm to the submitter if disclosed publicly. Examples of information that the department normally treats as proprietary, if requested and not already in the public domain, include trade secrets concerning the production process, production and distribution costs, terms of sale, individual prices, and the names of customers and suppliers.

33. Proprietary treatment

If a party requests proprietary treatment of information, and if the department agrees that the information is proprietary, the department will protect the information from public disclosure. If the department does not agree that the information is proprietary, it will return the information and not rely on it in the proceeding, unless the submitter agrees that it may be made public. The department will disclose proprietary information only to the U.S. International Trade Commission and U.S. Customs Service officials, and, under limited administrative protective orders, representatives of interested parties. (Section 777[b] of the act. See also *administrative protective order.*)

34. Rebates

Similar to discounts, rebates are reductions in the gross price that a buyer is charged for goods. Unlike discounts, rebates do not result in a reduction in the remittance from the buyer to the seller for the particular merchandise with which the rebate is associated. Rather, a rebate is a refund of monies paid, a credit against monies due on future purchases, or the conveyance of some other item of value by the seller to the buyer after the buyer has paid for the merchandise. When the seller establishes the terms and conditions under which the rebate will be granted at or before the time of sale, the department reduces the gross selling price by the amount of the rebate. (See also *direct versus indirect expenses* and *discounts.*)

35. Similar merchandise

In deciding which sales of the foreignlike product to compare with sales of the subject merchandise, the department first seeks to compare sales of identical merchandise. If there are no sales of the identical foreignlike product, the department will compare sales of the foreignlike product similar to the subject merchandise. The similar foreignlike product is merchandise that is produced by the same manufacturer in the same country as the subject merchandise, and that, in order of preference, is either (1) similar to the subject merchandise in component materials, use, and value; or (2) similar in use to, and reasonably comparable with, the subject merchandise. (Section 771[16] of the act. See also *foreignlike product* and *identical merchandise.*)

36. Subject merchandise

Subject merchandise is merchandise under investigation, and sold in, or to, the U.S. (Section 771[25] of the act.)

37. Technical service expenses

Technical service expenses are typically incurred when a producer provides technical advice to customers that are industrial users of the product. Generally, the department considers travel expenses and contract services performed by unaffiliated technicians to be direct expenses. The department treats as indirect expenses salaries paid to the seller's employees who provide technical services.

38. Third-country market

When the department cannot use home market sales as the basis for determining normal value, one of the alternative methods authorized by the antidumping law is the use of sales to a third-country market, for example, export sales of the foreignlike product to a country other than the United States. Generally, in selecting a third-country market to be used as the comparison market, the department will choose one of the three third-country markets with the largest aggregate quantity of sales of the foreignlike product. In selecting which country, the department will consider product similarity, the similarity of the third-country and U.S. markets, and whether the sales to the third country are representative. (Section 773[a][1] of the act. See also *home market* and *viability*.)

39. Verification

To establish the adequacy and accuracy of information submitted in response to questionnaires and other requests for information, the department conducts an examination of the records of the party that provided the information and interviews company personnel who prepared the questionnaire response and are familiar with the sources of the data in the response. This process is called verification. The department must verify information relied upon in making a final determination in an investigation, or in an administrative review when revocation of an antidumping order is properly requested. The department must also verify information submitted in an administrative review if an interested party so requests and no verification of the producer or exporter had been conducted during the two immediately proceeding reviews of that producer or exporter, or if good cause for verification is shown. (Section 782[i] of the act.)

40. Viability

To calculate normal value based on sales in the home market, the department must determine that the volume of sales is adequate in that market and that a "particular market situation" does not make their use inappropriate. To calculate normal value based on sales in a third-country market, the department must make the same determinations with respect to sales to the third country, and the sales must be "representative." These determinations establish whether a market is viable. The department normally finds sales to be adequate if the quantity of the foreignlike product sold in the market is 5 percent or more of the quantity sold to the U.S. In unusual situations, the department may find that sales below the 5% threshold are adequate, or that sales above the threshold are not. Also in unusual situations, the department may apply the 5% test on the basis of value rather than quantity. The terms *particular market situation* and *representative* are undefined in the statute. A particular market situation might exist, for example, when there was a single sale in the comparison market that constituted 5% or more of the quantity sold to the U.S., or when government control of pricing is such that prices cannot be competitively set, or when there are differing patterns of demand in the U.S. and the comparison market. (Section 773[a][1] of the act.)

Index